KINSHIP IN ACTION

SELF AND GROUP

Andrew Strathern
and
Pamela J. Stewart
University of Pittsburgh

Prentice Hall
Boston   Columbus   Indianapolis   New York   San Francisco
Upper Saddle River   Amsterdam   Cape Town   Dubai   London   Madrid
Milan   Munich   Paris   Montreal   Toronto   Delhi   Mexico City   Sao Paulo
Sydney   Hong Kong   Seoul   Singapore   Taipei   Tokyo

Editorial Director: Craig Campanella
Editor-in-Chief: Dickson Musslewhite
Publisher: Nancy Roberts
Editorial Assistant: Nart Varoqua
Director of Marketing: Brandy Dawson
Senior Marketing Manager: Laura Lee Manley
Marketing Assistant: Pat Walsh
Managing Editor: Maureen Richardson
Production Project Manager: Barbara Reilly
Senior Operations Specialist: Sherry Lewis
Operations Specialist: Cathleen Petersen
Media Director: Brian Hyland
Media Editor: Rachel Comerford

Manager, Rights and Permissions: Charles Morris
Cover Manager: Jayne Conte
Cover Designer: Suzanne Behnke
Cover Art: P. J. Stewart/A. Strathern Archive
Full-Service Project Management: Shiny Rajesh, Integra Software Services, Ltd.
Composition: Integra Software Services, Ltd.
Printer/Binder: RR Donnelley & Sons Company
Cover Printer: RR Donnelley & Sons Company
Text Font: 10/12 Garamond

Credits and acknowledgments borrowed from other sources and reproduced, with permission, in this textbook appear on appropriate page within text.

Library of Congress Cataloging-in-Publication Data

Strathern, Andrew.
   Kinship in action : self and group/Andrew Strathern and Pamela J. Stewart.
     p. cm.
   Includes index.
   ISBN-13: 978-0-13-184484-1 (alk. paper)
   ISBN-10: 0-13-184484-9 (alk. paper)
   1. Kinship. 2. Family. I. Stewart, Pamela J. II. Title.
GN487.S764 2010
306.83—dc22

2010020495

10 9 8 7 6 5 4 3 2 1

Prentice Hall
is an imprint of

ISBN 10:   0-13-184484-9
ISBN 13: 978-0-13-184484-1

To P.B. and T. ragl

CONTENTS

PREFACE

Kinship has made a comeback in anthropology. Not only is there a line of noted, general, introductory works and readers in the topic, but theoretical discussions have been stimulated both by artificial conception technologies and by reconsiderations of how to define kinship in the most productive ways for cross-cultural comparisons. Kinship studies have moved away from the minutiae of kin terminological systems, and the "kinship algebra" often associated with these, to the broader analysis of processes, historical changes, and fundamental cultural meanings in which kin relationships are implicated.

In this changed and changing context, we bring together in this volume a number of interests and concerns, to provide pointers for students, as well as for scholars, in the field of study. First, throughout the book, we take an explicitly processual approach. Kinship formations cannot be understood without exposition of structural frameworks, but these frameworks have also to be seen as historically situated and either potentially or actually changing because of their vital roles in larger processes. Second, from this processual vantage point, we examine the definition of terms such as "kinship" and the issues of filiation, descent, marriage, adoption, and the like. Third, our approach is invariably ethnographic. We seek not simply to illustrate our propositions with examples, but to draw the propositions from the case histories themselves. Fourth, and finally, we have deliberately often deployed materials from field areas where we have ourselves worked or the broader regions to which these areas belong, including the Pacific (especially Papua New Guinea), Europe (especially Scotland and Ireland), and Asia (Austronesian Southeast Asia, China, and Taiwan). This choice has of course not been exclusive. We take examples from all and any areas where relevant materials abound, and our scope is intended to be global, although in no way designed to be encyclopedic.

By using materials from works of fiction, we wish to indicate that fiction is also made out of process and can tell us much about historical patterns and themes of kinship-based relations. We have chosen illustrations of this point from Scotland and France, for instance, just as our other cases are drawn from places such as New Guinea: Whether already familiar to the readers or not, each example from fiction carries its relevant messages about succession, competition, desire, envy, and marriage, that belong to the ethnographic domains of life.

Our aim has been to explain the materials verbally, without recourse to kinship charts. These can be useful, of course. Sometimes they can also be confusing, so we have sought to make our discussions intelligible in their own terms. This means that we have avoided, as far as possible, language that is overly abstract or rarefied, while presenting the complex debates in the field.

Detailed information about kin terms in the two areas of Papua New Guinea which we have frequently alluded to in the book is given in an appendix, along with some remarks about the significance of kin terms in general (see Appendix 1).

The title and subtitle of this book represent different facets of the same approach. "Kinship in Action" stands for our interest in process. "Self and Group" indexes some of the major debates on ideas of personhood that have emerged in discussions on kinship in social contexts. Throughout, we have also tried to bring together concerns derived from British, European, and North American traditions of analysis in the field, recognizing, for example, the importance of the work of both Meyer Fortes and David Schneider (to take two prominent names). In particular, as readers will perceive, we have discussed how many of the fundamental and deeply insightful ideas of Fortes can be released from their historical identification with "structural-functionalism" and brought to life again in contemporary contexts. With this book, we commemorate those who, like Meyer Fortes, have become ancestral figures and provide a platform for those whose work has yet to come. Long may kinship studies live and flourish.

Andrew Strathern and
Pamela J. Stewart
Cromie Burn Research Unit
University of Pittsburgh
November 2009

ACKNOWLEDGMENTS

The idea for this book has been with us for many years. We have been interested in the topic and the fact that kinship studies have become more popular over the last two decades. Many years of teaching on kinship in a number of countries have also contributed to this volume.

We have included materials on kinship in many of our writings (e.g., Strathern and Stewart 2000a, 2000b, 2004), and we have had opportunities to discuss our work with colleagues when we were visiting scholars (e.g., University of Queensland, Brisbane, Australia; University of Otago, New Zealand, where we have worked on the copyedited chapters of this book in February 2010; Institute of Ethnology, Academia Sinica, Taiwan; Dong-hua University, Hualien, Taiwan; International Institute of Asian Studies, Leiden, The Netherlands; Minpaku, National Museum of Ethnology, Osaka, Japan; and the University of Aberdeen, Scotland).

We wish to thank the Office of Dean N. John Cooper, Faculty and School of Arts and Sciences, at the University of Pittsburgh, for long-standing support of our research and publication work. Thanks go to Ms. Catherine Rodgers for typographic assistance on sections of this book. We also thank everyone at Prentice Hall, especially Nancy Roberts, for their assistance and efforts in the production of this book. The extensive peer review of this manuscript has helped to strengthen it and we thank the five anonymous commentators for their suggestions. After our revisions and as this book goes to press, April 2010, the names of four of these evaluators were revealed to us by Prentice Hall. We thank them here: Dr. Richard Feinberg, Kent State University; Dr. Paul Sillitoe, Durham University; Dr. Julie David, California Baptist University, Orange Coast College; Dr. Michael McDonald, Florida Gulf Coast University.

Over the years, we have worked with many people around the world, from remote villages in Papua New Guinea to large cities in Europe, and we thank them all for their discussions and kindness.

References

Strathern, Andrew J., and Pamela J. Stewart. 2000a. Kinship and Commoditization: Historical Transformations. Special Issue of *L'Homme* on kinship [2000]. No 154/155, April/September 2000, 373–390.

Strathern, Andrew J., and Pamela J. Stewart. 2000b. Creating Difference: A Contemporary Affiliation Drama in the Highlands of New Guinea. *The Journal of the Royal Anthropological Institute* 6(1): 1–15.

Strathern, Andrew J., and Pamela J. Stewart. 2004. *Empowering the Past, Confronting the Future, The Duna People of Papua New Guinea.* For, Contemporary Anthropology of Religion Series. New York: Palgrave Macmillan.

ABOUT THE AUTHORS

Pamela J. Stewart and Andrew Strathern are a wife-and-husband research team with a long history of joint publications and research. They are based in the Department of Anthropology, University of Pittsburgh, and are also Visiting Research Fellows and Visiting Professors, Department of Anthropology, University of Durham; Visiting Research Fellows in the Research Institute of Irish and Scottish Studies, University of Aberdeen; and have been Visiting Research Fellows at the Institute of Ethnology, Academia Sinica, Taipei, Taiwan, over many years. They have published many books and articles on their research in the Pacific region, especially in Papua New Guinea, Europe (primarily Scotland and Ireland), and Asia (mainly in Taiwan and China). They are the editors of the *Ritual Studies Book Series*, the *Medical Anthropology Book Series*, the *European Anthropology Series* and the *Anthropology and Cultural History in Asia and the Indo-Pacific Series*. They are also the long-standing co-editors of the *Journal of Ritual Studies*. Their co-authored books include *Witchcraft, Sorcery, Rumors and Gossip* (2004) and *Empowering the Past, Confronting the Future* (2004). Their co-edited books include *Asian Ritual Systems: Syncretisms and Ruptures* (2007); *Exchange and Sacrifice* (2008); *Religious and Ritual Change* (2009); and *Ritual* (2010). (A list of their recent writings can be found at http://www.pitt.edu/~strather/sandspublicat.htm).

CHAPTER 1

Introduction

"Kinship" is a term with a wide range of meanings. These meanings vary in their scale of reference from the most intimate and immediate social ties in familial contexts to the broadest of ethical connotations in ethnic, national, or universal domains. Anthropologists and other social scientists study the full range of these meanings. In particular, they study kinship on a cross-cultural and worldwide basis. The discipline of cultural anthropology may be said to have partly taken its professional shape from the middle of the nineteenth century onward with theories of the significance of kinship in the long-term history of human society. Kinship was often seen simplistically in evolutionary terms as a progression from "primitive" to "civilized" forms of society. While a concern with evolution remains important in some regards, few scholars today would make such a classification central to their discussions of kinship.

Instead, the dominant focus today is on how themes of kinship-related behavior fit into social processes. We can identify historical transitions in different ways of behaving toward kinsfolk. What is of enduring significance is the question of how persons relate to one another in group contexts, hence the subtitle of this book: *Self and Group*. By pairing these terms, we do not intend to suggest that the "self" is intrinsically separate from the "groups" to which people belong, but that there is always a relationship at work. Few people live without some sense of belonging, thus the theme of "no person is an island." Yet, people are never entirely subsumed within their groups, even if this is a prominent ideological theme in their culture.

It is the intertwining of self and group that interests us and this intertwining can imply conflict as well as cooperation. Frequently, it can exhibit both of these features simultaneously. A classic example from kinship theory is that of the relationship between siblings, perhaps most notably same-gender siblings. The sibling bond is often viewed as the symbol of unity and solidarity. Sisterhood and brotherhood may be seen as models for cooperative, even altruistic, behavior. Nuns are often said to be sisters in Christ; and phrases such as joined in sisterhood

Meticulously decorated male dancers at a *moka* celebration, Mount Hagen, Papua New Guinea. They beat long hourglass drums. Their curved wigs are made of human hair. The rows of sticks at their necks represent numbers of goods given in *moka* to exchange partners. The expensive feather plaques on top of their wigs are constructed from various bird feathers and represent the network of kin who have made it possible for them to be worn. Their wives manufacture by hand their elegant front aprons. Each dancer is both "self-produced" and "produced by the group."   (Photo: P. J. Stewart/ A. Strathern Archive)

and the brotherhood of man are seen as uniting ideals. Other examples include the theme song for the European Union and an often-quoted segment of a poem by the Scottish poet Robert Burns: "And man to man, the world over, shall brothers be for all that."[1]

Despite this rhetoric, the sibling bond is also associated with inveterate competition, jealousy, and conflict. In some cultural contexts, this view is expressed in myths and folktales; in others, it is strongly present in psychological and psychiatric theories that purport to explain, as myths do, why such conflict occurs. A frequent theme in myths from New Guinea in the Pacific is the conflict or competition between elder brother and younger brother. Quite often, the younger brother is portrayed as more resourceful, spirited, intelligent, or endowed with good fortune than the elder brother, even though the elder brother has the advantage of age and experience and authority over his younger sibling. Complex messages about how this conflict plays out in actual social life are dramatically portrayed in stories of this kind.

In discussing the behavior of young children within the family, the Melpa-speaking people, who live in the Mount Hagen area of the Highlands of Papua New Guinea, say that children may be *wölik* (jealous, competitive) with one another, trying to get the better of each other in terms of access to special treatment within the family context; often the conflict is about food. In a similar vein, child psychologists in the United States and Britain point out how children compete in various ways to get the attention of their parents; for instance, if one child is favored, the other may throw a tantrum.

EARLY STUDIES

Historically, the study of kinship was central to the development of anthropology. Nineteenth-century theorists founded their notions of how human society began on ideas about how kinship operated. Theories of early matriarchy (rule by women, as "mothers" in society) and matrilineal descent (the practice of determining group membership by genealogical ties traced through women as mothers) are one example of this type of theorizing, associated with J. J. Bachofen and Robert Briffault. According to these theories, mother-right or matriarchy was the earliest form of social organization, based on the "natural" aspects of birth, and notions of paternity and father-right deriving from it came later, displacing mother-right either peacefully or by force.[2]

Another theory, put forward by J. F. McLennan in 1865, suggested that in early human societies there were forms of "group marriage," in which sets of young women and men were married collectively.[3] Such theories were supposed to explain the existence of classificatory systems of kin terminology, in which many people might be designated with terms that appeared to translate as *father*, *mother*, *brother*, and *sister*. Actually, no such hypothesis of origins is needed to explain these usages, since they are tied to group structures in which all persons are classified under a set of kin terms, expressing their political and economic standing in relation to one another. In other words, such terms are classificatory devices expressing values of solidarity or cooperation. They do not imply group marriage, nor do they indicate that people make no difference between their immediate parents and siblings and others. Quite the reverse: People do make clear distinctions. At the same time, these classificatory relations are not to be seen as fictional. They express real values and are underpinned by general notions of shared substance, whether in terms of "blood ties" or in some other way.

It was Lewis Henry Morgan, an American lawyer, who brought together systematically a great wealth of information from across the world about different patterns of kin terms and classified these into a concise set, based on paradigmatic cases from particular areas. Morgan began his scholarly quest partly out of his interest in the practices of the Iroquois people in North America, who followed rules of matrilineal descent but had also built up a powerful league of related groups in opposition to the colonists from Europe. "Iroquois" patterns of terminology for cousins still form one of the technical terms for kinship systems today.[4]

Morgan, like others, was interested in the supposed transition from classificatory to descriptive terminology systems. Classificatory systems were seen as earlier forms, giving way to descriptive usages as societies developed a greater awareness of differentiation between individuals. ("Descriptive" here means that people trace kin ties through specific genealogical links and do not lump persons together simply by virtue of their group membership.) Morgan's own classificatory endeavors provided some fundamental baselines for future work, whether scholars followed his evolutionary narrative of transitions or not.

A stress on looking at kinship primarily through the study of kin terminologies led to highly specialized and technical studies that could sometimes obscure how kinship relations operated in practice, or "on the ground," as it is often put. Theorists made kin diagrams, but these seemed to be "up in the air." How did they relate to what people were actually doing? The same reactions emerged from another series of studies that started from the notion of marriage as a form of alliance between groups, based on the avoidance of incest and the institutionalization of exogamy (i.e., "marrying out" beyond some range of kinship ties). Given its initial impetus in the nineteenth century by Sir Edward Burnett Tylor, with his aphorism "marry out or be killed out," during the twentieth century this approach found its greatest exponent in Claude Lévi-Strauss, who concentrated on "elementary systems" in which people married different categories of cousins. This might be exogamy, that is, marrying outside of one's descent group, but it was still marrying kin rather than nonkin, hence the term "elementary," as opposed to "complex" systems in which people married nonkin and so expanded and diversified their networks of kin, perhaps at the expense of solidarity between kinsfolk in the same group.[5]

Lévi-Strauss's powerfully synthetic and analytical expositions, expressed in his 1949 book *The Elementary Structure of Kinship*, were followed by a long list of ethnographies exploring his propositions in great depth and analyzing how such "elementary" systems worked in practice—usually they were found to be rather "complex"—and whether the systems should be described as prescriptive (i.e., bound by a clear rule) or preferential (i.e., a given form was preferred for some categories of marriages but not for all). These debates, like those regarding kin terms in general, became very abstruse and technical. While kinship was still regarded as a central topic in anthropology, debates on it were again becoming arcane and hard to follow. As a consequence, the popularity of kinship as a topic taught to university undergraduates declined by the 1970s and 1980s.

THE REVIVAL OF KINSHIP STUDIES

Today, however, kinship studies have been enjoying a revival. Why is this? One simple reason is that kin ties remain important in every society and no matter what the ethnographic topic is, sooner or later this becomes evident to the investigator. Kinship has always been more than the study of kin term patterns or patterns of marrying kin, since it is a context in which many people's personal, emotional, and economic lives are played out. While exploring broad topics related to contemporary life, anthropologists have found that kinship, far from fading away, keeps coming back, in transformed but still highly relevant ways.[6]

Another reason for the revived strength of kinship studies is that technological advancements in society, coupled with changes in attitudes and norms regarding sexual behavior, have posed in a new way fundamental questions of what constitutes kinship: questions which in their own ways anthropologists and others have always been engaged in investigating. For example, aspects of biotechnology which have split the functions of sexual reproduction in ways not possible before: through in vitro fertilization and sperm banks, as well as egg extraction, fertilization, and implantation in surrogate mothers.[7]

As we have seen, in early theories of kinship, motherhood was considered to be the "natural" and indissoluble bedrock of kin relations. There could be arguments about paternity, and many dramas have been based on this point, but not about maternity. The new distinction between the biological mother as the provider of the egg and the birthing mother who carries the child in her womb has introduced a different dimension to motherhood. The division also leads to possibilities of ambiguity and conflict, as for example, when a woman agrees to carry a child for another in return for a fee, and then after the birth is unwilling to give the child up, on grounds that it is biologically part of herself.

WHAT IS KINSHIP?

If we look at these cases from a historical perspective, we can see that complications of this sort are not entirely new, but that biotechnology places them closer to the heart of the reproductive process in contemporary societies. The basic issue is one that has caused much ink to be spilled in anthropological writings: What is kinship? Each society may have somewhat different definitions, and these differences turn on a limited number of issues. Is kinship something that is purely ascribed or can it be at least in part achieved in practice? Is it based fundamentally on biological ideas of reproduction or can it be based on a wider set of ideas about shared substance? Do we see extended definitions of kinship as based on metaphorical usages or simply on different criteria of how people may regard one another as kin?

In one model, kinship is seen as founded purely on biological notions, expressed in terms of ideas about "blood" or some other substance viewed as transmitted by biological reproduction. In another model, it is seen as based on codes of role-based behavior, such as nurturing, sharing food, caring, socialization, and general social support. The former model can be said to be status based and to rely on an ascriptive mode of eligibility; the latter is role based and obviously depends on achievement, or people living up to a "code of conduct," as the anthropologist David Schneider put it. In practice, kinship systems tend to be compromises between these two opposite models. It is precisely because there are such compromises that issues of definition arise and are irresolvable unless we recognize the multiplicity and variability of relationships that belong to the domain of kinship.[8]

There are theoretical reasons why kinship systems work in this complicated way. Human behavioral patterns are organized around an interplay between genetic and environmental constraints and opportunities. Humans act as they do partly because of their genetic makeup and partly because of how they perceive advantages for themselves. Over the long term, this interplay revolves around issues of adaptation. Not all behavior is adaptive, and some is quite maladaptive, but in viable groups there is a balance, with a net tendency toward adaptation over time. Adaptation requires flexibility. If patterns are too rigid, this becomes a constraint. If patterns are too fluid, social order suffers. In practice, all behavior is a compromise. It is unsurprising therefore that this should hold for the domain of kinship. Adherence to clear norms of marriage and filiation (the assignment of children to parents) gives order within communities; but if these rules are followed too rigidly, there may be too many or too few people in a given group or network. Mechanisms are developed, therefore, that enable people to shift across networks of filiation. One prime example of these is the institutions of fosterage and adoption, which are based on the idea that kinship can be achieved.

Fosterage does not imply that the original biological filiation is denied; instead, parentage is in a sense shared. The foster parents nurture and socialize the child, while the biological parent or parents are still recognized and may retain rights over the child. The child may eventually return to its biological parents. With adoption, as it has been legally defined in Euro-American contexts, there is a more definite separation and cutting off from biological parents, and the adoptive parents are given a fuller role. Even here, it is interesting to note that as children grow up, they may learn that they were adopted and may seek to find out about their biological parentage. Such a quest is based on the ideological primacy given to biological ties, which is clearly inscribed in the ways that the law ordinarily works. In societies in which there is a more balanced relationship between biological and social ties, this kind of opposition tends not to occur. In Pacific Island societies, children may be looked after and brought up by a range of kin, and ties between families are strengthened by this sharing of children between them. Therefore, such ties are created not only by marriage but also by the circulation of the products of marriage, that is, children.

In such cases, it is clear that a child may have more than one "mother" or "father" and parentage is shared on the basis of ascription/achievement. Arrangements of this kind tend to occur most often between families that recognize extended kin ties between themselves. That is, the sharing of children most often occurs among preexisting networks of kin and therefore new kinship does not have to be created out of nothing. People who are already distant kin can become close kin through the sharing of children; and this is facilitated by the use of classificatory kin terms among the families involved.

Therefore, whereas complexities in filiation have been brought into Euro-American consciousness by biotechnology and new forms of family groupings, comparable complexities have been practiced within other kinship systems for a long time. Basically this is because kinship is not just a way of classifying people, but rather a way of organizing action. While in some ways it may be significant on a daily basis, in others it may surface only at certain times of social importance, notably in life-cycle events. As might be expected, these are the events related to the creation, development, maintenance, and termination of kin ties themselves: birth, marriage, the advent of children, and death. These events are the basis of the elementary structures of kinship as they are exhibited in contemporary society, as well as across cultures, and are thereby the means through which kinship itself is reproduced. They are also profound carriers of social values in general, tying people into legal, political, economic, and religious institutions which ensure that the so-called "domestic" realm is actually an integral part of how the wider society operates. This is most obviously shown, perhaps, when the personages involved are politically important, for example a monarch or a president. But it is also the case with an ordinary individual, since every celebration of a marriage or a birth and every recognition of loss at a death bears on itself the stamp of wider community or societal regulation.

MOBILIZING KIN

In some societies, particularly those in which wider relations of kinship are operative, the mobilization of kin may also be important in many contexts other than those tied to the punctuations of the life cycle. Here is where the kinds of groups anthropologists are known for writing about come in. Most prominent among them are descent groups, defined in terms of normative rules of membership: patrilineal, with rules of membership through paternal ties; matrilineal, through maternal links; and, less commonly, cognatic, through either paternal or maternal connections. Mobilization can also occur through kindred ties, ties traced out to a range of cousins from a particular individual or set of full siblings, or through a mixed strategy of using ties of descent and networks of kin ties beyond the descent group.

When does mobilization take place? It happens in times of danger and crisis, in times of celebration, and at a more everyday level, in the context of work projects and communal decision making in general. In precolonial times, in the New Guinea Highlands, for example, fighting and threats of fighting were prime contexts of mobilization. In the area of Mount Hagen in Papua New Guinea, clan groups—whose members claimed common descent, held a common territory, and married only outside of the clan—were centrally important.[9] Within each clan-based community, sets of kin from different subgroups came together during fights, mustering at a ceremonial ground where a particular leader and his immediate kin lived, often with a cemetery for their dead at the back of the leader's gathering house. Each fighter would bring his own weapon, perhaps a long spear, bow and arrows, or a stone-bladed battle axe. They would charcoal their faces and wear perhaps a cassowary plume on their heads. For large-scale fights, some men would bring heavy shields behind which they could advance. Leaders had no particular authority to require warriors to gather, but they could harangue and encourage them once they had assembled. Adherence to the clan, rooted in idioms of patrifilial (paternal) kinship, was given as the sufficient reason why people would engage in fighting. In practical terms, they would either have to fight or be defeated and possibly driven from their territory, even if this were only temporary. As with a modern nation-state, they felt that they had to defend themselves if attacked, and if they initiated a fight, they had to fight to win.

Interestingly, in spite of the idea that all able adult male clan members who were co-resident should join in any fight, no-one was expected to attack or kill a close relative on the other side. Stereotypically, this was supposed to particularly apply to kin on the mother's side. Balancing the emphasis on paternal ties, ties with mother's kin and clan were seen as exceptionally strong in interpersonal terms. Killing mother's kin was believed to invite their ill will and in effect their curse, and the same held reciprocally. Given that clans were exogamous, marriages and the maternal ties they brought in their wake ensured that hostilities could not be too severe between intermarrying groups. In Mount Hagen, such ties were bolstered further by the idea that affines (in-laws) and cousins linked across clan divisions should exchange wealth with each other. Exchanges of wealth (pigs, shell valuables, etc.) bolstered interpersonal kin ties and also fostered good political interrelations at group levels. While clear distinctions were made between politics and interpersonal kinship in some ways, in practice they were related. The field of kinship was thus dynamic and pervasive in social processes generally, extending from contexts of conflict to those of reintegration and positive exchanges.[10]

It is commonly thought that this kind of integration between the personal and the political aspects of kinship is particular to the societies anthropologists customarily classified as "tribal societies." However, this view needs to be modified, for two reasons. First, the "tribal societies" themselves are, and in many cases have been for a long time, incorporated into wider domains of politics and economics, propelling them into complex situations of change that alter the relationship between interpersonal and political dimensions of behavior. Second, in state-based societies, there is actually an integrative relationship between the personal and the political and legal domains. The clearest illustration of this is the fact that what we call "the family" and may look upon as a "naturally" constituted unit arising out of sexual reproduction is actually a legally and politically constituted entity subject to renegotiation and redefinition over time. Of course, the family does in part arise precisely out of sexual reproduction, and this is true everywhere. But the specific form it takes varies considerably, leading to confusions about the meaning of the term "family" itself. And these variations are a matter of custom, law, politics, and religion, or most broadly culture.

FAMILY

In everyday usage in Euro-American societies, the term "family" can refer to different entities, coded in terms of the status/role distinction we have mentioned earlier. It can refer to the classic nuclear family, defined in terms of a couple (male and female) and their biological offspring, as well as to the extended family, with a three-generational extension, including grandparents. It can be broadened to mean essentially a network of kin spreading over several nuclear families (the expanded family) or extended further to include anyone brought into the incorporative and supportive domain defined by the idiom of biological ties but essentially referring to co-residence or other forms of solidarity.

We have heard it applied by university administrators to the concept of a university seen as a network of people rather than as a legal and administrative structure. This particular usage is interesting because it provides a parallel with the way some terms are used in politics. When stress is placed on the wider community of people, the term used is "nation," which in etymology refers to ideas of connectedness ultimately rooted in kinship; where the emphasis is on formal structures, the term used is "state." The composite phrase "nation-state" puts these two separate ideas together, implying that they are different dimensions of a single complex phenomenon. This binding together of terms also indicates that there are ways in which nation relates to state and vice versa. The nation, like a university, is sometimes imagined or expressed as though it were one large family. Even sets of allied nations can be referred to in this way. "Family values" may be ideologically brought forward as the basis of "national values." But the family in its narrower or more specific sense is itself regulated in various ways by state laws that define the family as a legal structure. In this sense, the family is founded on a state-recognized form of licensed sexual union between people. In a monogamous union, this bond is notionally exclusive. Transgressing this exclusivity may lead to civil or criminal sanctions and may also be grounds for divorce.

Divorce itself is a legal act, hedged about with all kinds of complex legal stipulations. The children of the union, if any, are defined in legal terms that specify legitimacy. The rights of people to benefits, maintenance, and compensation, and their ability to represent each other or to control each other in various ways, are all legally set out. Whether people follow all these rules is another, interesting, question, but it is separate from the rules themselves (a circumstance that fed into sociologist Emile Durkheim's famous definition of his topic as social facts that have to be understood in themselves "as things"). Sex enters into marriage, but sex and marriage are separate processes: Premarital and extramarital sex are problematic arenas that have surrounded the legally and morally permitted arena of marriage itself; and not all persons are permitted as sexual partners, still less as marital partners.

Incest rules prohibit sexual relations between close kin, especially between siblings or between parents and children, a practice that has long exercised theoreticians. None of these rules are universal, but exceptions to them are rare and require particular explanations such as the constraints of dynastic succession (as in the case of royal sibling in-marriage in ancient Egypt). Sometimes various people are permitted as sexual partners before marriage, but not as marital partners. Among the Trobrianders of Papua New Guinea, as studied in the early part of the twentieth century by Bronislaw Malinowski, classificatory clan sisters and brothers could have sexual relations, but marriage had to be exogamous, outside of the clan. This category of behavior had its own term, *suvasova*, distinguishing it from others. It was in stark contrast with the rigid prohibition of sexual relations between immediate brothers and sisters, a prohibition made more poignant by the founding myth of "love magic" (the magic of sexual desire), which was based on a story of brother–sister incest. As Malinowski pointed out, all this reflected the paradox of Trobriand ideas of conception and descent: The brother found his social continuity in some ways through his sister's marriage because of the rule of matrilineal descent, but he was prohibited from any sexual contact with her. Children were seen as reincarnated spirits of the mother's matriline; yet it was important for children to have a legitimate father, and this had to be through marriage. Fathers were not thought to contribute to the initial coming into being of their children but they were thought to mold the child in the womb so it would resemble them. Therefore, a Trobriand child was supposed to resemble its father and never its mother's kin. Clearly a vocabulary based on notions of genetics and conception will fail to comprehend the specifics of such a cultural system of ideas. Still, the general analytical point holds: Just as in state-based societies, in the Trobriands "the family" was a legal concept.[11] This fundamental point is what underlies the controversy in the United States, the UK, and other places regarding the legal definition of marriage itself.

MARRIAGE

Same-sex partnerships have forced a crisis on the institutions of state and federal governments. Sexual and reproductive unions outside of marriage are customarily or traditionally penalized and stigmatized in many societies. Some benefits in marriage will not be available to people outside of marriage even if they are close, faithful, and long-term partners. Such partners cannot be regarded as "next of kin" in circumstances of illness, death, or burial. The prominence given to marriage is reflected in the fact that if you are married your marital partner is usually expected to be named as your "next of kin" (confusingly in a way because spouses are not usually consanguineal kin at all: this in turn reflects the conflation of consanguineal kin and in-laws in Euro-American usages). Marriage trumps consanguineal kinship here, but in the absence of a legal marriage, consanguineal kin who have not been close to a dying person may have more say in the after-death events than a long-term co-resident partner.[12]

The contemporary inequities of this situation are due to changes in patterns of sexual relationships and also because the law is premised on a strong privileging of ties geared to legitimate biological reproduction. This privileging also underlies people's desire to have biological offspring, on which huge amounts of effort may be expended. If one of the core purposes of marriage is to produce biological offspring of the marriage partners, same-sex marriage may appear as a contradiction in terms. Same-sex partners can bond but this bond by itself cannot produce offspring. But if marriage is seen more as a companionate relationship, encompassing exclusive sexual relations but going beyond these, and as not having to involve the reproduction of biological offspring, same-sex partners may acquire a case for marrying. In complex urbanized societies, marriage has already undergone a partial redefinition of this sort within heterosexual unions. Numbers of children born and raised in middle-class families have tended to drop and the overall rate of reproduction has also dropped. Effective forms of contraception have enabled sex without an ensuing pregnancy. People live longer and expect to remain sexually active longer. All of these factors have tended to separate marriage from reproduction (just as sex is analytically separable from marriage). The recent revolution in same-sex sexual practices came on the heels of all these attitudinal and behavioral changes in heterosexual contexts. Interestingly, in terms of the study of processes of social change, the next step was that same-sex partners who formed lasting commitments wished to see these recognized in symbolic or cultural terms, as well as legally.

Cultural recognition, while at first given grudgingly to new practices, can be gained gradually. Legal recognition raises the bar, however, and issues over it can lead to intra-societal conflict. This is why the struggle in the United States and the UK, for instance, heightened when same-sex union advocates began demanding that they be allowed to have marriages recognized by the state. Neoconservatives, tied to Christian conservative traditions, began to fight a rearguard action against this demand. Massachusetts recognized same-sex marriages, provoking the federal administration to support the idea of marriage as a union between two people of opposite sex, by further strengthening the 1996 Federal Defense of Marriage Act (Public Law no. 104–199, 110 Stat. 2419). Again, interestingly, this was a defense of basic cultural classifications and symbolic values. Authorities had already granted certain legal privileges both to common-law heterosexual "marriages" established by cohabitation and to same-sex couples. What was resisted was the idea that same-sex unions could be called "marriages" as such. Nothing could show more clearly that certain ideas about kinship and marriage lie at the heart of the very symbolic constitution of states themselves.

The state claims the right to determine and uphold these basic values and to regulate any changes in them. Therefore, the "state" and the "tribe" act in one and the same way with regard to how kinship is acceptably configured. In the past, an issue such as same-sex marriage could hardly have entered into political consciousness. It was taboo, comparable to incest. People might engage in such acts, but as a result they were inevitably stigmatized. The same has held, however, in other contexts such as interethnic relations, but has changed over time. Generally, issues of various kinds have been flagged under the rubric of basic human rights. By claiming normality for themselves, same-sex partners align their cause historically with the causes of racial equality and gender equality, and they identify their recognition with the idea of a "progressive" society at large.

Kinship terms are one of the basic means whereby kinship values are transmitted. In systems where there are wide classificatory usages, these terms also enter into the political realm; however, when kin terms are restricted to the three-generational extended family, and beyond that chiefly to first cousins, the domain of kinship appears to have shrunk. Perhaps this is why it is so difficult for students unfamiliar with tribal organizations to grasp the significance of all the complicated terminological systems previously discussed by Lewis Henry Morgan and his successors in the field of kinship studies.[13]

Our own basic point has been different: The domain of kinship relations may appear to have shrunk from one viewpoint, but it remains tied into the larger structures of society and is itself a crucial component of these. The contemporary arguments about marriage clearly show this to be the case. Throughout this book, we will return to this theme of how kinship is interwoven with other societal practices.

Why study kinship today? Because it is everywhere around us and is a part of our lives, now, as it was in the past, in many societies around the world, from Scotland to New Guinea. It has also entered into many creative works of art, including ones that we could call ethnographic, such as the novels of Sir Walter Scott, who lived 1771–1832. Scott's novels often exemplify the intertwining of kinship and marriage with politics in Scottish history, and we end this introductory chapter with a "case history" from one of his novels, *The Fair Maid of Perth*, or *St. Valentine's Day*, first published in 1831.

THE FAIR MAID OF PERTH

The fair maid of Perth in Sir Walter Scott's romantic novel of that title is Catharine Glover, daughter of Simon Glover, in the city of Perth during the time of Robert III of Scotland, who ruled from 1390 to 1406. The novel portrays Catharine as possessing a beauty that made her an object of attention in the society. Various men are depicted as being enamored by her. These included the following: David, the Duke of Rothsay, son of King Robert himself; "Conachar," a young Scottish Highlander who is employed as an apprentice in Simon Glover's household but later is revealed to be Eachin MacIan, chief of Clan Quhele and son of Gilchrist MacIan, who had been sent into refuge with Simon owing to adverse omens surrounding his birth; and Henry Wynd or Gow, a blacksmith and armorer, who is also a noted fighter and warrior much respected by the people of the city. Simon favors Henry as a spouse for his daughter Catharine, but she is uncertain whether she wishes to marry at all.

Catharine is deeply religious and affected by the teachings of Father Clement, a Dominican priest who is critical of the laxities of the church in his day, its accommodations to pre-Christian ideas, and its complicities in politics. The fates of the three men enamored of her—the Duke of Rothsay, "Conachar," and Henry Wynd—are skillfully interwoven by the author until the end of the story, where Henry and Catharine are united in marriage after the tragic deaths of the other two suitors.

One axis on which the story turns is the romance of Catharine and these men of different status linked by their admiration for her. The city of Perth itself is pivotal in the novel and is emblematic of the whole of Scottish society at the time. It stands near the foothills of the Highlands and is the site of mediation between the proud Highlands chiefs and their clans and the solid citizens of Perth, who represent Lowlands values and pay allegiance to civic government and the monarch himself.

The second axis of the novel reaches the international level—the troubled and ambiguous relationship between Scotland and England. Independence, reaffirmed by Robert the Bruce's victory over Edward II of England at the battle of Bannockburn in 1314, requires constant vigilance along the Scottish Borders. The King has arranged for the betrothal of the daughter of the Earl of Dunbar and March, whose lands lay near the Border country with England, with his own eldest son, the Duke of Rothsay, in order to cement an alliance that would help to protect Scotland. The King, however, is much influenced by his brother the Duke of Albany, who makes it known that whichever noble house offers the largest dowry payment would win marriage with the King's son and heir. The Earl of Douglas, a redoubted warrior and also a guardian of the borderlands, contests the betrothal of Rothsay to the Earl of March's daughter. Douglas is also close to the throne himself since he is married to the eldest daughter of the King. Son-in-law to the King, Douglas seeks to make his daughter the King's daughter-in-law. The Duke of Rothsay would thus marry his own niece, his sister's daughter. (Dynastic unions often involve such close relatives marrying, unions which ordinarily would not be countenanced.)

Douglas offers a larger dowry than the Earl of March and induces the King, via Albany, to break the marriage contract and have Rothsay marry his daughter, Marjory Douglas, whom Rothsay does not wish to marry. Dynastic intrigues and competition come into conflict with personal feelings. Rothsay spurns Marjory, the competition between Douglas and March flares, and the security of Scotland as a kingdom is threatened. March gives signs of changing sides and betraying Scotland to the English crown, checked only by fear of Douglas.

Rothsay, portrayed as a feckless young man, fails to woo Catharine and is later betrayed and tricked by his uncle, the Duke of Albany, in league with the Earl of Douglas. He is kept a prisoner and starved in the castle of Falkland in Fife. Finally, he is murdered in a bid to subvert succession to the throne. The Duke of Rothsay is thus a victim of dynastic politics.

Conachar, the young Highland chief, is similarly caught up in the violence of politics, but in a different way. His father, Gilchrist MacIan, dies just at the time when a severe conflict is in progress between his clan, Clan Quele, and Clan Chattan. In Walter Scott's account, the Highland clans as a whole are dissident within the kingdom and the conflict between these two major clans threatens to spill over into the Lowlands. The King does not command the military force to subdue the Highlanders. It was, according to Scott, Rothsay himself who suggested that the dispute between Clan Chattan and Clan Quele could be settled by arranging a duel between their champions. This is duly set in hand, and Conachar is required to take a leading part in the duel. He is terrified in battle and flees, later committing suicide by leaping over a cataract after confessing his cowardice to Catharine, who is sheltering in the Dominican Priory at

Perth. Conachar is caught in the inexorabilities of clan politics, enmeshed with those of the monarch, and dies.

The deaths of Conachar and Rothsay precede the success of Henry in winning the hand of Catharine. Simon Glover's "commonsense" preference thus wins out, while the intrigues of the court and the clan vengeance of the hills bring his rivals to their deaths. As readers of the novel, we see how politics, kinship, and marriage are all intertwined, while the romance of Henry and Catharine carries on through the narrative as a whole.[14]

Conclusion

Terms such as "kinship," "marriage," and "family" carry complex meanings, and these meanings also vary cross culturally. What we call kinship touches on the biological aspects of reproduction at one end of a continuum and at the other end broadens out into social relations, politics, and the nation. Kinship relations are often highly regulated, and what they regulate also varies. As the narrative from Scott's novel shows, the courtship of one young woman could involve dynastic plots and regional animosities. In the end, however, Catharine marries locally.

Questions to Consider

1. What are the most productive ways to define kinship?
2. How are familial relations often bound up with politics and state structures?

Notes

1. The European Union theme song emphasizes one of the core intentions behind the genesis of the Union itself, the creation of peace between former enemies at the heart of Europe, stemming from the two world wars of the twentieth century. Hence the choice of Beethoven's Overture from his ninth symphony, "Alle Menschen werden Brüder" ("All men shall be brothers"). The vernacular Scots of the quotation from Burns is, "And man to man the world o'er shall brithers be for a' that." The title of the poem is "A man's a man for a' that." Burns lived 1759–1796.
2. Johann Jakob Bachofen, *Myth, Religion, and Mother Right* (Princeton, NJ: Princeton University Press, 1967); and Robert Briffault, *The Mothers* (New York: Macmillan, 1927).
3. John Ferguson McLennan, *Primitive Marriage* (Chicago, IL: University of Chicago Press, [1865] 1970).
4. See Lewis Henry Morgan, *Systems of Consanguinity and Affinity of the Human Family,* Smithsonian Contributions to Knowledge no. 17 (Washington, D.C., 1871); and *League of the Iroquois,* (New York: Corinth, [1851] 1969). For a discussion of Morgan's work, see Thomas R. Trautmann, *Lewis Henry Morgan and the Invention of Kinship* (Chicago, IL: University of Chicago Press, 1987). For a deeply thought-out overview of kinship studies in the domain of British social anthropology,

see Meyer Fortes, *Kinship and the Social Order: The Legacy of Lewis Henry Morgan* (Chicago, IL: Aldine, 1969). Appendix 1 in the present volume has further details on kin terminologies, with some details from the Hagen and Duna areas of Papua New Guinea.

5. Claude Lévi-Strauss, *Les Structures élémentaires de la parenté* (Paris: Presses Universitaires, 1949). On Tylor's ideas in general, see Sir Edward B. Tylor, *Primitive Culture* (London: J. Murray, 1871). Appendix 2 in the present volume presents a more in-depth discussion of the topics of incest prohibition and exogamy, including more details on Malinowksi's findings.

6. Some studies on this theme are Peter P. Schweitzer, ed., *Dividends of Kinship: Meanings and Uses of Social Relatedness* (London and New York: Routledge, 2000); Janet Carsten, ed., *Cultures of Relatedness: New Approaches to the Study of Kinship* (Cambridge: Cambridge University Press, 2000); Janet Carsten, *After Kinship* (Cambridge: Cambridge University Press, 2004); Robert Parkin and Linda Stone, eds., *Kinship and Family: An Anthropological Reader* (Oxford: Blackwell Publishing, 2004); and Michael G. Peletz, "Kinship Studies in Late Twentieth-Century Anthropology," *Annual Review of Anthropology* 24 (1995): 343–372. For a study of historical changes in kinship in Europe, see Jack Goody, *The Development of the Family and Marriage in Europe* (Cambridge: Cambridge University Press, 1983). For a recent cross-cultural overview, see Maurice Godelier, *Les Métamorphoses de la Parenté* (Paris: Fayard, 2004).

7. See Hal B. Levine, "Gestational surrogacy: Nature and culture in kinship," *Ethnology* 42, no. 3 (2003): 173–185.

8. David Schneider himself criticized what he saw as a Eurocentric analytic bias in the definition of kinship relations. Although his criticisms did not destroy the cross-cultural basis of studying kinship, as a mode of relationship between people founded on notions of shared substance, his critiques forced anthropologists to think more carefully about their usages of the term as a cross-cultural universal. See David M. Schneider, *A Critique of the Study of Kinship: A Cultural Account* (Ann Arbor, MI: University of Michigan Press, 1984). For discussions of Schneider's ideas on this point, see references given in note 6 above and also: Ladislav Holy, *Anthropological Perspectives on Kinship* (London: Pluto Press, 1996); and Richard Feinberg and Martin Ottenheimer, eds., *The Cultural Analysis of Kinship: The Legacy of David M. Schneider* (Urbana: University of Illinois Press, 2001), especially R. Feinberg's Introduction, pp. 1–32, in that volume and Robert McKinley's, The philosophy of kinship: a reply to Schneider's "Critique of the Study of Kinship," pp. 131–167, in the same collection. For a study of the processes whereby senses of kinship are established in role-behavior, see Signe Howell, "Kinning: The creation of life trajectories in transnational adoptive families," *Journal of the Royal Anthropological Institute* 9 (2003): 465–484.

9. See Andrew Strathern, *One Father, One Blood* (Canberra: Australian National University Press, 1972) for a detailed exposition of this aspect of social life in Mount Hagen, based on fieldwork in the colonial period, 1964–1965.

10. For an account of ceremonial exchange relations in Mount Hagen, incorporating earlier analyses and discussing the transformations of exchange in colonial and postcolonial times, see Andrew Strathern and Pamela J. Stewart, *Arrow Talk: Transactions, Transitions, and Contradiction in New Guinea Highlands History* (Kent, OH: The Kent State University Press, 2000).

11. On the Trobriand concepts of kinship and sexual practices, see Bronislaw Malinowksi, *The Sexual Life of Savages in North-Western Melanesia* (New York and

London: Harcourt, Brace, Jovanovich, 1929). Malinowski's report that the Trobrianders were "ignorant" of physiological paternity led to a huge controversial literature. The work of Annette Weiner, based on later fieldwork in the same local area where Malinowski made his investigations, did much to clarify this topic. See, for example, Annette Weiner, *The Trobrianders of Papua New Guinea* (Fort Worth, TX: Harcourt Brace, 1988). Weiner's work also contributed significantly to studies of gender and kinship, on which in general see Jane F. Collier and Sylvia J. Yanagisako, *Gender and Kinship: Essays Toward a Unified Analysis* (Stanford, CA: Stanford University Press, 1987). For a wide-ranging review of questions regarding incest, see Bernard Vernier, *La Prohibition de l'Inceste* (Paris; L'Harmattan, 2009).

12. See, for example, Kath Weston, *Families We Choose: Lesbians, Gays, Kinship* (New York: Columbia University Press, 1991); and Marilyn Yalom and Laura L. Carstensen, eds., *Inside the American Couple: New Thinking/New Challenges* (Berkeley, CA: University of California Press, 2002).

13. For example, in British social anthropology, Alfred Reginald Radcliffe-Brown, *Structure and Function in Primitive Society* (London: Cohen and West, 1952); and in American cultural anthropology, George Peter Murdock, *Social Structure* (New York: The MacMillan Company, 1949).

14. As in other novels of Scott, for example, *Rob Roy* and *The Heart of Midlothian*, the theme of hostility in Highlands–Lowlands political relations in Scotland is portrayed as mediated by ties of kinship, friendship, and romance.

CHAPTER 2

Life Cycles

LIFE CYCLE AND FAMILY: BASIC CONCEPTS

Everyone goes through birth and death and in many societies people are expected to marry and reproduce. The phrase "life cycle" stands for the concept that family structures are replicated over time by the process of reproduction. In this sense, kinship networks are seen as sets of interlocking families. Writers on kinship signal this interlocking process in its simplest form by speaking of "the family of orientation" and "the family of procreation." The former is the family a person is born into, and the latter is the family that the person is involved in procreating. The person in focus here (the "ego" in kinship charts) is the link between these two "families." Here "family" is restricted to the two-generational sense, but all kinship systems recognize at least three generations, indicating the linkage between "orientation" and "procreation." In other words, grandparents are recognized universally. Often they play important roles in terms of social-ization, child care, or even authority in extended families, where grandparents and their married children continue to live in the same household. Grandparents and grandchildren are sometimes linked in kin terminological systems by self-reciprocal terms, expressing an intimate correspondence between them (for examples, see Appendix 1). Friendship and bonding between children and their grandparents also led anthropologists to speak of the "alliance" between alternate generations as contrasting with the "opposition" between adjacent generations (i.e., parents and children.)

The emergence of the "nuclear family," or the family of parents and children living separately from grandparents and other kin, is often associated by sociologists with the breakup of rural communities and the migration of people as industrial workers to towns and cities, which gained momentum in Europe in the nineteenth century. But family relations in the broader sense persist even when family members do not reside in the same household. They may live nearby, for example, and visit often. Grandparents can help with child care if they live near enough or can visit regularly, or if children can stay with them. These kinship ties can be operative even if the wider communities into which they were once set no longer exist or are much reduced.

The idea of the life cycle, then, contains within it two elements. One is the sense of continuity over time contained in the interlocking of the generations. The other is the perception that each generation repeats the structures begun by the previous generation. The nuclear family one is born into is repeated in form by the nuclear family one creates through marriage. Of course, the repetition is a formal one. It does not preclude changes in habits, values, attitudes, or expectations. In any case, this idea of life cycles depends on the imputed facts of birth, reproduction, and death. This is why these universal events are generally not left to happen by themselves. They are regulated, and they are ritually marked. In human societies everywhere, rituals are important as prime indicators of social processes and cultural values. In anthropology, therefore, a good deal of attention has been paid to the rituals surrounding life cycles, as we have defined these.

MARKING BIRTH AND MAKING IDENTITIES

Birth is a physical event. It is, however, an event that is usually a part of a much more elaborate set of cultural processes. In many societies, it is supposed to occur only within the context of a prior marriage. In such cases, the birth of the first child also marks the beginnings of a new nuclear family. It is for this reason that, in many cases, the firstborn's birth is given special importance, and firstborn children may also have to observe special taboos in relation to their parents. This is highly likely in family systems in which the eldest child is expected to succeed to a position of authority in the household or in the extended family. This syndrome is most marked where succession of this kind runs through males, from father to eldest son, and significant material assets are involved, or a responsibility for sacrificing to the spirits of ancestors in the male line devolves upon successors.[1]

This circumstance of succession to authority, as well as the inheritance of property and obligations that go with it, is called *primogeniture*. Its opposite, succession by the youngest child, is *ultimogeniture*. In aristocratic families in Scotland, the rules of succession caused a big divide between the eldest son and his junior male siblings. The eldest son was expected to succeed. His juniors had to find something else for themselves to do. Robert Louis Stevenson's novel *The Master of Ballantrae* explores the ramifications of such a rule in the context of one family and its fortunes in the seventeenth century. The idea of succession by the eldest son was so deeply entrenched in society that even if a junior were, in practice, to succeed to a title, it was still felt that the rightful owner of the title "the Master" was the elder.[2]

Birth, then, is an event that takes place in strongly marked cultural settings and has implications for other social relations, most immediately in terms of the creation, through it, of parenthood, but also the creation of *siblinghood*, that is, a position among a potential or existing set of sisters and brothers. Like parenthood, siblinghood is an important basis for ideas about social relations in general. Siblinghood contains two different ideas, which are partly in contradiction with each other. As children of the same parents, full siblings can be seen as equals. But their birth order, and/or their gender, may make them quite unequal. Siblinghood thus represents a tension between equality (and with it an idea of solidarity and support) and inequality (with its connotations of potential rivalry and hostility).[3]

Mythologies around the world often depict this ambivalence of relations between siblings, as well as forms of relations between parents and children. The depiction of a duality between positive and negative affect, or amity and enmity, love and hostility, is one that inheres particularly strongly in the sphere of kinship, although it also appears across the spectrum of human social relations. Myths sometimes depict relations in ways that provide warnings against mistakes in kin relations or in marital relations. For example, as we have noted in Chapter 1, younger sons may be depicted as smarter than elder sons, even though elder sons are expected to be preeminent. Or married persons may be warned of dire consequences if they ignore the wishes of their wives/husbands.[4]

Given this state of affairs, birth rituals often mark out the importance of the event, not just for the parents but for the wider social networks thought to be involved. And because of the importance of the life cycle to the reproduction of social relations generally, religious practices are often brought into play to signify these wider connections. Christenings are a case in point. For example, through the act of marking a child's forehead with holy water taken from a font (a ritual pool) in a consecrated building (the church), a priest or pastor/minister, as an authorized practitioner, inducts a child into "the greater family" of the deity and a congregation, in the presence of witnesses who include the parents, other kin, and friends. In the Catholic tradition, godparents chosen from the community, who may or may not be also already kin, are explicitly and publicly announced on this occasion to indicate this widening of the bonds of kinship beyond the confines of the immediate nuclear family; they have to ritually signify their agreement to take up this role by their presence, if possible, at the christening itself, and also customarily by offering gifts to the child.

Godparents also represent one of several possible ways of augmenting or supplementing relations of kinship by consanguinity or birth, thus creating a wider network of support for persons as they grow up into adult life. Godparenthood relations tie children not only into the community of the church but also into the community at large. Ladislav Holy, in his textbook *Anthropological Perspectives on Kinship* (published by Pluto Press, London 1996, p. 166), provides some useful references on this phenomenon. Holy points out that godparent relations are like those of "created kinship" in Truk, Micronesia, where people who do not share substance nevertheless treat one another as kin. The point can be taken further, because there is more than one way of creating shared substance, for example, by sharing food, or sharing in a ritual act of baptism, as in the case of godparents.

In other traditions around the world, there are analogous ways of marking the event of birth. The marking may not happen at once, however. In some instances, people may wait to see if a child will survive before it is given a name, for example. Names, in turn, may be drawn from ancestral contexts and may indicate particular kinship identities. Naming gives a child a place in society, and combinations of names given to an individual express or create different aspects of identity. It is at baptisms that a child born into some Christian traditions is formally given its name in a religious context. But each child in a state-regulated society tends to have its identity and name fixed also by registration at a local government office, giving notice of who the parents are declared to be and the place of birth, the date of birth, and the name of the official who has certified these elements as factual. Birth certificates are like internal passports: They give the child entry into the secular world ruled by government and law, just as a passport, containing similar information to the birth certificate, is a mode of entry into an international world beyond the state. Birth certificates, or their equivalents, are often needed as forms of validation of who a person is; they are tied into, and depend specifically on, the context of kinship.

In clan or kin-based nonstate societies, there is no direct equivalent of legal registrations of births, but there are ways of identifying a child as a potential member of a community beyond the immediate family. In the Mount Hagen area of Papua New Guinea, the father of a child was formerly expected to take the afterbirth and part of the umbilical cord and bury these in the earth in or near to his settlement, and to plant a cordyline bush or banana stock on the spot, surrounding it with a small fence of stakes. Through these vital repositories of the mother and the child itself, the child was said to be rooted in the clan area of its birth, and thus to have claims on the clan land and the resources of its kin networks. The site was known in the local Melpa language as the *uklimb kut*, "the navel trench," or also the *kangambokla te pakla*, "the feces fence of the children," since the child's feces, again remnants of itself and its mother's milk, were for some time thrown into the space behind the fence, contributing to the growth of the plant within it and also, as people explained, preventing roaming pigs from inappropriately consuming the feces. The father was expected to construct the "navel trench" quietly and privately, but nevertheless his act established the identity of the child within the clan.[5]

NAMES AND NAMINGS

Names may carry considerable significance within the biographical history of a group. In the Pangia area in Papua New Guinea, children might be given names commemorating and expressing grief over the deaths of leading persons in their community.[6] Children born around the time of the death of such a leading person within the kin network might all be given different names improvised to recognize the death, so that their names become a register of a particular event in history, projecting its memory and significance forward into their own lifetimes. The references in the names would not necessarily overtly mark grief. They might, for example, refer to a flower that sprang up near the person's grave. But they all were intended to convey grief, and so can appropriately be called *penthonyms* (sorrow-names).[7] In other cultures, naming children directly after someone who has passed away has a similar intention.

In Pangia, there was another naming feature that was directly tied with kinship and the life cycle, as well as with marriage practices. When an eldest child was born, the parents afterward were referred to in third-party reference as "father of so and so" or "mother of so and so," marking their new status. Even after subsequent children were born, the parents were referred to with reference to their eldest child, whether this child was male or female. If the father had, as was sometimes the case in leading families, more than one wife, the firstborn child of each wife tended to be identified through its mother rather than the father, thus differentiating each woman's childbearing status from the others and placing the firstborn children accordingly. These usages are called *teknonyms*.[8] Interestingly, in Pangia the children were not called "son of so and so" or "daughter of so and so." The teknonyms picked out the parents, indicating that the birth of the child established their permanent status as such.

These names also functioned in reference, thus making them like titles in community discourse. Through habitual usage, they could also be extended over time to direct address—an idiosyncratic development since the forms of "father" and "mother" used in them were reference, not address, forms. Thus, the term of address for father is *arai* and for mother *aũwa*, both usually prefixed with the term for "my" (*anu*), becoming by assimilation *angarai* and *angaũwa*. But the teknonymic forms retain the reference terms of *erene* and *nine,* respectively, prefaced by the name of the child in question. The teknonym is thus formed out of the personal name (or *autonym*) of the child with the reference form of the term for father or mother, depending on which parent is being referred to.

Details of this kind may seem complicated to describe. But they are a part of daily habitual usage in communities in which kinship status and local society status are closely tied together and in which parenthood is a stage of life that is important for the constitution of the group. Naming practices in these cases tie self and group together. This is not in essence different from the Euro-American practice of tying personal names with surnames. The surname does not pick out a specific parent, but it does pick out a certain ancestral line. And becoming a parent for the first time is widely seen as a kind of initiating process into a stage of adulthood that leads to a new status in the community as a whole, beyond that of being simply "adult" or holding "citizenship."

Personal names given at birth are not necessarily permanent in all cultural settings. They tend to become fixed in bureaucratic circumstances where the names on the birth certificate remain permanently on record. Outside of this context, peer groups often give their members nicknames, marking them out as both individuals and members of a small in-group. In small-scale societies, with strong face-to-face relationships, stages and events in life may be accompanied by name changes. Among the Duna people of Papua New Guinea, parents might change a child's name if it became sick, and divination suggested that some of its ancestors were hostile to it because of the imputed wrongdoings of its senior kin.[9] The divination was conducted by sacrificing a pig and pouring blood from its nose into a shallow bark container. An expert looked into the fluid and determined signs of a dead kinsperson who might be responsible for making the child sick. To mark the occasion, and to remove the ghost's attention from the child, the parents might give the child a new name at this time. In Hagen, a comparable but different tactic was employed in one case: a mother who had lost her earlier children to illness named her next son *Andakit*, meaning "bad grandfather," to shame the spirit into letting the child be.

Names, of course, change in other circumstances as well. In Papua New Guinea, when people join a Christian church as adults, they are given an adult baptismal name reflecting their new identity. Often this also reflects the particular denomination of church they are joining. The Catholic practice of naming children after the names of saints, for example, leads to this kind of result.[10] In parts of Europe, there is a custom whereby a woman is expected to change her surname to that of her husband upon marriage, something that remains customary but not obligatory. This practice must have derived from the old practice, stemming from Roman law, of considering that the wife is incorporated into her husband's social group.

MATURATION

Maturation and the attainment of adulthood, as some of our examples have shown, can be marked in various ways. In Pangia, as a child grew up, its parents were expected to make a constant flow of gifts to its mother's people, as the *opianango*, "the kin of bearing." These gifts were not simply obligatory payments. They were to repay the mother's kin for the blood that the mother had transmitted to the child, blood identified with her own line of kin, and for her nurture of the child. Without such payments, the mother's kin might withdraw their goodwill, and the child, it was feared, would not grow properly. It was not just the living kin who were involved. The ghosts, or ancestral spirits, on the mother's side were those who could make the child sick or halt its growth by entering into its liver and influencing its well-being. The gifts made to ward off such ill will functioned as sacrifices to these ghosts since they would often include pigs or pork, which could be used as offerings to the spirits. In kinship contexts, a range of payments and gifts can be seen in this way: as gifts that are also sacrifices.

In Hagen there were similar practices, still holding in the 1960s. Earlier, we have noted how a Hagen father was expected to make a ritual site for the navel cord of his wife's newborn child. While the child was dependent on the mother's breast milk for sustenance, the couple should not have further sexual intercourse, for otherwise it was thought that the father's semen might enter the mother's milk and would make the child sick. (This form of abstinence during a period of time after the birth of a child is technically called a *postpartum taboo*.) After two or three years, the child would be considered ready to be weaned from the breast, and when this was accomplished, the father's kin were expected to present pork to the mother's people to thank them for the mother's "work" in nurturing the child. This gift was called the *wakl te kng*, "the pig of the child's feces," since the feces were said to contain mother's milk, and when the child's diet changed, its feces would also be altered.

A leading Hagen man might increase the amount of pork given beyond a minimal amount required, and the mother's kin might later respond with a return gift, thus building up a partnership around this point in the child's life cycle. Gifts of this kind formed a part of an extensive relationship of exchanging wealth between two leading men among the Kawelka people in Hagen, Ongka and Ndamba, in the 1960s and 1970s.[11] One of Ongka's wives was the daughter of one of Ndamba's wives.[12] This was Rumbukl, a forceful and able person, and her own active involvement in producing pigs for exchanges was the mainstay of this relationship, which developed out of her giving birth to a son, Namba.[13]

These "thanksgiving" gifts could, then, be integrated progressively into political contexts, transcending their original interpersonal kinship meanings. A son made the focus of these gifts could also expect to go to the mother's kin and ask for some wealth goods (valuable shells or small pigs) with which to begin his own entry into adult exchanges. In Hagen, there were no formal practices of initiation into adulthood (at least none that had survived through to the 1960s).[14] A boy began life in his mother's house, the "woman's house" (*manga ambnga*), and would stay there after he was weaned until about 10 years of age, when he would be encouraged to get some food and sleep in a small compartment in his father's "men's house" (*manga rapa*), nearby to his mother's house, perhaps just a grassy yard space away from it. The family and visitors or other kin would often in any case eat food from a shared earth oven in which vegetables and pork (on occasion) were steamed for communal consumption. A child could easily run from one side of the yard to the other, so a transition from the women's to the men's house was not difficult. (If the husband was *polygynous*, i.e., had a number of wives concurrently, each wife had her own women's house tucked away in a small location of its own, affording her some privacy and allowing the husband to visit also without being seen by everyone.) Moreover, a mother could still bring food to the doorway of a men's house for the husband and any of her sons if she chose to do so.

In Hagen, then, the typical transition of a boy to life in the men's house was gradual and unproblematic. At no stage was the boy definitively removed from the former context of his life. For girls, there was no residential break at all, since a girl stayed with her mother and from an early time learnt tasks in the house and the gardens. Girls were involved in planting, weeding, and harvesting sweet potatoes, which were washed in a stream and separated into smaller tubers—to feed raw (or sometimes cooked) to the pigs—and larger, better specimens—to bake in ashes or steam in the earth oven for the family and kinsfolk to eat. Men's and women's houses were built from timber and bark with roofs thatched by means of strong sword grass (*Imperata cylindrica*), which grew in fallow garden areas. Fires were always kept smouldering or with hot ashes in them, and sweet potato snacks could be prepared at any time, including by children.

The male leader Ongka has given an account of his childhood at Mbukl, the place to which his father's family had fled as a result of warfare in their old territory further south. Ongka makes it clear that childhood could be a time of play and fun (Strathern and Stewart 2000: 11–18, for reference see note 11). Some of the games mimicked adult activities, such as divining the cause of sickness, or finding small rodents and making an earth oven to cook them, saying they were pigs. Girls and boys helped each other to make model pigs out

An intimate moment in an extended (polygynous) family, Mount Hagen, Papua New Guinea. A man divides out parts of a slaughtered pig to be prepared for cooking. Vegetables lie in a metal dish. A small child looks on. Men and women of a family cooperate in sorting out the meat for distributions on occasions like this where social ties are strengthened and reaffirmed.   (Photo: P. J. Stewart/A. Strathern Archive)

of mud and play-acted killing and eating them. Ongka's accounts are charming and amusing. He notes, though, that after a while he grew tired of playing with mud pigs, and he recounts how:

> I asked my father to make a bow for me so I could go hunting small birds. The white men had not come at that time [the first explorers from outside arrived in Ongka's world in the 1930s]. We had to make things with stone tools, with just ordinary stones! [The outsider explorers later brought steel axes and other steel tools with them as trade goods.] . . . Well, my father made a bow and arrows for me,

Sides of cooked pork laid out for distribution at the settlement of a leader, Mount Hagen, Papua New Guinea. The man smiling is an in-law of the leader. Distributions of pork are central to the maintenance of peaceful social life among kin.   (Photo: P. J. Stewart/ A. Strathern Archive)

and I cut myself some branches to make a bird-blind. I had a pronged arrow strung ready and waited for birds to come. When I got my first bird I was delighted (Strathern and Stewart 2000: 1).

Onkga's account of this period of his life deals with his acquisition of skills. Even though the Hagen people have depended on sweet potato gardening for several hundred years, and horticulture in general may go back as far as 9,000 years BP,[15] there was still in the 1960s a delight in forest craft and forest lore in the northern part of the area where Ongka grew up, with thick stands of forest on the mountain slopes just to the north. The forest was an area for boys to learn such hunting skills, while girls specialized in gathering wild foods and especially in catching small frogs along watercourses within clan territories, searching for these by night along with adult women, who lit their search by means of burning torches of cane-grass. In both cases, then, the forest and wild areas were arenas in which boys and girls found pleasant food-getting diversions and learnt skills, as they gradually grew up into puberty with its physiological changes.

In many parts of New Guinea and in a great many of the areas of the world studied by anthropologists, this gradual easing into maturity did not hold. Instead, at some point either or both genders were inducted into special rituals called *puberty rites* or *initiation rites*. Puberty rites, as the name suggests, were performed at or around the time of puberty, most commonly for girls at first menstruation, which is in most cultures given some ritual recognition and entails girls learning how to manage their menstrual flows. Menarche for a girl unequivocally marks the possibility that she can become pregnant and bear a child. It does not necessarily mean that for that reason she is entitled to do so, but her potentiality to do so is signaled. In first menses rites, girls may be instructed on how to deal with their future sexual and reproductive activities, and in particular whether they can or cannot enter straightaway into these. Often, but by no means always, the right (or obligation) to do so is linked to becoming married. For boys, puberty rites as such are not so marked, but in some cases in New Guinea, rites of seclusion for boys were explicitly designed to apply magic to them to make them grow (mature). This was so for the Duna people, as we describe later.

"Initiation rites" is a broader term, always having to do with initiation into adulthood, and for boys it is especially connected with the assumption of statuses within the wider kin-based community beyond the immediate family. (This may be the case for girls also.)[16] Earlier theorists in anthropology, interested in psychological explanations, spilt much ink hypothesizing that young boys became attached to their mothers in circumstances where men and women kept separate houses and that initiation rites, sometimes accompanied by harsh actions, were "necessary" to break these attachments and force the boys into an adult male world. Ideas about the dangers of female menstrual blood were said to be a part of the means whereby such a separation was pressed on boys. Boys' initiation rites sometimes did indeed involve physically harsh tests and painful operations such as circumcision (the removal of the foreskin or prepuce from the penis) or subincision (the cutting of a slit on the underside of the penis). Examples of these two practices came from the Maasai people of Tanzania in East Africa and the Australian indigenous people, for example, the Arunta (Aranda/Arernte).[17] However, it is not necessary to suppose that these practices met any psychological requirement to break a boy's whole relationship with his mother or to resolve a cross-sex identity complex. Instead, they should be seen as projecting the boy into a world of male activities and labors, especially and prominently warfare, which could be demanding on their courage and endurance. This was true for the East African cases, in many of which (e.g., the Maasai)[18] boys would be initiated into a particular *age-set*, or group of boys all initiated at the same time across a number of families and neighborhoods, and each of these age-sets belonged at any given time to a particular *age-grade*, or named level of life-cycle status such as "youths" or "warriors." Beginning as "youths," each age-set would progress to "warriors" and then to "married men" and "elders." Age-sets are ways of aggregating youths across family lines, like classes of children in schools in the Euro-American education system. Age-grades mark how the life cycle is formally demarcated and coordinate people's entry into each grade, ending with elderhood and death.

The age-set/age-grade phenomenon is probably correlated with pastoral societies in East Africa and with their practices of mobilizing large numbers of warriors. The phenomenon is political and outside of the framework of kinship and descent. In New Guinea, initiations were organized directly by kin groups and were part of the wider structure of kinship itself. They were particularly marked in the Eastern Highlands of Papua New Guinea where warriorhood was important in precolonial times and clans or wider groups such as *phratries* (sets of clans claiming common ancestry) or *tribes* (alliances of clans that may or may not claim common ancestry) were often at odds with one another and where exchanges of wealth between groups were not so highly developed as they were, for example, in Hagen to the west.

Growth rites for boys, found in populations from the Enga area west of Hagen as far as the Duna, had a different purpose and represent an interesting cultural development outside of warfare. Although warfare was a part of life in these societies too, rituals of seclusion for boys were to make them grow into young men who would be attractive to girls and to make them strong enough to handle the supposed rigors and hazards of sexual activity, which, it was thought, could be physically depleting for them. Among the Duna, the seclusion house was called the *palena anda*, "the house of ginger" (i.e., magic house). Senior bachelors, devotees of a Female Spirit known as the Payame Ima, and related to the boys in general as their paternal uncles, immediate or classificatory, taught the boys magic to make their skins or bodily surfaces good, that is, healthy with a layer of fat beneath the skin. They also taught them magic to make their hair grow long, combing it and clipping it to make wigs that the boys could wear when, after some months, they would ceremonially exit from their secluded life. On their emergence, predictably, they looked bigger and more handsome. They could now take part in courting occasions (*yekeanda*) at which they could play songs to girls on their mouth harps and girls responded with mouth-bow music, passing on verbal messages through the inflections of the music itself (a practice found developed to a high degree also in Pangia).[19]

Practices of this kind were not secular. They all had to do with spirit forces and their influences on life, as well as with kin relations. One of the Eastern Highlands people of Papua New Guinea, known as the Siane, had particularly elaborate first menses rites for girls, as a prelude to their entry into courting practices.

R. F. Salisbury, who studied the Siane in the field in 1952–1953, shortly after colonial administration began there, noted that a girl's first menses were "treated as a form of pregnancy," in which she gave birth only to blood. This blood was seen as belonging to her father's line and had to be "birthed" in the father's clan place. (This is analogous to the cordyline planting ritual in Hagen discussed earlier.) Men sang courting songs to the girl while she lay behind a fence of aromatic branches in her mother's house. After six evenings, older wives married into the clan gave her knowledge of adult life as a woman, and a senior man handed over ancestral spirit to her in the shape of sugarcane for her to eat. Next day, she cooked and ate a special meal, gave a part of it to the singers, and for the next two months she was expected to stay in the village in a woman's house shared by nubile, unmarried girls who could entertain courting visitors. A special version of this ritual was performed for a girl who by kinship rank was considered the "oldest sister" of a small lineage (Salisbury 1962: 73–74).[20] This "oldest sister," Salisbury says, symbolically represents the whole lineage and is described as the "house post person" of the group (p. 75). The central house post is seen as holding up the whole house. In the same way, the sister holds up the whole clan by means of her female fertility, even though among the Siane descent is traced through males. Apart from this striking point, the example shows us again an intersection between the individual, the family context, the clan, and the life cycle.

We deal with marriage itself, the outcome of courting, in a later chapter. The life cycle, punctuated by birth, maturation, marriage, and reproduction, ends with death, and it is at death that sets of kin are elaborately mobilized. Death may also mark a crucial point of transition between the generations.

A funeral among the Duna people, Papua New Guinea. Women and children cluster round the place where the coffin will be placed. Women do the major mourning, including the singing of laments, at Duna funerals. Men dig the grave and make the wooden coffins and grave supports. In the background are banana plants, fruit pandanus, grassland, and forest. Graves are made in garden sites. The dead still belong with the living, although their spirits are sent away by mourning songs to the high limestone rocks above the settlement levels.   (Photo: P. J. Stewart/A. Strathern Archive)

Death is, of course, an occasion for formal grieving. While a new child represents a gain for the group, a death is a loss, and the loss is felt most keenly by those who have lived close to the deceased, who in many instances are also their kin. With the dispersal of kin and kin-based groups that results from travel and employment, kinsfolk may not have stayed close to the deceased; but they still may be expected to come to the funeral. This is as true for contemporary Euro-American societies as it is for the small-scale groups of Papua New Guinea, some of whose members may be away in employment or study elsewhere. A funeral, even more than a marriage, is expected to mobilize kin. Whatever their practical relationship with the deceased, the death is thought to obligate them to come and "pay their last respects." Kinsfolk may ask to see the deceased before the body is interred or cremated. At one funeral in Hagen in the 1970s, a longtime local evangelist for the Lutheran Church died, and one of his sons, who was studying in the capital city Port Moresby far away, was not able to get to the funeral quickly. He arrived after the body had been placed in the coffin (an introduced Christian practice) and went into a paroxysm of grief, pounding at the coffin and demanding that it be opened up so that he could see his father's body. He also wanted to know why people did not wait for him.

Kinsfolk come to a funeral to mourn, but they come to do more than mourn. A death may precipitate a family conference about what is to happen to property, how to interpret or respond to a legal will if there is one; how to handle the funeral itself, who is to speak and what they will say; how to put on a funeral feast. The funeral must recognize and produce closure on one set of relationships while opening up and renewing others. Kin should show solidarity in mourning but may quarrel over what to do when the funeral is over. Sometimes the question of cause of death is important, and not only in cases of sickness, suicide, or murder. In New Guinea, many deaths can be attributed to acts of sorcery or witchcraft, and the surviving kin seek to find out who has committed such acts. There are also regular death-payments to be made regardless of the cause of death, principally, like other life-cycle payments, to mother's kin, who may arrive at the funeral protesting at the death and blaming the father's kin for not preventing it. A death can therefore be expensive, with death duties payable to maternal kin rather than to the state. If the deceased person held a number of positions or offices, successorship to these has to be decided, and may be important, as in the case of the pope or a reigning monarch. All in all, death requires both the recognition of loss and the need to repair it, and it brings crucially into focus the contingent character of intergenerational ties of kinship. No wonder that the first task is to admit the death itself and achieve closure.

Among the Duna, this closure was achieved in two ways. First, the kinsfolk had to be able to see the body. (This seems to be a universal wish, so that the knowledge of a death can be certain and proper mourning can be carried out.) One leader declared, "If I do not see my sister's body, I will think she is still alive. She must be brought here and buried at my place, so

I have her nearby." The second part of his statement indicated how closure is also effected by burying the body in the right place, the home place, for without this order cannot be reestablished. Actually, among the Duna, as in other cases, disputes could arise about who could have the body and where it should be buried. These disputes arose out of the importance of ties on both mother's and father's side in the Duna system of kinship and descent, which was *cognatic*. Kin on either side might claim the body, to keep it on their own land. The spirit, *tini*, was also enjoined in women's elaborate and moving mourning songs to fly away and take up a new abode in rock shelters high up in the forests of the group territory. Both the body and the *tini* spirit were to be retained within the kin group. A married woman's body might be claimed by her husband's group. Even so, a ritual could be performed to bring her spirit back to her natal place if it was said to be unhappy at the husband's place and was causing people there to be sick. Kin groups thus consist of both their living and their dead. While this specific structure does not hold everywhere, people often remember their ancestors, visit their graves, regard them in general as a part of their lives, and in some cultures consider that they visit them in dreams and continue to affect them, bringing good or bad fortune. A kind of "life" goes on in the life cycle beyond "the grave."[21]

Two children carry large pumpkins home to be cooked by their families in the Duna area, Papua New Guinea. The girls pass by sweet potato plots and a small set of circular plantings of peanuts (a recent introduction). Duna girls learn early on to help their mothers with gardening tasks and carrying food home. Pumpkins were also introduced to the Duna in colonial times. They are a very popular food, usually cooked in earth ovens.   (Photo: P. J. Stewart/A. Strathern Archive)

Three young girls, siblings of an extended family, at a cooking of pork among the Duna people of Papua New Guinea, set in a secluded area away from the possibly envious looks of witches. The girls are happy at the prospect of food cooked in the earth oven. Location: Hagu settlement.   (Photo: P. J. Stewart/A. Strathern Archive)

Conclusion

In this chapter, we have taken a brief look at a few features of the life cycle to which everyone is subject. At each stage, we have tried to show the social involvement with kin and some special features of how that involvement is played out: at birth, by ritual inductions such as baptism and naming; the creation of a link with place, shown at various stages (e.g., the cordyline planting ritual in Hagen, Siane first menses rites, places of burial among the Duna); in maturation, with the linkages between family and community, and in the special institutions of puberty, growth, and initiation rites; and at death, with the need to achieve closure on some fronts of kin ties while reorganizing these in other ways. While many of our examples have drawn on cases from our own work in Papua New Guinea, much of what we have written applies more widely, and students or readers of the book could think further about this by asking themselves how the life cycle is symbolized in their own society and how kin relations are linked during the life cycle to wider social institutions, for example marriage and the birth of children.

Questions to Consider

1. Why do you think rituals are often performed to mark stages in the life cycles of kin?
2. What do names and naming practices do in the sphere of kinship? Think both of your own experience and the cross-cultural context.

Notes

1. See, for example, Meyer Fortes, "The first born," in *Religion, Morality, and the Person: Essays on Tallensi Religion*, ed. J. Goody (Cambridge: Cambridge University Press, 1987), 247–286.
2. Robert Louis Stevenson, *The Master of Ballantrae* (London: Cassell, 1889).
3. See references to siblinghood in Meyer Fortes, *Kinship and the Social Order* (Chicago, IL: Aldine, 1969).
4. See Pamela J. Stewart and Andrew Strathern, *Remaking the World* (Washington, D.C.: Smithsonian Institution Press, 2002), 98–99.
5. See Pamela J. Stewart and Andrew Strathern, *Humors and Substances: Ideas of the Body in New Guinea* (Westport, Bergin and Garvey: Greenwood Publishing, 2001), 92–94.
6. The people of Pangia District in the Southern Highlands Province of Papua New Guinea speak the Wiru language. See Jeffrey Clark, *Steel to Stone* (Oxford: Oxford University Press, 2000); and Andrew J. Strathern, "Wiru and Daribi Matrilateral Payments," *Journal of the Polynesian Society* 80, no. 4 (1971): 449–462.
7. See Andrew Strathern, "Wiru Penthonyms," *Bijdragen*, Deel 126 (1970): 58–74.
8. See Rodney Needham, "The system of teknonyms and death-names of the Penan," *Southwestern Journal of Anthropology* 10, no. 4 (1954): 416–431, for an exposition on the interrelations of naming practices and kinship among the Penan people of North-Western Borneo.
9. See Pamela J. Stewart and Andrew Strathern, *Remaking the World* (Washington, D.C.: Smithsonian Institution, 2002), 85.
10. In the Mount Hagen area of Papua New Guinea, an early Lutheran missionary-linguist, Hermann Strauss, developed an ingenious practice of adapting the original personal name of a convert by giving a Christian meaning to it. Thus, for example, the name Kuri, meaning "white bird of Paradise," became Kur-iti, "a witness" (to the Gospel).
11. See Andrew Strathern and Pamela J. Stewart, *Collaborations and Conflicts: A Leader Through Time* (Fort Worth, TX: Harcourt College Publishers, 2000).
12. As a "big-man," or leader, among the Kawelka, Ongka had a number of wives, who helped him to raise pigs as forms of wealth and provided connections of alliance for him to their natal kin.
13. Rumbukl and Namba both predeceased Ongka and were given honorific decorated sites for their graves, Rumbukl at Kuk where Ongka had moved back to his father Kaepa's original place, and Namba in the place Mbukl at the head of an old Kawelka ceremonial ground, where he had originally been brought up. Kawelka history is discussed in Andrew J. Strathern, *One Father, One Blood* (Canberra: Australian National University Press, 1972). Rumbukl's grave is illustrated on p. 138 of "Collaborations and Conflicts."
14. Hermann Strauss (with Herbert Tischner), *Die Mi-Kultur der Hagenberg Stämme* (Hamburg: De Gruyter, 1962), 319–322, refers to certain practices as "initiation" in Hagen, pointing to the induction of boys into ritual events and the first cutting of their hair and forming of head-wraps. For an extensive discussion of related questions, see Pamela J. Stewart and Andrew Strathern, *Gender, Song, and Sensibility: Folktales and Folksongs in the Highlands of New Guinea* (Westport: Praeger (Greenwood Publications), 2002), 165–210. For an earlier discussion centered on the Hagen area, see Andrew Strathern, "Flutes, birds, and hair in Hagen, Papua New Guinea," *Anthropos* 84 (1989): 81–89.

15. See Andrew Strathern and Pamela J. Stewart, eds., *Kuk Heritage: Issues and Debates in Papua New Guinea* (Pittsburgh, PA: University of Pittsburgh, 1998). For an earlier account, see J. Golson, "The Ipomoean revolution revisited: Society and the Sweet Potato in the Upper Wahgi Valley," in *Inequality in New Guinea Highlands Societies*, ed. A. Strathern (Cambridge: Cambridge University Press), 109–136 (reissued with new Preface by Andrew Strathern and Pamela J. Stewart, 2009).

16. For an early discussion of girls' initiation rites among the Bemba of Zambia (Africa), see Audrey I. Richards, *Chisungu: A Girls' Initiation Ceremony among the Bemba of Zambia* (London: Tavistock, 1982). For a set of studies from the South-West Pacific, see Nancy C. Lutkehaus and Paul B. Roscoe, eds., *Gender Rituals: Female Initiation in Melanesia* (London and New York: Routledge, 1995).

17. See, in general, on masculinity among the Maasai, the historically nuanced account by Dorothy L. Hodgson, "Once Intrepid Warriors," in *Gendered Modernities*, ed. Dorothy L. Hodgson (New York: Palgrave, 2001), 105–145. On the Arunta, see the early classic study by B. Spencer and F. Gillen, *The Aranda* (London: Macmillan, 1927).

18. See Paul Spencer, *The Maasai of Matapato: A Study of Rituals of Rebellion* (Bloomington, IN: Indiana University Press, 1988).

19. On Duna growth rituals for boys, see Pamela J. Stewart and Andrew Strathern, *Gender, Song and Sensibility*, chap. 7, esp. (Westport: Praeger (Greenwood Publications), 2002); also A. Strathern, *Empowering the Past* (New York: Palgrave Macmillan, 2004), 40, 52, 75, 94, 166.

20. Richard F. Salisbury, *From Stone to Steel* (Melbourne: Melbourne University Press, 1962). See also Richard F. Salisbury, "The Siane of the Eastern Highlands," in *Gods, Ghosts, and Men in Melanesia*, ed. Peter Lawrence and Mervyn J. Meggitt (New York: Oxford University Press, 1965), 50–77. For a reanalysis of the Siane materials, see Andrew Strathern and Pamela J. Stewart, "Cults, Closures, and Collaborations," in *Women as Unseen Characters*, ed. P. Bonnemère (Philadelphia, PA: University of Pennsylvania Press, 2004), 120–130 (for the ASAO); and Pamela J. Stewart and Andrew Strathern, "Power and Placement in Blood Practices," ed. Janet Hoskins, special issue, *Ethnology* 41, no. 4 (2002): 349–363. See also Thomas Buckley and Alma Gottlieb, eds., *Blood Magic* (Berkeley, CA: University of California Press, 1988).

21. See Pamela J. Stewart and Andrew Strathern, "Cosmology, Resources, and Landscape: Agencies of the Dead and the Living in Duna, Papua New Guinea," *Ethnology* 44, no. 1 (2005): 35–47.

CHAPTER 3

Concepts in Reproduction

BIRTH AND SOCIAL REPRODUCTION

Poetic and literary writings often capture one moment in the drama of life, the pain of the birthing process itself and the apprehension of danger in the world at large as opposed to the temporary security of the mother's womb; the pathos of the human child, unable to fend for itself, needing care, and not yet fully "developed." Images of this kind are diagnostic of deep feelings about "the human condition," and they concentrate on the parent–child bond, which is sometimes cited as the central one in kinship ties.

Such images exist and are appealed to in all societies. The basic processes of the life cycle are thought to underpin social continuity in general. Social reproduction in a wider sense, of course, includes other things. It implies cultural continuity in practices, values, and attitudes that depends on socialization and explicit teaching. It also implies continuity in major institutions such as the family itself, for example, continuity in its form and how it is embedded within wider structures. The heated contemporary debates and struggles within the United States regarding same-sex marriages result from pressures to change the gendered form of the family and the resistance to those pressures. And since same-sex marriages do not involve couples who could reproduce their own offspring without recourse to some other source of fertility, the implications are considerable. (We should notice, however, that this is not uniquely so, since adoption and the use of sperm or egg donors or surrogate wombs objectively involve the same sorts of processes.)

Concepts of reproduction, then, are vital to society but vary considerably. As such concepts sometimes focus on notions that may be labeled as "biological," they tend to be taken for granted, or, as anthropologists have put it, they are *naturalized*, while in fact they are culturally specific, at least in certain

Among the Duna people of Papua New Guinea, a young woman with two children, one a relatively newborn infant. Two other women of the locality sit nearby. Women with children continue to do their ordinary work of gardening, and carry both children and food in capacious netbags which they manufacture themselves from plant fibers.   (Photo: P. J. Stewart/A. Strathern Archive)

regards. William Blake's poetic image of the child leaping actively out of the womb grants an agency and individuality to the figure of the child, which represents one part of the ideas regarding birth (Blake, "Infant Sorrow," 1979). But immediately following this is his depiction of the child as a helpless and shadowy being requiring care for it to become fully "human." These two elements of individuality and dependency are replicated in many cultural settings, including those in New Guinea.

Concepts of reproduction can also be considered cultural *ideologies*, that is, as ideas that are reinforced by sanctions and upheld as dominant and correct in the society. Classifying these ideas as ideology shows their importance in shaping society's major institutional forms. (We use the term "society" here as a shorthand for social organization at large, not as a bounded entity that is fully homogeneous or centrally governed. By "Hagen society," for example, we refer to social arrangements that hold, or held, widely in the cultural-linguistic-geographical area we identify as "Mount Hagen," with some 80,000–100,000 speakers of related dialects.)

Anthropologists began to think about notions of reproduction as ideologies, or sometimes as "religious dogmas," after they realized that there can be problems in referring to such notions simply as beliefs. This is because it is hard to know what any one individual may personally "believe," but it is possible to observe what ideas are publicly supported, given value, and are adhered to in situations of conflict. These contexts, then, can stand proxy in our enquiries for "beliefs." However, we need not throw out the concept of "belief" entirely here. It is useful as a marker of personal or collective commitments in cases other than those where people's actions are a result of sheer coercion (see Kirsch 2004). With these points in mind, we return to the controversies about notions of kinship among the Trobrianders of the southeast coast of Papua New Guinea, discussed in Chapter 1.

TROBRIAND CONCEPTS OF REPRODUCTION

The case of the Trobrianders, first widely brought to attention by Bronislaw Malinowski, illustrates how anthropological findings have from time to time gained publicity because of their apparent challenge to cultural presuppositions. (Margaret Mead's writings about sexual practices and norms in Samoa also had the same effect, giving rise to a great deal of controversy, see Freeman 1983.) Malinowski's findings about Trobriand ideas of reproduction, which apparently suggested that they dispensed with the idea of biological fatherhood, were considered challenging.

In fact, this interpretation of Malinowski's findings was based on a misundertanding which arose from thinking that reproduction stems from an exclusive moment of conception. This is the form of thinking that has come to be the folk or popular model in Euro-American contexts, based on the findings of biological science. In this model, the moment of the union of sperm and egg is seen as the moment of conception and is ineluctable in its implications. This folk–scientific amalgam has been reinforced by DNA-based science. Its form is quantitative, suggesting that each parent contributes half of the genetic materials for the child; the contributions are also seen as qualitatively different but of the same genetic "kind." People are thus initially seen as made out of units called "genes" and sets of genes, which entail phenotypic results or characteristics as the person grows and matures. Of course, even in this biological model many Euro-Americans say they believe that the conception was made possible through cosmological interventions, for example, "by the grace of God."

Trobriand ideas are quite different from this genetic notion. They are directed firmly toward the affiliation of children to their mother's lineage or subclan (the *dala*), which is important in the constitution of Trobriand society

(Weiner 1988). They do not depend, however, on ideas about the body in isolation from the spirit world, as in a purely biological model. Instead, children are thought to result from the voluntary entry of a spirit child into the mother. The spirit is always one that belongs to the woman's *dala*. After a person's death, he or she is thought to become a spirit and travel to the land of the dead, the island of Tuma. The spirit, once there, may grow old again, then slough off its skin and be renewed. In order to be reborn into the society of the living, the spirit has to travel across the surface of the sea and enter a particular woman of its subclan. After it is lodged there and the mother becomes aware of it, she continues to have intercourse with her husband, whose substance and actions of intercourse are held to mold the fetus so that when the child is born it will resemble him as the father. If we count the entry of the spirit child into the mother to be the moment of "conception," then, clearly husbands have nothing to do with this. The process, thus far, is autogenic and cyclical within the matri-lineage. But after this point, the father has an important role to play in giving an individual appearance to the child, by means of actions which are sexual but are best thought of as ways of feeding the fetus and making the child grow in his image. The child begins as a matrilineal spirit but emerges from the womb with the imprint of its father upon its body, including the face. Since "face" and personhood are strongly linked in many New Guinea cultures, the father has a significant and permanent tie with the children of the mother, provided it is he who has had regular intercourse with her. The claim of the father is therefore every bit as "biological" as that of the mother, whose initial tie with the child is actually based on the recycling of spirit in her matrilineage.

Earlier misunderstandings of the Trobriand case were based on the idea that the role of "biological father" was not recognized, because the father played no role in "conception." The mistake here lies in the unthinking applica-tion of the ethnocentric concepts of "biology" and "conception" in accordance with an exogenous folk theory. Trobriand ideas of conception and biology, in a broader, less ethnocentric, sense, clearly reveal different but complementary roles for mother and father in the creation of a child, and Trobriand social practices reinforce this point (Weiner 1988: 51–65). The Trobriand case strongly reaffirms the robust quality of the concept, first introduced by Meyer Fortes, of "complementary filiation" (Fortes 1969: 98): in cases where descent and group membership are strongly affirmed as belonging to one side of a person's kin universe, for example on the *matrilineal* side, with ties traced exclusively through mothers, personal ties are also strongly affirmed on the other side. Putting this into technical terms, in the Trobriand case, descent is clearly and strongly matrilineal, but this is balanced by *complementary patrifiliation*.[1]

At one stage, the debates about Trobriand kinship were couched in terms that compared Trobriand ideas to the notion of "virgin birth" (Leach 1969). Nothing could be further from the actual situation. Virginity is not valued by the Trobrianders in this way. Young people begin (or began, until the influence of Christian churches deepened among them since the 1980s) their sexual lives before marriage and pursue these vigorously. After marriage it is a different matter, and we have already seen why. Since fatherhood is important for the society at large, the best way for a couple to ensure a mutual commitment to their child is to restrict their sexual intercourse exclusively to each other. This explains why premarital sexual relations can be multiple, while in marriage this is no longer normatively permitted. The following might be an answer to why in the time of Malinowski, the primary fieldworker in the Trobriands from 1914 to 1918, unmarried girls apparently did not often become pregnant: It is possible that this was because by the time of their menarche they tended to be married anyway, and menarche might be later than in the case today, as a result of dietary and other lifestyle changes.

IDEAS OF REPRODUCTION AND SOCIAL STRUCTURE

The Trobriand case, discussed above, makes it clear that concepts regarding reproduction may closely mirror social structure. Here we use the term "social structure" to refer to the basic social divisions and groupings within the society at large. Given that these divisions among the Trobrianders are organized matrilineally, the idea that the spirits of the matrilineage are recycled through the bodies/wombs of its women over time obviously fits with a strong emphasis on matrilineal ties.

Not all matrilineal systems, however, depend on such a notion of reincarnation. And notions about sexual activity and reproduction may be quite similar, whether descent in terms of group membership is traced through females (matrilineally) or males (patrilineally). Douglas Oliver ([1955] 1967: 69–70, 170) made a detailed ethnographic study of the Siuai people on Bougainville Island, which is a part of Papua New Guinea. The Siuai trace descent matrilineally. He tells us that the Siuai considered the fetus to be "formed out of the sexual fluids (*kosi*) of both mother and genitor [the putative physical father]. A man's fluid is stored inside his penis until emitted; it contains some of his strength (*itikaivo*) along with some of the material that goes into making his blood" (Oliver 1967). If a man engages in too much intercourse and is weakened by this, he can regain strength by eating coconuts and fresh almonds (p. 70). Ten to fifteen acts of intercourse in a single menstrual cycle are said to be enough to begin a fetus: The fluids turn into blood and form the nucleus of a heart. After this, the prospective mother declines any further intercourse because this might harm the fetus. Instead of the man's semen, her own blood, no longer discharged in menstruation, goes to build up the child (p. 70).

Interestingly, Oliver's informants told him that the initial process of building up a child in the womb can only be conducted through intercourse with one man. If more than one man is involved, their fluids cannot combine, it was said, and so no fetus would be made. When an infant is born, both its body and soul are weak, and the link between them is thought to be fragile and has to be strengthened by care and nurture over time (1967: 70).

Oliver comments, "The child . . . is therefore a true product both of mother and genitor, formed of materials from both their bodies" (1967: 70). He also notes that Siuai think "a girl cannot bear children until she menstruates," and "this can occur only after she has begun to copulate" (p. 71).

These notions clearly delineate physical roles in the creation of a child that belong to both women and men. Similar notions are common in many societies where the dominant perspectives of descent lean on the patrilineal, rather than the matrilineal side, as is the case for the Siuai. Meyer Fortes' ideas are again helpful in understanding why this can be so. Fortes (1969) distinguishes clearly between *filiation* and *descent*. *Filiation* is the tie between parent and child; *descent* is the tie between the child and the larger group to which it belongs in cases where this is ideally determined by a line of descent from an ancestor. What we call "conception" ideas may refer to either or both of these domains. Siuai ideas, as sketched above, seem to relate clearly to the realm of filiation, without reference to descent. Trobriand ideas, by contrast, combine elements of descent and filiation: the maternal tie is linked to descent, the paternal one to filiation.

Concepts of reproduction may be difficult to describe. Anthropologists have adapted terms like "descent" and "filiation" from ordinary English usage and given them more technical meanings, as we have just seen. The term "kinship" itself has complex layers of meaning, as we pointed out in Chapter 1. The Trobriand case shows that we have to be careful about what is perceived to be "biological." One anthropologist, David M. Schneider, used another Pacific Island case to challenge the generalization of the connection between "kinship" and physiological ideas of procreation as basic to it.

Schneider took materials for this discussion from his and others' study of people in Yap Island in Micronesia.[2] He worked through a number of indigenous terms of social groupings. Central to these terms was the idea of the *tabinau*. The *tabinau* was a term applied to a co-residential landholding unit whose members worked with and took care of each other. Women were born members of a particular *tabinau*, but they were also said to become members of the *tabinau* into which they married and with which they resided and worked after their marriage.

When marriage entails the wife leaving her natal place and living at the husband's place, it is said to be *virilocal*. More complicatedly, it may be *patrivirilocal*, that is, residence is with the husband's father's group. If the *tabinau* is seen as a local kin group focused around males, this is the residential situation found on Yap. The term *tabinau* is often used with more than one strict meaning. In some contexts, it refers to members strictly by descent; in others, it extends to include in-married spouses. Schneider himself notes this possibility (1984: 21).

One of the features of the *tabinau* that is commonly found cross culturally is that each *tabinau* possesses a stock of personal names which "are given to the children of women who marry men of the *tabinau*" (Schneider 1984: 22). In fact, a child should be given the name of its paternal grandfather (to use this way of referring to the relationship) by the decision of *tabinau* elders, and after that divination is performed to see if this ancestor agrees with the name being bestowed in this way (p. 22). Names are selected in this way particularly for the elder male children. The *tabinau* spirits are called the group's *thagith*. Naming practices clearly delineate *tabinau* membership and associate it with the ongoing tutelage of these spirits.

Yapese ideas about conception changed over time with increasing American influence. Schneider wrote that "in 1947–48 when I worked on Yap I was assured by those who were knowledgeable . . . that coitus had nothing to do with the conception of children" (1984: 28). He goes on: "The decisive element was that the *tabinau* spirits (*thagith*) of the husband's *tabinau* interceded with a spirit (*marialang*), and this spirit accomplished the pregnancy by assigning a spirit to form the child in the mother's 'stomach' " (p. 28). Schneider does not elaborate on what kind of spirit the *marialang* was thought to be, but he speaks generally of "nature spirits" with which the *thagith* interceded via a diviner on behalf of humans, so we may assume that the *marialang* was one of these nature spirits, a part of the overall Yapese cosmos.

The Yapese idea that "conception" is the entry of a spirit into the mother's womb exactly parallels Trobriand notions, although in a context which, using other terminology, we would recognize as patrilineal rather than matrilineal. But the Yap situation was made even more complex by the fact that the children of sisters of the *tabinau* were described as its *mafen*, and these children also held custodianship rights over the *tabinau* land. An in-marrying woman who had children was the point of creation for a new small set of maternal kin (her children) constituting what was called a *genung* group. These children's rights to hold the husband's *tabinau* land were contingent on the agreement of the *tabinau's mafen*. In practice, the rights were gained not simply through the maternal or the paternal tie but by work. Access to land and succession to headship in the *tabinau* were gained in exchange for work (Schneider 1984: 29). If the mother and her children did not work in this way, they could be removed from *tabinau* land. And if a woman left her husband's *tabinau*, she was not allowed to take her children with her. The children belonged to the *tabinau*. She was no longer called by the title *citiningen* of these children, which we would be inclined to translate as "mother." Instead, either the next wife or the sister of the husband she left would gain the title of *citiningen* (p. 30).

This "traditional" Yapese situation (i.e., the one holding in 1947–1948 in Schneider's account) clearly presents a number of challenges to what we may call the equation of social and biological kinship, a challenge that Schneider puts forth more generally in the bulk of his 1984 book. The central claim, that coitus and "conception" were not seen as connected, is the same as we found for the Trobriands. But there was no notion, according to Schneider, corresponding to Trobriand ideas of fatherhood, that a father's substance molds or creates the appearance of the child. Schneider is in fact silent on this point. When it comes to "motherhood," however, he is a little more explicit. Although he has argued that the title of *citiningen* can shift from one woman to another in the *tabinau*, he also writes, "coming from the same belly remains explicit in the cultural conception as something which entails special bonds of warmth, love, loyalty, respect, trust, and mutual help" (1984: 79). An adopted child does not lose its relationship with the woman from whose womb it came (p. 79): a point that surely modifies Schneider's observation that a divorced woman cannot take her children with her and someone else becomes their *citiningen*. Clearly, *citiningen* is one of those words that can mean more than one thing, like *tabinau*. This mother–child tie might then be taken as emblematic of personal kinship relations in Yap, just as the *tabinau* is emblematic of the idea of the group. The core of kinship would, then, be the mother–child tie. The *tabinau* itself is more like a legal or political-economic structure, buttressed by ideas of locality and spirit power.

As a footnote here, Schneider notes that the next fieldworker on Yap, David Labby, found that 20 years after his own work Yapese ideas had apparently changed. "Now the view was that the man planted the seed, the woman being like a garden: the seed had to be nurtured and tended and this took place in the woman, the garden" (p. 28). Where did this idea come from? It is not an American idea. It is apparently an endogenous Yapese creation, and perhaps it was based on a set of latent or alternative notions previously present in the way the Yapese talked about the world (what anthropologists have called *muted discourse*).

One strong impression that we gain from the discussion of the *tabinau* is that it was basically a legal structure, perhaps designed to protect land rights in a situation of potential land shortage on a small island.

LEGAL CONTEXTS

Writings about kinship in general show the same duality that we have just seen in the Yapese case. From one viewpoint, kinship looks like a legal system; from another, it looks like a set of emotional predispositions. This duality is catered to by the distinction that Meyer Fortes made between the *politico-jural* and the *domestic* domains of social life (Fortes 1969). While the distinction has sometimes been criticized as being too rigid (because these domains are in practice intertwined) or perhaps even ethnocentric, it remains a generally useful way of thinking about data on kinship.

The distinction holds across a wide range of societies. Societies without centralized or state control, such as that of the Trobrianders or the Yapese, of course did not have, prior to colonial control, systems of law administered by overall authorities. They did have ideas of binding customs, with social or spiritual sanctions to support them. The Trobriand *dala* (see Section "Trobriand Concepts of Reproduction") and the Yapese *tabinau* (see Section "Ideas of Reproduction and Social Structure") were legal structures. We may sometimes forget that this point is just as true for what we call "the family" in Euro-American contexts. The family may be underpinned by ideas of love and trust (or undermined by their opposites, hate and distrust), but in the society at large it too is a legal structure, with political and economic ramifications. Since families are normatively expected to form households and households may have to have a legally representative or responsible person recognized as "head of household," we can see already that the categories of the state impinge on the structure of the family. Gender may be at work if the head of household is expected to be male, in the old Roman-derived pattern of *pater familias* ("father of the family").[3]

Family structure may depend generally on the status of the parents in marriage, and marriage is fundamentally a legal contract. This is precisely what distinguishes it from sexual cohabitation, even though such cohabitation is in another sense supposed to be central to the marriage relationship. Marital partners acquire rights and duties in relation to each other that set the relationship apart from other social ties. These rights and ties pertain most often to children, property, and finances, during the lifetime of the marriage or the lifetime of the partners. But such rights and duties are also greatly influenced by wider features of society. As anthropologists are fond of pointing out, hunter-gatherer modes of economic subsistence do not lend themselves to elaborate forms of enduring property rights. Instead, the duties of spouses to each other are set into a network of wider kin ties and are related to the overall food quest.

Food quest, division of labor, gender relations, and kinship obligations all tend to go together. If most gathering is done by women and most hunting for animal meat is done by men, each partner to a marriage contributes a different kind of food to the family. A much-studied case of the phenomenon is that of the !Kung San people of the Kalahari Desert in Southern Africa. Women gather nuts and dig for roots, providing most of the staple food for their immediate families. Men hunt for large animals, such as varieties of antelope or deer known as impala and kudu. When a man captures such an animal, he must distribute a good portion of its meat to his wife's family, and this pattern continues into the life of the marriage as a whole. This is a type of *brideservice*. The meat, however, does not go exclusively to the wife's natal family. It is likely to be shared out widely among the members of the small, co-residential band of kinsfolk, who move across the land in search of food. The hunter who gives gifts of meat strengthens his marriage, as well as his bonds in the small community to which he belongs. Generous giving brings prestige. But for a young husband it is in the first place an obligation to his wife's family. The band does not possess elaborate personal property or fixed places of dwelling. "Inheritance" of property is not important, then. What is important is that both girls and boys should get to know their environment well, as the source of their livelihood. Knowledge is the most important possession, and it is gained gradually by practical experience and living with the band. The nuclear family is closely merged with the wider band (Stockard 2002: 19–22). Stockard, who draws in her account on the firsthand researches of others, points out that while a father-in-law must depend on his younger son-in-law to provide him with good meat, the son-in-law expects to learn about the territory where he will hunt from the father-in-law, because he has moved to live near his in-laws in order to carry out his brideservice. Meat and knowledge are thus exchanged, and this exchange takes the place of inheritance.

Brideservice societies are often contrasted with those where *bridewealth* is important. Bridewealth is wealth paid by a groom's kin to the bride's kin, in association with the expectation that the bride will come and work at the new husband's place and on land to which he has access. Brideservice entails a kind of *uxorilocal* residence, that is, with the wife's kin; bridewealth, and the inheritance of land and other rights via the husband-father in the family, often goes with virilocal residence. All of these arrangements constitute the basic legal structure that provides a road map for any given marriage.

The more the inheritable wealth involved, the greater the stress on the parceling of it out among heirs and the greater the potential competition between siblings when each can claim a part of the wealth. The ability of a parent to make a will can complicate matters further. A typical pattern in the class-based, wealth-acquiring capitalist societies of the United States and Europe can be found in the disputes that may arise out of a will. A parent or parents may have worked hard to acquire wealth and may be reluctant to see it thoughtlessly squandered (as they see it) by "spoilt children." Such cases often hit the news. From Nashville, Tennessee, the *New York Times* (Wednesday, February 16, 2005, pp. A1 and A15), reported on a case where a businessman who had made his money out of oil, real estate, and the financing of auto sales wished to keep the inheritance of his wealth away from his children, regarding these as spoilt and ungrateful (p. A1). Unfortunately for him, the solution he worked out backfired. He had left the estate to a foundation that his younger wife would run (p. A1), and that would be devoted to helping poor and deserving young people in Tennessee generally. However, his wife and he both died unexpectedly in an accident, and control over the foundation fell into the hands of a long-standing female assistant, who was then said to have misused the monies and who did actually move the foundation out of Tennessee altogether. The total amount of money at stake was said to have been some $100 million when the businessman died, but the amount currently left was unclear. The ex-assistant and foundation manager was reported to have been paid more than $4 million since the time of the couple's death (p. A15). One old associate of the businessman commented that the deceased magnate's ghost must be very upset (p. A1). Curiously, the newspaper article makes no further mention of the children. More often, in such cases we read of children contesting a parent's will in order to try to get some of the wealth for themselves. The case also shows that while parental love is supposed to be natural and the norm, there can be severe hostility and alienation between parents and children.[4]

NEW REPRODUCTIVE TECHNOLOGY

The mention of what is "natural" reminds us of the great range of issues that have arisen from the introduction of new ways of reproducing humans. The demand for such ways is clearly based on a powerful motivation, the desire for children, typically on the part of heterosexual couples who are unable to achieve such reproduction through their own sexual partnership. We do not need to decide whether this motivation is "natural" or "cultural." It is clearly in every case both: The near-universality of the motivation is evidence for a cross-cultural tendency that is supported by both biology and culture. At the same time, there is equally strong cross-cultural evidence of hostility between parents and children, as exhibited in the case from Tennessee noted earlier.

In spite of this, the desire for children "of their own" has led couples in the United States and other countries to expend considerable resources on methods such as in vitro fertilization, whereby an extracted egg is united with sperm in a laboratory context and then reintroduced into the woman. Reproductive technology has become big business, and it is based mostly on the notion that the ideal form of reproduction (implicitly the one that is closest to the values of the society) is one in which the sperm and egg of a married couple are united to form the child: The biologically based nuclear family of procreation.

If this ideal were not in play, the demand for expensive technology would not exist. Couples might take on children conceived by others and bring them up as their own. David Schneider's arguments about "kinship" in Yap were based precisely on a situation in which "kinship," as he put it, was more about doing than being (Schneider 1984: 72); more about action and process than about essentialized given attributes stemming from birth itself. The Yapese example, if we follow Schneider's account, was an extreme one, in which what we call "kinship" was in large part (though not entirely) an achieved rather than simply an ascribed status. Or, if status was initially ascribed via motherhood and residence, it still had to be affirmed by continuous work and support. In the practical world that people in the United States live in the same situation also holds. The real-life relations of kinship depend on how ties are maintained.

The difference between the Yapese situation in Schneider's time and the United States lies in the legal baselines on which the system is founded. The baseline for the Yapese appears to be performance, whereas for the United States it appears to be genetically tested biological connection. The reason why the Yapese case could operate as it did is fairly clear. Yap is a small island in Micronesia within the Pacific region, with a fairly high population density, a hierarchical organization of groups, and land parceled into small units with very careful control over their use. Marriages take place between these small groups, so that in one way or another everyone is tied in with everyone else. Whether they call each other "kin" or not, they are bound together by multiple ties of solidarity in dense social networks. There is a strong backdrop of local "being," then, that frames Yapese "doing." In the United States at large, none of these conditions hold. People move about, members of families are physically and socially separated and may belong to different social classes, religious, or political parties, for example. The whole emphasis of the society is on "doing" and achieving, as well as on multiple social distinctions that divide and individuate people. The backdrop of the society at large is based on "doing." Against it, the "being" of kinship is ideologically picked out and emphasized precisely because it is in contradistinction to this backdrop. The two "societies" or "societal cases," then, are opposites. In Yap, "kinship' ties are in effect strong and extended, but in the United States, they are not; but instead "biological connection" and "the family," seen as unchangeable, are privileged. "Family values" and "Thanksgiving Day" rituals emerge from this foregrounding of biological connection. By the same token, legal battles in real life as well as on endless TV drama shows featuring forensic methods (e.g., *CSI Miami*) quite often turn on the proof or disproof of biological connection. A diplomat father, for example, protects his criminal son with immunity from prosecution until the agents pursuing the son are able to obtain a sample of the diplomat's blood and find by a DNA test that the "son" is not related to him biologically—thus imputing a problem between the diplomat and his wife, for the son is hers but not his. Although the son may still be legally protected by his mother's marriage to the father, the father is upset and repudiates him, enabling his arrest to take place. This kind of scenario, with its proverbial overtones, is represented in folk discourse by the dictum "It's a wise son who knows his own father" (and here emphasis on the father–son dyad shows the gendered character of historical practices of inheritance and succession).

By implication, the folk saying also suggests that whereas paternity may be biologically uncertain, motherhood is always clear, and not only clear, but also indivisible. It is, however, exactly this indivisibility of biological motherhood that has crumbled in the face of a further development of reproductive technology in the form of the surrogate mother, the "birthing mother" who receives an implanted fertilized egg from another woman and then grows it in her womb with the purpose of handing over the baby to the woman whose egg was used, ordinarily in return for a fee. "Fatherhood" can be split between a biological *genitor* or procreator and a "social father" or *pater*, who looks after the child and brings it up, usually in the context of marriage. But motherhood was supposed to be the fundamental tie of kinship, buttressed by strong sentiments (as it appears to be in Yap). The advent of the surrogate mother changed this, splitting motherhood not into a social versus biological mother but into two kinds of biological ties, that of the "egg mother" and the "birth mother." The egg mother becomes more like a female version of a male sperm donor. She gives the needed substance (already fertilized in some chosen way), but after that does not bear the literal burden of growing the child with her substance inside herself. The child is her external, not internal, child. Further, an ineluctable bond is turned into a source of transaction. This again puts the egg mother in some ways in a similar position to a man who pays bridewealth for a woman who will bear "his" children. Moreover, the transaction may not be secure. The birth mother, influenced by her experience of carrying the child in her womb for nine months, may in the end want to keep the child. The anthropologist Robin Fox has devoted a lengthy chapter of his book *Reproduction and Succession* to the case of "Baby M," which is yet another scenario of divided parenthood (Fox 1997: 53–125).

Here, the scenario was that a married couple who were childless had made a contract with a woman (herself married with two children) to bear a child for them through insemination with the sperm of the husband. The husband had apparently been left without any familial relatives as a result of the Holocaust, and he wanted a child as a descendant of his own "blood." The prospective birthing mother was to be paid a fee of $10,000 and the lawyer who drew up the contract was given $7,500. The agreement was made in 1985 and was called the Surrogate Parenting Agreement (Fox 1997: 54). The birthing mother agreed within this contract that "in the best interest of the child, she will not form or attempt to form a parent-child relationship" with the child she was intending to bear for the childless couple. However, the birthing mother was not willing or able to give up the baby girl whom she bore in March 1986. The contracting couple then used the police and judges to forcibly obtain possession of the child after the birthing mother and her husband had fled with it. The case eventually came to court, with the issue of determining whether to privilege the contract or the birthing mother's feelings for her child: In other words, which of these two principles—"law" and "motherhood"—should prevail. On the legal side, it was not clear if the contract could be upheld, because surrogate parenting lay outside of the definitions of the law in general at that time; on the kinship side, the question was whether the birthing mother, regardless of the source of the sperm, always has an overriding "natural" right to keep her child if she wishes to. The complications of the case threw conventional notions about the law and about biology out of kilter. Regardless of the contract, did the "natural" mother also have an overriding right against the "natural" father, for example? The possibility of making transactions of a commercial and legal kind over "natural" processes of reproduction seems to have been confusing to the legal apparatus at the time.

In effect, this concern about whether a baby can be bought and whether a legal frame can be put on natural processes appears odd when it is considered on a more cross-cultural basis. As we have argued earlier, in many, if not all, societies, "kinship" is an amalgam of legal rules and biological processes, the inscription of culture on biology, as well as the cultural definitions of biology itself. The old tag from Roman law, which Fox quotes (1997: 55) *pater est quem nuptiae demonstrant*, "the socially recognized father is the one who can show that he is married to the mother," indicates this point clearly within the European traditions. Roman law did distinguish between the *pater*, the social father, and the *genitor*, the presumed biological father, in cases where these were not one and the same. But, in the absence of any argument about such a division, the law assumed that marriage, a legal contract, gave a man the right to social fatherhood of children borne by the wife. By the same token, however, if the *genitor* was not the husband of the mother, the status of the child could be affected. "Kinship" privileged a legal status, but it could also privilege a natural status. Ideally or normatively they should go together. New reproductive techniques disaggregate the factors involved in parenthood in new ways; but the possibility of disaggregation exists in many systems in which such reproductive techniques are unknown.

In the first trial on the Baby M case, the judge decided in favor of the contract and the rights of the "natural father" as against those of the "birthing mother." This decision was later struck down by the New Jersey Supreme Court (Fox 1997: 115), on grounds that "motherhood" cannot be extinguished by a contract and that the contract itself was therefore not valid. The Supreme Court, however, gave custody to the contracting couple while giving visiting rights to the birthing mother: In effect, recognizing the rights of both sides to the dispute and separating "custody" as an issue from the fundamentals of "kinship" (p. 119). (This case is revisited in Chapter 8.)[5]

ADOPTION

Our discussion in the previous section should be taken in tandem with the question of adoption discussed here. Adoption, like the issue of surrogate parenting, deals with a division between "natural" and "legal" parenthood. Classically, the imagery involved is that of a "natural" mother, bearing a child in circumstances perceived as nonviable for the child's future, giving it up for adoption. In a system that is based, paradoxically, *both* on ideas of "natural" ties *and* on ideas of the primacy of "law," this can lead to problems on many sides, when "the law" and "nature" are not fused together.

Add to this the importance placed on the nuclear family as the prototypical form of kinship or household organization. This is a cultural doctrine that has grown up or evolved historically in Euro-American society over a number of centuries and has been accentuated since industrialization and the expansion of the middle classes. The "prototypical" form is in fact a product of history, and it has impacted attitudes toward adoption. In effect, practices of adoption have resembled the struggle between a birthing mother and the contracting couple, discussed earlier. In excluding the mother (and by secondary implication, the genitor) from pursuing contact with, or rights over, her adopted child, the law has decreed that the child must unequivocally "belong" to a recognized suitable "family." It goes to make up an essential, desired part of that new family, and it cannot also be a part of any other family. It must grow up thinking that it belongs to its adopted parents as in fact its natural parents: "art" not just imitating but taking the place of "nature."

Emotional problems are practically guaranteed if the child discovers it has been adopted and has not been told this before. Given the cultural stress on "nature" as a basis of relationship, the child may begin a quest for its genetrix (genetic or birthing mother) and may feel that it was all along a secondary element in its adoption family. This, in itself, may ignore the fact that the bonding of an adopting couple with their adopted child, if the child is adopted when an infant, may be every bit as "natural," that is, based on experience, as the bond of gestation and birthing. The child feels itself denied of some of this "natural" heritage; the adopting parents are equally denied the "natural" dimension of their parenting experience with the child through the nemesis of genetics. The reality of the dilemmas involved is indicated, as with other issues we have remarked on, by their repeated appearance in popular television shows, one theme of which is "a mother (i.e., a genetrix) always knows her child"; and a child will always seek its mother and a mother will always seek her child. (Note the emphasis on the mother: "the mother knows her child because it was one with her inside her" is the form of symbolism that is at work. No such intuitive predisposition is attributed to the genitor.)

These dilemmas are created as much by the legal and cultural form of adoption, in the United States, for example, as by people's natural predispositions (see discussions in Modell 1994, 2002). From a cross-cultural and anthropological viewpoint, it is interesting to note how the dilemmas involved are mitigated or practically disappear when the social forms of kinship and the articulations of social versus biological parenthood are arranged differently. In particular, it is also important to realize that in several cultural contexts the whole idea of what constitutes the "physical" realm differs from the idea that the physical and the social are separate realms of being. The world is often conceived of as a *cosmos*, in which all elements have their shared place, rather than being divided into "environment" and "human society," seen as entities of a different kind. This point may seem a bit obscure because it has become habitual to make a distinction between the social and the environmental domains as a result of the procedures of natural science, which have fed into cultural contexts generally. So it is important to realize that many peoples around the world have historically operated with the opposite view, linking humans intimately to their physical life-world.[6]

We will look at some examples of "adoption" from different places, concentrating on the Pacific region, where much work on this topic has been done. We first take a case study from the Eastern Highlands of Papua New Guinea, among the Kamano people, as studied by Elizabeth Mandeville (Mandeville 1981). The Highlands region was entered by explorers only in the early 1930s, and while many changes ensued, especially after 1945, kinship patterns in the 1960s and the 1970s were relatively unaltered from precolonial times. Mandeville points out that transfer of children between families was common enough, leading at times to disputes between the natal and the adoptive parents (1981: 229). As she uses the term, "adoption" here refers to the voluntary transfer of children from one family to another by a special contractual arrangement, and not necessarily triggered by deaths of parents or marital infertility. Among the Kamano, she notes, "some kin statuses carry with them the right or duty to care for orphaned or otherwise distressed children" (p. 230). So, if such kin activate this duty, she does not call this adoption. Nor indeed, we may add, is it "fosterage." It is more like custody or guardianship automatically falling to next of kin, as a kind of succession.

This special contractual arrangement resembles contemporary Euro-American patterns in relation to adoption. But an additional feature of the Kamano case makes a clear difference: When a Kamano child is adopted, its natal parents do not lose all their rights or ties with it (Mandeville 1981: 230). In the 1970s, the Kamano lived in small villages with "up to a few hundred people" (p. 230), and although people tended to live with agnatic kin (i.e., ones related through males), they were also quite mobile, in response to disputes, warfare, and the availability of land elsewhere. Children whose parents died were generally cared for by close agnatic kin within their village, although a mother's brother might also take up this role in accordance with his obligation "to supervise the health and general well-being of his sister's children" (p. 231). We see here a distinction between the collective claims of a set of agnates, probably within the village, and the individual claims of a maternal uncle, probably (though not necessarily) belonging to another village.

Mandeville further distinguishes between the following "transactions in parenthood" (1981: 231): "guardianship, coparenthood, succession to parenthood, assumption of parental rights by grandparents, provision of quasiparental care [i.e., fosterage], and adoption" (p. 231). As can be seen from her list, the first four types of "transaction" fall within the sphere of previously existing kin ties that carry a potentiality of care for children. "Guardian," however, had a special meaning in the case of a girl. Her birth parents were not permitted in custom to play active parts in her puberty rituals or marriage, so that these occasions were managed by a designated guardian couple. In the 1970s, bridewealth payments were rising and parents tended to appoint close agnates to take on this role of guardianship. The rise was due to the colonial introduction of Australian state money into the economy (via wage labor and cash cropping). Similar processes occurred everywhere in the Highlands whenever cash was introduced alongside, or in replacement of, the shell valuables traditionally employed in bridewealth. Parents wanted close agnatic kin to be guardians so that the new valuable, money, would be kept in the family.

The role of guardian was assigned soon after the birth of a child but would not come into play until the child grew up. Adoption, too, was arranged at birth, but in this case it came into effect quickly. The adoptive mother would breast-feed the infant if she was able to do so and otherwise would take the child after it was weaned, having helped to look after it meanwhile (Mandeville 1981: 234). If the transfer did not work out, the adopters might choose simply to be co-parents (p. 234).

It is interesting to note here that although adoption was in practice distinct from the other variants of child caretaking, Mandeville reports that the Kamano did not make a sharp verbal distinction along these lines. Instead, they stressed that all of the various arrangements were "normal" ways of sharing children among people (1981: 234).

In spite of this stress, it is clear that there was some ambivalence about the idea of making information about an adoption publicly known. The adoption of a young child might be kept quiet, Mandeville writes (1981: 235), although in a small village we might expect it to be noted and to enter into local gossip. However, when the adoptee had grown up with the adopters, there was little secrecy. Early secrecy was about strengthening the adopters' position, which was potentially vulnerable.

Given the observation about mother's brothers made earlier, it is not surprising to learn that kin on the mother's side (matrilateral kin) were "by far the most frequent adopters" (Mandeville 1981: 237). This was especially true for the adoption of girls. Agnatic kin were more willing for girls to be adopted than boys, especially since colonial control (p. 238). Colonial influence was at work here; perhaps boys were seen as newly important because of their role as potential wage earners, although in precolonial times they would also have been important as warriors-to-be. The practice of guardianship over female children would encourage their adoption away from their natal agnates, but only if the agnates agreed to this, because an adopted girl's bridewealth payments would be made at least in part to her adopting kin at marriage, we may suggest.

What was adoption about among the Kamano? It was not about creating political alliances between villages. Villages were often at enmity with each other, and they were not bound together by elaborate exchanges. Mandeville suggests that adoption was "about love" (1981: 240). Asking for and giving a child was a mark of affection. Also "women separated from their kin" were happy to be "given a brother's child to look after" or to send one of their own children back to their natal place (pp. 240–241). These details reveal two significant points. First, adoption was very much women's business, motivated by female concerns and feelings. Second, it operated at an interpersonal level as a kind of compensatory mechanism for the *lack* of political alliances between intermarrying groups. In both regards, it was an interpersonal rather than a political process.

Moreover, the rights of natal kin were not annulled by adoption, and adoption meant that natal kin would continue to look after and make gifts to their child, and would be angry if this was denied to them. In some ways, natal kin ties retained primacy. For example, an adopted child would observe the same rules against incest as his or her natal siblings but could marry freely within the adoptive group (Mandeville 1981: 241). In fact, such a marriage was sometimes approved of as a way of strengthening the adoptee's attachment to the adopting group (p. 242).

The rationale the Kamano give for adoption is highly significant. "Food creates flesh," the Kamano say. Food-giving and the power to make people grow literally can create "consubstantiality," the sharing of substance (see A. J. Strathern 1973). Adopters therefore stress their role in food-giving (p. 242). Publicly, their role is supported; privately, people recognize that natal parents may eventually want to get their child back (p. 243). Interestingly, the context of food-giving can be ambivalent. When adoptees grow up, they sometimes leave because they are afraid that people might feed them "poison," that is, might make sorcery on them through food. Such a fear correlates again with the lack of alliance between villages. It also resonates with ideas about sorcery throughout the Highlands of Papua New Guinea. In Mount Hagen, a euphemism for saying that someone was killed by sorcery (*kopna*, "ginger") is that "he/she ate food" (*röng nurum*). Kinship-by-blood and kinship-by-food both operate together among the Kamano, and adoption is a marker both of the flexibility of ideas about identity and of a certain baseline privileging of blood ties, though without much concern for elaborate genealogies. The Kamano case also reinforces the point that a term like "adoption" cannot be given an a priori set of characteristics but must be explicated from within the cultural realm under discussion, as Esther Goody did in her study of "child exchange" among West African people (e.g., the Gonja) (Goody 1982). And in general, the question of adoption underscores the need to have a broad definition of the term "kinship" itself, one that recognizes elements derived from both birth and nurture, and also recognizes that the combinations and weightings of these principles are variable and complex (Marshall 1977; Terrell and Modell 1994).

Marshall, for example, has stressed the importance of action and experience in the Trukese case in Micronesia (Marshall 1976). He identifies "sharing" as its most distinctive behavioral index and notes that in Truk the same criterion holds between "friends," who model their relationship on that of "siblings" (Marshall 1977: 649). *Any* relationship has to be sustained through nurturing, no matter how it is initially defined (Marshall 1977: 651; cf., in general, Mauss 1990). Here, then, nurturing and performance are preeminent; but the model on which "sharing" is based is expressed in terms of siblinghood, with its implication of a blood tie (Marshall 1981).

A case study from another Trukese area strengthens both these observations by Marshall and the particular conclusions we have drawn here from Mandeville's Kamano study. Juliana Flinn (1985) studied Pulap, an atoll island in the western Truk area, in 1980–1981. Here, adoption took place only between kin. A person would adopt only someone classified as a sibling's child. In contrast to the Kamano case, descent in Pulap was reckoned matrilineally. Sisters by the same mother would adopt each other's children, thereby strengthening their internal solidarity in the close matrilineal group (p. 95). However, there was a further preferential form whereby a woman would adopt a child of her brother, from outside of her matrilineage, thereby strengthening a patrilateral tie (i.e., through the brother) that otherwise might remain rather tenuous (p. 95). Flinn argues that in this case the adoption strengthens intergroup solidarity (1985: 95).

This seems to be in general correct. We may, however, suggest that this solidarity remains on an interpersonal and familial basis rather than being political. This was our conclusion from the Kamano study by Mandeville. It is pertinent to place the Pulap example in a comparative context. We have seen earlier how significant patrilateral ties can be among the Trobrianders, who practice matrilineal descent as the Trukese do. Such patrilateral ties take on a group aspect at Trobriand funerals, when the paternal kin act as "workers" for the funeral's "owners," the matrilineal kin. Perhaps adoption on Pulap could become the vehicle for setting up political cooperation also. In the reverse case of the Kamano, who practiced patrilineal descent, adoption strengthened sentiments of solidarity with the mother's kin; but political fragmentation precluded it having further effects.

On Pulap at the time of Flinn's study, adoption was very common: In her sample of 233 children of elementary school age or younger, 123 were adopted (1985: 96). Five out of these 123 were adopted by non-Pulapese (p. 103, n. 5). Of the remaining 118, 71 "were adopted by members of the father's matrilineal descent group" (p. 100). The reason given was "a desire to assure that the child will not forget the father's descent group" (p. 100). As in the Kamano case, the usual way to seek an adoption was to ask the mother for the child soon after its birth (p. 100).

Similarly to the situation in the Trobriands, there is an institutionalized context for the interpersonal ties between a woman and her brother's children. All those whose fathers are of a particular matrilineage are said to be the "children of the descent group"; and the matrilineage can call on its "children," to help in many tasks, such as making a feast for visitors or building a house-roof. The "children," in fact, should come without being asked. They also have certain rights in their father's descent group's property, such as land and canoes. By showing their concern, the "children" also gain prestige (Flinn 1985: 99). Yet the relationship is fragile compared to that between matrilineage members. It depends greatly on a continuing series of gifts. Land given to these "children" can be reclaimed if its recipients fail to meet obligations. Flinn argues that adoption can strengthen these potentially fragile ties, because the adopted child retains ties with both sides and as adoption is "jurally inclusive" (Flinn 1985: 100, quoting Brady 1976: 16–17). Today, adoption may perform a new but analogous function, since a man who is away from home as an urban wage earner can adopt one of his sisters' children, fulfilling his obligations as a sibling and strengthening his claims to land he himself has received from his matrilineage at his marriage but is not currently using.

How exactly, then, does adoption strengthen such ties? In two ways, we can suggest. First, the kin on either side will do their best to stay on good terms because of their mutual interest in the "transferred" child. Second, when the child grows up, he or she may act as a go-between for the kin, having a feeling of affiliation to both sides. The child is in a way like a "pledge" between them, a guarantee for good behavior between exchange partners.

Conclusions

This chapter discussed notions of kinship and the life cycle, beginning with birth and social reproduction. When we move from birth to broader notions of social reproduction and cultural context, we find that the meanings of kinship become more complex. It is these complexities that we have explored, for example, among the Trobrianders and in the Yapese case, as studied by David Schneider and used by him in his campaign against kinship as "genealogy." While Schneider's views on Yapese ways of thinking about relationships problematized the theory of kinship in "traditional" anthropological contexts, recent developments in reproductive technology have similarly problematized them in practice in the Euro-American context. A balanced overall viewpoint on these problems needs to recognize that different, but by no means infinitely numerous, principles may be at work in the definition of kinship. Characteristically, there is an interplay between ideas founded on birth and on nurture. Our final section on "adoption" shows that the same interplay is involved in cases of "child transfer." Systems that stress "blood" ties have the greatest problem with adoption, where it is regarded as a suppression of birth in favor of nurture; this type of problem does not arise in the more performance-based and "jurally inclusive" Pacific Island systems. This might be due to the prevalence of broad kin ties in the Pacific Island systems and their relatively narrow scope in Euro-American contexts.

Questions to Consider

1. What suppositions by anthropologists have underlain the debates on the definition of kinship? How can such debates be resolved?
2. How does the case of practices of adoption help us to think about cross-cultural variability in kinship relations?

Notes

1. The concept of complementary filiation was important to Fortes's overall view of kinship and descent structures. Whereas descent, if socially important, was most often traced unilineally, that is, on one side of ego's kinship universe and through single-gender links, filiation was always, or nearly always, bilateral: that is, recognized on both sides. Taking the example of the Ashanti people of Ghana, among

whom descent is matrilineal, Fortes wrote, "What really underlies such institutional patterns is a basic structural feature of unilineal systems. The descent principle is normally, probably invariably, counterbalanced by the principle of complementary filiation" (Fortes 1969: 98). The descent rule stipulates, in Fortes's analytical scheme, the side of law, while the complementary filial rules specify "sentiment, morality, and equity" (p. 98). The side which does not count for the reckoning of descent is called "complementary" because the values expressed through it complement those defined by descent. There is, of course, filiation on the descent side as well, but filiation on the nondescent side is the kind called "complementary." Our usage here thus reflects exactly both Fortes's usage and the ethnographic materials on the Trobriands as reported by Malinowski, for example, under the heading "sociological paternity" (Malinowski 1932, *The Sexual Life of Savages*, pp. 203–210). This note is included in response to a request for clarification of the "correct" meaning of "complementary filiation," from one of the anonymous peer reviewers of this book. Whether there is a single "correct" meaning of the term is another matter. We wish here simply to indicate how it fits the context of Fortes's work.

2. As another peer reviewer of our manuscript reminded us, Schneider drew some of his ideas for his revised account of Yapese "kinship" and social structure from the fieldwork findings of his student David Labby. Schneider records the history as follows: he refers to "work that I did, beginning in 1947–1948 on the island of Yap in the West Caroline Islands and wrote up as my doctoral dissertation in 1949 and continued later in a series of publications from 1953 to 1962. This description is compared with a quite different description, the key element of which was first developed by Dr. David Labby as a result of his work on Yap more than twenty years later," referring to Labby's 1976 book *The Demystification of Yap*, The University of Chicago Press. Here, Schneider also notes that he took into account work by Lingenfelter, Kirkpatrick and Broder (1976), and Marksbury in constructing this revised account (Schneider 1984: 5). Labby himself (1976: Acknowledgments) declares that his work "has essentially been a continuation of what he [Schneider] began" and acknowledges a general debt to Schneider as one of his former professors when he was a student at the University of Chicago. So there is a long intertwining of their ideas and mutual influence on each other.

Schneider goes on to note that Labby found out that "instead of land being transmitted in a patrilineal line, it was transmitted instead from one *genung* (crudely glossed for the moment as a matriline) to another." (Schneider 1984: 8). Schneider tells us that he is reluctant to use the term "matriline" here and that a *genung* transmits an estate of land to another, but "not by inheritance at all" (1984: 8). Labby actually develops a speculative historical reconstruction of how the patterns of landholding which he elucidated could have come about through the parceling out of an original matrilineally constituted estate into smaller matriestates associated with the phenomenon of a male matriclan member remaining on his natal land and his wife coming to join him and being allocated a part of his matriclan land to use for food production. He further suggests that this innovation could have emerged from the historical adoption of taro cultivation (Labby 1976: 114ff.). Taro was a basic staple, but taro gardens were also ranked in terms of their status, and they required intensive garden work. In these circumstances, control over taro gardens may have gradually shifted into the hands of men, who would then form a patrilocal group, giving rise to the appearance of the *tabinau* when both Schneider and Labby worked on Yap.

It is notable here that Labby, in pursuit of his avowedly Marxist (or materialist) analysis, was quite happy with the use of the terms "matrilineal" and "matriline," with which, by contrast, Schneider expresses dissatisfaction, because he became resolved to expel all "conventional" usages from his own analysis. Labby also used the spellings *ganong* instead of *genung* and *tabinaw* rather than *tabinau*. We follow Schneider's spellings here simply because they have been established in the literature.

Labby's suggestions about historical changes in the kinship/descent system of the Yapese may be further related to his report that fatherhood was now represented as "planting the seed" in the mother. Such an ideology would fit with the putative shift from a strongly matrilineal form to one with a patrilineal emphasis. From early days, Marxist analysts have been keen to suggest historical transitions of this kind. Such a project, however, lies quite outside of Schneider's own project of debunking the idea of kinship based on genealogy as a general concept. If, by contrast, we take Labby's ideas seriously, we can also suggest that the naming practices within the *tabinau* take the place of ideas of patrifiliation, or rather that they constitute exactly what Malinowski called "sociological paternity."

Schneider's viewpoints generated a great deal of comment, and his supporters, who see themselves as his successors, tend to regard his work as creating a watershed between the "old" and "new" ways of looking at kinship. The various essays brought together in Richard Feinberg and Martin Ottenheimer's edited book *The Cultural Analysis of Kinship* (Urbana and Chicago: University of Illinois Press, 2001) provide useful appreciation and criticism of Schneider's work. Martin Ottenheimer's own chapter in this book, on "Relativism in Kinship Analysis" contains many sensible points, in particular when he remarks on "Schneider's error: the Absolutism of Cultural Relativism" (Schneider 1984: 199). Here he is referring to Schneider's claims that "kinship" was a category imposed on societies through a Eurocentric model of biologically based ties, and that each culture's own models should be studied, with the result that there would be no overall model of kinship (1984: 120). Ottenheimer comments that this viewpoint is absolutist, privileging each cultural difference without regard, presumably, for many obvious overall cultural similarities. We may comment further here that much of this debate turns on what we mean by "biology" and "genealogy." The exchange between Schneider and Akitoshi Shimizu is illuminating in this regard. See Shimizu, "On the Notion of Kinship," *Man*, n.s., 26 (1991), and Schneider's response in *Man*, n.s., 27, no. 3 (1992): 629–631, and Shimizu's further reply *Man*, n.s., 27, no. 3 (1992): 631–633.

Recent ethnographic studies support the view that there is a need to be flexible in one's use of the term "kinship." Isabella Lepri remarks at the end of a discussion on kinship among the Ese Ejja of northern Bolivia that for these people "kinship is about sharing substance and sharing life, and that relatedness derives from both birth and conviviality . . . In Ese Ejja kinship reckoning, performance and filiation, what is processual and what is given, are not mutually exclusive and are equally important" ("The meaning of kinship among the Ese Ejja of Northern Bolivia," *JRAI* 11, no. 4 (2005): 703–725, 720).

3. For a study of aspects of ancient Roman kinship practices, see Maurizio Bettini, *Kinship, Time, Images of the Soul*. Trans. John Van Sickle (Baltimore and London: Johns Hopkins Press, 1991), 1–112.

4. A case from the Bronx in New York City was reported in *The New York Times* (Monday, March 30, 2009, p. A24), in which a son, with the help of his mother, excluded his two sisters from their share in their father's estate of some 100 properties

in the city. The sisters did not discover the situation for almost 30 years, and stumbled on it only when one of them came across some information while studying real estate in a night course. The father had left a simple will leaving a third of his estate to his wife and dividing the remaining two-thirds equally among his three children, with a trust fund to be established for the two daughters until they were 23. The discovery of the will led to a complex and bitter legal struggle, and competing versions of the truth. One of the sisters commented, "The deepest hurt came from my mother's role in the conspiracy. A mother is supposed to protect her child. The life my father wanted for us would have been very different."

Wills and inheritance can make all the difference to a person's material status in life, as our own fieldwork in Scotland and elsewhere has brought home to us. Siblings may deceive one of their number if they are "in the know" about a will and the other is not and meanwhile trusts them to be honest, especially when they inform their brother or sister that a parent did not leave them anything in their will.

5. Sandra Bamford has brought together reflections on biotechnology and a discussion of her interpretation of ideas of reproduction among the Kamea, an Anga-speaking people in Papua New Guinea (Bamford 2007). Taking her cues from David Schneider's deconstructivist and Roy Wagner's reconstructivist work on kinship, Bamford argues that for the Kamea, sibling relationships are centrally important and these are indicated in the idea that siblings are *hinya avaka*, of "one blood" (2007: 61). She explains that "Like most Papua New Guineans, Kamea believe that repeated acts of sexual intercourse are necessary to create a child" (p. 60). Furthermore, "conception is said to take place when sufficient quantities of a man's reproductive fluids (*iya coka*) both mix with and are encompassed by the fluids of his wife (*panga coka*). This outer female covering will ultimately form the skin and surface blood vessels of the child while the father's semen contributes to the making of bones and internal organs" (pp. 60–61).

But, Bamford continues, this idea that both parents contribute to the substance of their children is not used by the Kamea "as a compelling feature of the parent-child relationship" (p. 61) and "Kamea do not equate the building of bodies with the building of social relations" (p. 61). In this regard, the Kamea would be quite unlike "most Papua New Guineans," even though their fundamental ideas of conception are very similar to those of other Papua New Guinea cases.

The heart of Bamford's argument is that Kamea siblings share blood and are in fact seen as "one blood," but are not said to be "one blood" with either of their parents. "Women bestow upon their children a horizontal type of relatedness that is imagined in terms of 'containment' rather than the lineal transmission of bodily substance" (p. 61).

This account can be compared with material from other Papua New Guinea cases. The Melpa also, for example, use the "one blood" idiom, and refer it primarily to connections through mothers. They extend it, however, to matrilateral kin connected by female links, described as *mema tenda wamb*. In other words, the idiom *is* extended. In the Kamea case, Bamford informs us that it is not. The idiom would be unique to each set of siblings by the same mother. Among the Melpa, a mother is not said to share all the same blood with her children; however, part of her blood comes from her own mother, and so on, but "blood" can also be referred to on the father's side, and so some of the mother's blood is not the same as that of her children. But if the children share anything from the mother, it *must*, in effect, be her blood. And if they get "bone" from the father's semen, is this bone not paternal? Classically, "blood" in Central Papua New Guinea Highlands cultures refers to maternal ties of filiation and "bone" to paternal ties of descent. Bamford notes that *tambuna* (ancestral) stories are cited to justify claims to tracts of land and that these land claims, not genealogical connections, are the basis of continuity in time. However, she also reports that the Kamea say, "men are expected to 'follow in the footsteps of their father'" (p. 39). It seems likely that whereas the Kamea do not invoke a strong descent model, they do go by a notion of cumulative patrifiliation. The Kamea narratives about ancestors (*tambuna, tumbuna*) establishing land rights by planting trees and crops are paralleled by many other cases, including the Duna people. Bamford's account makes the Kamea "different" from other cases; seen comparatively, they appear "similar" to others. Schneider himself noted that description can be led by theory: "Obviously, the theory and presuppositions which inform each description, the purposes of the description, the implicit premises which guide the transformation of the field materials into descriptions must differ in order for the descriptions to differ" (*A Critique of the Study of Kinship* 1984: 5–6). Quite so, and so indeed here as the ethnographer of the Kamea follows in Schneider's own footsteps and "creates" the Kamea on her way. For further studies in this same pathway, see Sandra C. Bamford and James Leach, eds., *Kinship and Beyond: the Genealogical Model Reconsidered* (New York: Berghahn Books, 2009).

6. Sara Dorow and Amy Swiffen have discussed emergent issues relating to transnational adoption practices, situating their discussion in the context of "new kinship studies" and also "in studies focused on the decentering and recentering of blood ties, gay and lesbian parenting and the hybridization of racial and cultural family identities" (Dorow and Swiffen, "Blood and desire: The secret of heteronormativity in adoption narratives of culture," *American Ethnologist* 36, no. 3: 563–573), 2009. These authors note the creativity and also the ambiguity inherent in people's attempts to mediate "forms of interplay between blood and social origins" in the adoption narratives they discuss (p. 573). Pacific Islanders have exercised their own creativity in this domain long before the advent of "new kinship studies."

References

Bamford, Sandra. 2007. *Biology Unmoored. Melanesian Reflections on Life and Biotechnology*. Berkeley, CA: University of California Press.

Blake, William. 1979. *Blake's Poetry and Designs*, ed. Mary Lynn Johnson and John E. Grant. New York: W. W. Norton and Co.

Brady, Ivan, ed. 1976. *Transactions in Kinship: Adoption and Fosterage in Oceania*. Honolulu, HI: The University Press of Hawaii.

Flinn, Juliana. 1985. Adoption and migration from Pulap, Caroline Islands. *Ethnology* 24(2): 95–104.

Fortes, Meyer. 1969. *Kinship and the Social Order. The Legacy of Lewis Henry Morgan*. Chicago, IL: Aldine Publishing Company.

Fox, Robin. 1997. *Reproduction and Succession. Studies in Anthropology, Law, and Society*. New Brunswick and London: Transaction Publishers.

Freeman, Derek. 1983. *Margaret Mead and Samoa: The Making and Unmaking of an Anthropological Myth*. Cambridge, MA: Harvard University Press.

Goody, Esther. 1982. *Parenthood and Social Reproduction*. Cambridge and New York: Cambridge University Press.

Kirkpatrick, John T., and Charles L. Broder. 1976. Adoption and parenthood on Yap. In *Transactions in Kinship*, ed. I. Brady, 200–227. ASAO monograph no. 4. Hawaii: University of Hawaii Press.

Kirsch, Thomas G. 2004. Restaging the will to believe. *American Anthropologist* 106(4): 699–709.

Leach, Edmund. 1969. Virgin birth. In *Genesis as Myth and Other Essays,* ed. E. R. Leach. London: Jonathan Cape.

Malinowski, Bronislaw. 1932. *The Sexual Life of Savages*. London: Routledge and Kegan Paul.

Mandeville, Elizabeth. 1981. Kamano adoption. *Ethnology* 20: 229–244.

Marshall, Mac. 1976. Solidarity or sterility? Adoption and fosterage on Namoluk atoll. In *Transactions in Kinship*, ed. I. Brady, 28–50. ASAO monograph no. 4. Hawaii: University of Hawaii Press.

Marshall, Mac. 1977. The nature of nurture. *American Ethnologist* 4(4): 643–662.

Marshall, Mac. 1981. Sibling sets as building blocks in greater Trukese society. In *Siblingship in Oceania,* ed. M. Marshall, 201–224. ASAO monograph no. 8. Ann Arbor, MI: University of Michigan Press.

Mauss, Marcel. 1990. *The Gift: The Form and Reason for Exchange in Archaic Societies*. Trans. W. D. Halls. New York and London: W. W. Norton.

Modell, Judith S. 1994. *Kinship with Strangers: Adoption and Interpretations of Kinship in American Culture*. Berkeley, CA: University of California Press.

Modell, Judith S. 2002. *A Sealed and Secret Kinship: Policies and Practices in American Adoption*. Oxford and New York: Berghahn Publishers.

Oliver, Douglas L. 1967. *A Solomon Island Society: Kinship and Leadership Among the Siuai of Bougainville*. Boston, MA: Beacon Press.

Schneider, David M. 1984. *A Critique of the Study of Kinship*. Ann Arbor, MI: University of Michigan Press.

Stockard, Janice E. 2002. *Marriage in Culture: Practice and Meaning Across Diverse Societies*. Fort Worth, TX: Harcourt College Publishers.

Strathern, Andrew J. 1973. Kinship, descent, and locality: Some New Guinea examples. In *The Character of Kinship*, ed. J. R. Goody, 21–34. Cambridge, MA: Cambridge University Press.

Terrell, John, and Judith Modell. 1994. Anthropology and adoption. *American Anthropologist* 96(1): 155–161.

Weiner, Annette. 1988. *The Trobrianders of Papua New Guinea*. Fort Worth, TX: Harcourt Brace.

CHAPTER 4

Groups

The relationships surrounding a particular person are one of the aspects of kinship. We speak of these relationships as the person's "egocentric kin network." Kinship diagrams often show how terms for kin work in a social context from the point of view of a particular individual, dubbed "ego" (the "I") or sometimes the "propositus" (the "person in question"), with relationships radiating out from the immediate parents and siblings of the person. A second aspect of kinship, however, is how kin ties build up into whole groups in accordance with rules and practices of social affiliation, or group membership.

These two aspects of the person's kinship universe, that is, the whole spectrum of their kin relationships, are connected because a part of this universe may also be a segment of a wider group defined according to some specific rules. Therefore, a person's definition of self tends to be closely bound up with his or her sense of group membership. In some societies there are no such large, recognized kinship groups, and all kin relations exist on a network basis. This is reputedly the case in contemporary Euro-American society, but ideas of "family" illustrated in "family trees" or genealogies may belie such a supposed absence of kin groups. Nevertheless, there is little doubt that over many hundreds of years in both Europe and America, kinship-defined groups have declined in significance or have disappeared, replaced by a narrower focus on "family" in the sense of the immediate two-generation or at most the extended three-generation family (grandparents, parents, and children).

Probably the term that lies closest to popular consciousness in the realm of wider kinship ties, linked to group notions, is the term "clan." People of the same surname who stick closely together may be described as "very clannish." The image of the clan is the epitome of the idea of the self closely bonded with the group. Further, within Euro-American society, the idea of the clan is most closely associated with sets of surnames that are seen as belonging to Scottish clans, stereotypically from the Scottish Highlands and their contemporary diasporic descendants. Clan societies, based on shared surnames, all over North America (the United States and Canada), attest to the ubiquity of historical memories and contemporary associative endeavors based on this social form of Scotland's past, inextricably identified with the originally Gaelic-speaking Highlands regions of Scotland as opposed to the Lowlands (where, however, many clan names and many "family associations" based on surnames are also to be found).

Interestingly, the Scottish Highland clan proves difficult to describe in systematic ethnographic, or anthropological, terms. In most places of the world where "clans" have been identified, they are technically defined in terms of what is called unilineal descent, that is, descent from a particular supposed founder through only one type of link—in the patrilineal case, the ties descend through fathers and sons; in the matrilineal case, through mothers and daughters.

THE SCOTTISH CLAN: A COMPLEX CASE

However, the Scottish clan does not correspond in any simple way to such precise rules of descent, largely because it was historically a conglomeration of families held together by allegiance to a chief who was seen to hold his title to land by a "feudal" tie to the monarchy. Families bearing different names were historically united through their allegiance to their chief and were over time amalgamated into the clan as a whole, as one of its "septs" (a term that seems to be cognate with "sects," meaning simply "a division"). By implication, the various septs of a clan are descended from those who were subordinate to the chiefly line and dependent on it for their patronage.

In other words, the Scottish clan was not in its essentials an egalitarian group whose members were defined primarily as co-descendants of a particular founder. It was more like a political alliance founded on patronage and protection. The contemporary clan associations preserve at least a part of this structure, since it is up to the hereditary chief of the clan to decide whether an applicant for membership of the association should be accepted, and membership of the association does not necessarily mean membership of the clan in a more narrow sense.

But what would this "more narrow" sense be? The Gaelic term *clann* simply refers to "children" or "family," without specifying a rule of membership. In practice, it appears that the two most obvious pathways of affiliation were via one's father or alternatively one's mother. Robin Fox, in his book *Kinship and Marriage*, accordingly classified the Scottish clan as "a form of cognatic descent group," that is, one in which ties of descent from an ancestor could be reckoned through either male or female links (Fox 1967: 159). He goes on to suggest that it "had a strong patrilineal tinge as is evidenced in the inheritance of surnames" (p. 159); that is, the inheritance of surnames through males. Then he adds: "Note that every true Highland Scot bears two names; his father's and his mother's"—which returns the description to the cognatic form. How do we reconcile these points with one another?

From Fox's discussion and from other evidence, it seems that we can resolve these issues first by taking a historical approach, and second by making use of structural models of cognatically defined descent groups derived from Pacific Island studies (as Fox 1967 also does). First, then, we can probably recognize that the early Scottish clan corresponded to a Gaelic, and thus Celtic, form found in Ireland, from which the Scots or "Scoti" (Latin term) had migrated first into Argyll on the western coast of the land and then into other parts of the north and east. When this migration happened cannot be pinpointed with complete accuracy. The historian Magnus Magnusson suggests that these Scoti, from the northern parts of Ireland, had been raiding and crossing over the sea and settling "for quite a long time" prior to around the year 500 C.E., when a more concerted movement took place from what is now Antrim in Northern Ireland into Argyll, according to a seventh-century Irish source. "These people were known as the Dal Riata," and they established a kingdom "which came to be known as Dalriada" (Magnusson 2000: 32–33). Norman Davies, another historian, tells us that Dal Riata was in fact the name of the original kingdom in Ireland, and that the name Argyll means Ar-gael, "the Eastern Irish." For some time, the Dal Riatans held power both in their Irish homeland and in Argyll, but in 637 C.E., their forces in Antrim were defeated in battle with another Irish high chief, the Ui Neill, and subsequently they had to consolidate their power base in Argyll alone (Davies 2000: 183–184). It was these migrants, then, who may have spread the clan system as they moved outward from Argyll and gradually came to dominate other populations around them, including the Picts, residential descendants of Iron Age populations. Since much of their history was bound up with warfare, we may suppose that the clans were fighting units, and that the institution of chiefship was enshrined in clan structures. All such systems tend to allow for new sets of people to be amalgamated into the political group, since they may be needed to help in military actions. On the other hand, if they become indigent, they may have to look to their chief for support, but if they are not in fact related to him, they may not be fortunate.

Gradually the immigrant Dalriadan Gaels insinuated or imposed themselves into the existing structure of leadership among the Pictish groups to their east and north. Kenneth Mac Alpin, the Gaelic Lord of Kintyre, whose mother appears to have been Pictish, succeeded in taking control of the Pictish lands and set up a new hereditary dynasty over both the Picts and the Scots (Davies 2000: 191). The joint kingdom became known as Scotia, although the whole wider area was also known as "Alba." Kenneth or Cenedd (the Gaelic form of his name) ruled from 840 to 857 C.E. Some of the major Scottish clans lay claim to descent from him or his children. Just as there were narratives that developed as the Scottish kingdom grew, laying claim to mythical progenitors of both the Scots and the Picts as a whole, individual clans traced themselves back to notable warriors or leaders. The Campbells of Argyll, for example, trace themselves to MacCailean Mor ("Colin the Great") of Lochawe, who was killed in battle in 1294 (and, incidentally, it is not clear whether these Campbells are of Irish descent or of the Brythonic Celtic stock resident in Alba before the arrival of the Scoti). The McGregors and McKinnons claim descent from Kenneth MacAlpin, and therefore identify themselves as "Scoti" in origin.

Celtic kings reigned in Scotia/Alba until the time of the historical king Macbeth, two centuries after Kenneth MacAlpin. Macbeth reigned from 1040 to 1057. He belonged (Magnusson 2000: 53) to "one of the three kindreds [i.e., clans] of Dalriada" or Argyll, who had extended their power to the northeast. He was in turn deposed and killed by Malcolm Canmore, the eldest son of King Duncan, whom Macbeth had killed in battle in 1040. Malcolm had fled to England on Macbeth's accession to the kingship. He came back with English support, arranged by Edward the Confessor; and Malcolm's second wife was Princess Margaret, who belonged to the old Saxon royal line (p. 63). Her two daughters married into the Norman aristocracy that ruled England after 1066; three of her six sons became kings of Scotland (p. 65). Davies notes that these kings became vassals to the English throne in the introduced Norman feudal system. They were also tied in by the dynastic marriage of one of Queen Margaret's daughters to Henry I, son of William the Conqueror (p. 69). The Scottish kings linked in this way to Norman power invited the Normans to serve in their armies and to settle in Scotland. David I, Malcolm's third son, was particularly active in this regard. He reigned from 1124 to 1153 and is seen as having brought together the Celtic and the Norman traditions, melding together the notion that all land belongs to the king and the Gaelic notion of collective clan ownership of land in the person of the chief. If chiefs are like vassals of the king, the kingship and the clanship systems are automatically connected. Hence the reference to "feudal" ties which we made earlier.

This sketch of the historical situation illustrates two points. First, and most generally, many of the institutions of kinship from different areas of the world do in fact have their own history rather than being evidence of unchanging "traditions." Second, in the case of the Scottish clan, in our view, its constitution from earliest times was affected by the significance of chiefship within it and the warlike character of social relations pursued by chiefs. We may classify the Scottish clan technically as a "cognatic descent group," as Fox rightly does (1967: 159, previously cited). Its dynamics, however, are to be understood in political terms. Further, two structural features are worth noting here. First, the so-called "feudal" system brought with it a preference for primogeniture, that is, succession to titles and property by the eldest son of a family. In the Celtic system, primogeniture did not hold. Instead, collaterals rather than immediate children tended to succeed; the group members had a say in it; and succession was sometimes determined by violence between rivals, as in the case of Macbeth mentioned earlier. Primogeniture obviated the potential instability of the Celtic system. It also created junior lines of descent cut off from major power. Second, wider political relations were structured or strengthened by royal marriages, as with the marriage of Queen Margaret's daughter to Henry I. It is likely that similar alliances were made between chiefly families in the older Gaelic system of clanship. Intergroup ties, then, are often crucially mediated by individual marriage alliances. The two aspects of kinship which we noted at the outset of this chapter—networks and groups—are in this way interrelated.

But how does this information compare with our knowledge about Pacific Island cases? Cognatic descent groups in a general sense are found across the

Pacific. They tend to be genuine kinship-based groups, that is, ones in which land and other rights are held collectively on the basis of descent. But they also show a certain structural asymmetry that mirrors the gender asymmetry in these societies. We take here a case with which we are familiar from long-term field-work, the Duna people of the Papua New Guinea Highlands.

COGNATIC GROUPS AMONG THE DUNA

The Duna are a people of the far western reaches of the Southern Highlands Province of Papua New Guinea. They number some 20,000 plus speakers of a single language, marked by dialect variations and historical ties with the language of the more numerous Huli-speakers to their southeast and the less numerous Bogaiya to their west. First visited briefly by Australian explorers in the 1930s, the Duna were not fully brought into the ambit of Australian colonial administration until the 1960s, when an airstrip and government post were established at Lake Kopiago. After Papua New Guinea's political independence in 1975, government patrolling decreased in intensity. Missions and churches were set up in the wake of early patrols and by the 1990s, Duna groups were all nominally Christianized. Expatriate missionaries, however, were few and far between. Quietly, the people reincorporated, while transforming, many of their earlier beliefs and practices into their lives.[1]

In addition, major features of social structure exhibited some apparent continuity with the past, even though the ritual underpinnings of these features were no longer in evidence. The basis of social structure among the Duna is the cognatic descent group. Each group has its own founding myth or narrative, usually traced to a spirit being or *tama* regarded as having considerable power and often as having traveled from some other locality to settle in the group territory. Although the group ideology is in the overall sense cognatic, two important characteristics give groups their organizational specificity. The first characteristic is that the group is seen as tied inextricably to a particular bounded territory (although the boundaries shift over time).

The usual way of referring to these groups does not indicate descent at all: the term is *tindi/rindi*, which means "ground/land" in the sense of lived space attached to a named category of people. The connection between people and land is made via the ideology of descent. And here the second characteristic comes into play. Although descendants via both male and female links are all potentially able to live on and claim a part of the *rindi* seen as a shared territory, agnatic descendants of the founder are said to have precedence in terms of control over the disposition of land use.

Agnatic descendants are called *anoagaro*, "man-standing," members, while persons belonging through female links are *imagaro*. *Anoagaro* descendants tend to provide leadership. They also tended in the past to control important ritual knowledge and practices to ensure the ongoing fertility and prosperity of the land. In the 1990s, when our fieldwork was carried out (spanning the period 1989–1999, with an earlier visit in 1970 when C. N. Modjeska was carrying out PhD research in the area, see Modjeska 1977), knowledge of the names of, and the invocations to, ancestral "ground-owning" male spirits was still restricted to agnates, or to a few individuals assimilated through long residence and cognatic ties; and this right to knowledge was seen as the ultimate legitimizing element in claims to each *rindi* area or group territory. Agnatic genealogies of descent from a founding figure were recited like a kind of essential backbone in *malu* or group origin stories. Agnates tended to be the custodians of these *malu*. It may be asked how knowledge of such origin stories could be kept secret or in the sole possession of agnates as such. For example, if the *malu* had sometimes to be recited, others beside agnates would hear them and possibly learn them. There are several answers to this question (which was posed by one of the peer reviewers of this book, probably based on experience with a different Papua New Guinea population in which cumulative patrifiliation was the predominant mode of affiliation to groups, and exchange relations defined individual prominence). First, the recitation of detailed *malu* requires considerable learning and storage in memory, more than could be exercised by an isolated hearing. Second, *malu* are taught by senior men to their juniors and full knowledge of them is acquired only gradually. Third, these operational circumstances go with the social fact that only agnates, and among these the agnates of leading families, are authorized to possess and transmit the *malu* of the group. Fourth, for the Duna, such narratives share an important form of social capital that leaders deploy on behalf of their groups, just as important as the deployment of pigs as wealth in exchanges. The narrative, however, cannot simply be produced, as pigs are, by the mixed labor of men and women. They belong to males, and authorized males at that, and the spirits of the land, it is thought, would not be happy if others presumed to invoke them or refer to them without having the authorized links to them. "Cumulative patrifiliation" would not do as a basis for this stipulation.

This distinction between agnates and others was not necessarily something that was made evident, or even came into play, in everyday life. It was more a kind of implicit, ongoing background, neither challenged nor greatly emphasized. Agnatic genealogies were personal possessions and tended to be the means whereby particular people tied themselves to the ancestor via many generations of intervening links, varying from 8 to 10 or 12 generations from the founder to senior men in the 1990s. Some ancestral male figures were also cited as the founders of segments of the *rindi*. These ancestors were in the past recognized also in the idea that after four or five generations, their petrified hearts would emerge from the ground in the form of black volcanic stones known as *auwi* (a term that also refers to the ritual domain generally). These stones were then made the focus of ritual activities in particular shrines within the *rindi* territory. While these shrines were largely destroyed or abandoned during the early period of missionization in the 1960s, many of the stones actually survived, being put aside in various nooks and crannies, and the names of the ancestors associated with them are still kept in memory in the group *malu* whose custodians are senior male agnatic group members and those whom over time they designate as the successors to their sacred knowledge.

While senior agnates were, and still are to a substantial extent, seen as the custodians of the cosmic principles of order that formed the basis of social structure (*rindi tse*, the root of the ground), social order was also pervasively founded on the conjunction of agnates and cognates within the group, and on the marriage ties that linked persons across group boundaries. The indigenous ritual cycle among the Duna was based on the perceived need to maintain the fertility and viability of each *rindi* group, and also of the *rindi* in the broader sense of the whole land. Rituals carried out to ensure these ends invariably required the cooperative activity of agnates and cognates together, and in many contexts also the cooperation of men and women, although much (but not all) important ritual knowledge and skill was usually vested in males. This male bias, as we may call it, was balanced to a certain extent at the cosmological level by the special prominence given to a category of female spirit known as the Payame Ima (Ima means "woman" in the Duna language; the meaning of Payame is not certain.) Within the Duna area where our research has been carried out, the Aluni Valley which runs westward to the Strickland River, certain groups' areas or parishes, as we call them, had their own versions of stories about this spirit. She was said to choose one of the agnatic men of the group to be her husband. Such a man would become a ritual expert, skilled at discovering witches in the community and at instructing youths in growth magic, enabling them to mature and find young women to marry (Stewart and Strathern 2002a, 2004).[2] The expert thus chosen by the spirit would not marry a human wife. To do so would risk the anger of his spirit wife and the loss of his powers. The Payame Ima was said to preside over the growth rituals for boys conducted in the *palena anda*, the "ginger house," a ritual enclosure made in the forest where the boys were secluded away from the settlements inhabited by men and women in families. It was her magic, putatively, administered by her human "husband," that helped to make the boys' hair grow so it could be shaped into a wig and to make fat develop under their skin so they would appear strong and healthy. Male well-being was thus seen to depend on the power of a spirit female (see also Biersack 1982 for a comparative case).

In terms of social relations generally, there was, and is, a great emphasis on giving recognition to both the father's and the mother's side in kin relationships. It is seen clearly on occasions of raising and disbursing wealth for life-cycle purposes, such as marriage or at death. Both father's and mother's kin contribute wealth in pigs and state money (previously valuable shells obtained in trade) to pay the brideprice on behalf of a youth for whom a bride has been chosen; on the bride's side, the wealth handed over is also distributed to her father's and mother's kin. (There is a special rule about this. In brief, "the daughter's brideprice repays that of the mother"; that is, the father of the girl being married takes a part of the brideprice given for her and with it repays those who contributed to his own brideprice a generation earlier.)

There is definitely a preference for marrying within a fairly close geographical area among the parish groups in the Aluni Valley. Close kin, defined as cousins up to about the third degree, are not supposed to marry. If a marriage is held to violate this notion, then the groom's family may be asked to pay an extra pig in the brideprice, known as the *hewa ita*, "pig of the sun," because the sun, thought of as a spirit agency overseeing morality, is held to be offended by the marriage. Sometimes a bride's people will demand a higher brideprice on the basis of an assertion, not always clearly agreed on, that somehow the prospective couple are too closely related. The emergent effect of these rules is that networks of intermarriage do not become too dense. On the other hand, the preference for marrying close by also has strong practical reasons behind it. After marriage, the bride is supposed to move definitively into her new husband's settlement, where she becomes an incomer under the surveillance of her mother-in-law. She is not supposed to go back and stay with her natal kin. If she comes from not too far away and a relatively friendly place, her kin may visit her and may see her at public gatherings and the small weekly markets or church services that are held on Saturdays and Sundays. In-laws also call on one another to help in various ways, which is made easier if they live nearby. Since a parish contains both agnates and cognates, as well as a number of other historically immigrant subgroups, some marriages occur within the parish itself; but this is not a result of any specific preference for this pattern.

In the precolonial past—that is, prior to the 1960s—members of different parishes were sometimes at enmity with one another and involved in bouts of physical combat that resulted in deaths. Agnatic leaders of the parishes influenced these fights, just as they influence the conduct and resolution of disputes nowadays. But instances of such warlike conflict did not necessarily mobilize all parish members. One man might be seen as the "root" or "cause" of the fighting (*wei tse*). This man might have been in a conflict over pig-theft, trespass, a sexual offence, insults, or any other matter with someone of another parish. (Within the parish, leaders would try to quell physical violence or contain it.) Each disputant would gather support where they could, both from within their parish and through other ties. Relationships of fighting could thus involve networks of kin in complex ways that actually inhibited the full-scale involvement of their parish groups although it facilitated spreading the effects of the conflict among a number of parishes. Fighting, therefore, did not define the parish as a corporate or collective unit. Compensation payments made for killings, or for the loss of life by one's allies in fighting, similarly had to be organized by the "root men" involved, in the first place as individuals. Leaders (*kango*), who might be polygynists (i.e., have more than one wife), would have a greater ability through their wealth in pigs to handle such compensation issues and so both to generate and to ameliorate conflicts (Stewart and Strathern 2000a).[3] Their wealth thus defined their positions as leaders within their parishes. Divinatory procedures to determine who in future would become a *kango* were designed to predict exactly this characteristic: who would become wealthy and thus able to contribute their wealth to social occasions. *Kango* were also expected to play a leading verbal part in compensation occasions by making speeches in elaborate and archaic stylized language expressing the meaning of a given payment. These speeches were called *tambaka*, a shortened form of *tamba haka*, "compensation talk."

The *anoa kango* ("wealthy man") among the Duna thus played a social role in some ways comparable to that of the Scottish clan chief, but in a much less hierarchical way. Duna society was not, and is not, in any way based on a principle of absolute command over land or military supporters. Much more room is given for individual, though socially influenced, choice among them. Agnatic genealogy, ritual knowledge, polygyny, and speaking abilities all worked together to give the *kango* an edge over others within his parish (however, not all *kango* had to be agnates). The position was not formalized nor was it subject to any clear rule of succession. While both the Scottish clan and the Duna *rindi* or parish group can be seen as basically cognatic with an agnatic "backbone" defining leadership, their underlying principles of political control and land ownership were markedly different. The wider historical and political circumstances always affect the actual operation of kinship "principles," as these two cases clearly show.

CLANSHIP AND EXCHANGE: OTHER CASES FROM THE NEW GUINEA HIGHLANDS

The Duna case is similar to that of some other Pacific Island peoples, notably the Choiseulese studied by Harold Scheffler (1965) and the Kwaio of Malaita, studied by Roger Keesing (1967, 1968). Both of these populations belong to the Solomon Islands, far from the Papua New Guinea Highlands, so the structural similarities between the cases are not due to historical contact or influences. Rather, they have to be viewed as the structural realizations of generative possibilities that exist in many contexts and result in permutations of social forms. When we examine other cases from the Papua New Guinea Highlands, we see that all these show an interplay between cognatic and agnatic ties of kinship and descent, but these elements come together differently in practice from the form that has developed among the Duna (which parallels most exactly, we should add, that of their immediate neighbors, the more numerous Huli-speakers who live to their southeast).

We take the case of the Mount Hagen area in the Western Highlands Province of Papua New Guinea to show the different arrangements of similar elements that we have referred to here. The Hageners are a much larger population than the Duna, with probably some 120,000 speakers today of the Melpa language, which belongs to a larger set of related languages separate from the languages spoken to their west, where the Duna live (Strathern and Stewart 2004: 10).[4]

Hagen groups are numerically larger than Duna parishes. The widest political group is the tribe, which may number more than 5,000–10,000 persons nowadays, although this applies to only a few, especially large groups in the central Hagen area where the land is most fertile and population density is heaviest.[5] Tribes are elaborately segmented into subgroups. The most significant subgroups are the clans, whose members maintain a common territory, defended in the past by warfare (as were Duna parishes), and recognize a rule of exogamy, that is, they do not marry within the clan itself (unless in exceptional circumstances). Clans were important as solidary fighting units during precolonial times (prior to the 1930s), and they remain significant as collective political actors today. Clan male leaders also tended to be polygynists, as with the Duna, but polygyny was more marked than in the Duna case and marriage was more definitely a vehicle for extensive political alliances. Most markedly, the Hageners developed an elaborate institution of competitive exchanges, known as the *moka*, which linked networks of prominent individuals and their groups in great cycles of exchange of wealth comparable to those practiced in the exchanges known as *tee* among the Enga people to their west (Feil 1984, 1987; Strathern 2007; Strathern and Stewart 2008).[6] Leaders were those who were not just wealthy in pigs and shells, but who deployed these in the *moka* in order to gain greater status through their achievements. The consolidations of groups around such leaders or *wuö nuim* led to a greater effective sense of collective sociality within the clan group in Hagen than appears among the Duna, coupled with a much greater emphasis on ongoing exchanges between groups.

Pigs lined up on a ceremonial ground in Mount Hagen, Papua New Guinea, to be presented to allies and affines in a *moka* occasion. Pigs are reared and fed largely by women's labor. Men give them away as prestige objects in local political events. Each pig has been marked with red ocher paint by its owners to signify its health and vitality. The pig is at the heart of Melpa "kinship," since as a wealth item it stands for the value inherent in a "person."   (Photo: P. J. Stewart/A. Strathern Archive)

Mount Hagen, Papua New Guinea. A man helps his kinsman to don the elaborate decorations for a *moka* dance. Eagle and red bird-of-Paradise feathers are among the brilliant feathers in his headdress. Family members sit in a small clearing near the ceremonial ground where the dance for the *moka* will be held.   (Photo: P. J. Stewart/ A. Strathern Archive)

Early explorers and Australian colonial officials came to Hagen in the 1930s, and administration was consolidated in the 1950s, followed by the establishment of local government councils and early occasions of voting for a nascent House of Assembly in the 1960s. Independence in 1975 brought with it a full-scale parliament of Papua New Guinea as a whole and Hagen leaders were from early on prominent in national politics. Economic development, based largely on cash cropping from the cultivation of coffee, began to take off in the 1960s. Lutheran and Catholic pioneer missionaries came along with the government personnel, and after World War II resumed their activities in force. By the 1960s, most people could be described as nominally Christian, although degrees of adherence to Christian practices varied widely.

The Australian colonial officials sought early on, first to contain, then to suppress indigenous warfare, which was a vigorous part of political action in the past. Following this period of "pacification," as it is conventionally called, there was a great efflorescence of exchange activities. This was fuelled by two main causes. First, the Australians brought in large numbers of the shells valued as prestigious objects by the Hageners, especially pearl shells, and used them to pay for local labor, food, and access to land on which to build airstrips and government and mission stations. These shells came from the far distant marine areas off the coast of the island. They were obtained cheaply there, but were objects of great value in the central mountains far from their sources. In colonial times, they had trickled in through indigenous trade routes. Now there was a sudden influx. Second, with warfare temporarily ended, many deaths had to be paid for and alliances renewed, and the new wealth was put to work for these purposes. Moreover, with pacification, marriage ties could be extended beyond a narrow range. Leaders acquired more wives. New exchange links grew up. The system expanded exponentially. Groups were consolidated around these extended patterns of exchange. There was no such history among the Duna, for whom effective administrative control came much later and the inflation in the supply of shells was much smaller. Hagen became a center of both political and economic development. The Duna area has by contrast so far remained a backwater in terms of political interest and involvement in national affairs in general.

How does this historical information relate to patterns of kinship and marriage? In Hagen, there was a greater development of political groups and exchange relations prior to "first contact" with the world outside of New Guinea. Tribe membership and clanship were strongly marked as signs of identity. While among the Duna an individual leader might be recognized as the "root man" of a fight, in Hagen this term came to be applied to whole clans as collectively responsible units (even though, in practice, things often happened through the instigation of individual leaders). Alliances between groups were more stable, and more propped up by intermarriage and exchanges of wealth. These patterns were if anything further intensified by the advent of pacification. Within the clan, kinship terms referring to relations with "fathers"/"sons"/ "brothers," and "sisters"/"daughters"/"mothers" became strongly entrenched (see Appendix 1).

This consolidation of terminology was accompanied by a consolidation of descent ideologies regarding the clans and tribes. Each tribe has an origin myth, and each clan recognizes a specific narrative expressing its distinctiveness within the tribe. Complex oral histories indicate that many clans have come into being and either died out or have been incorporated as subgroups within more successful or dominant clans. Historical realities reveal a flux of identities from the past. But the colonial period partly froze these complexities derived from the times of warfare in the past. Consequently the clan emerged as a more stable unit. And within this emergence agnatic genealogies of origin perhaps became more fixed and definite. The earlier detailed ethnographic accounts of Hagen, written in

German by Lutheran missionaries, reveal a society in which a patrilineal ideology was uppermost; and we suggest that in certain regards, this ideology was strengthened rather than weakened through pacification and the expansion of exchanges.[7]

Patrilineal ideology was modified in practice, however, in a number of ways. As with the Duna, many people became affiliated to groups through their mothers. Group members who belonged through their fathers were (and are) described as *wuö-nt-mei*, "born of men," while those belonging through their mothers were *amb-nt-mei*, "born of women." These two categories operated differently from their apparently similar analogs among the Duna. In the Duna case, discussed earlier, the categories "man-standing" (*anoagaro*) and "woman-standing" (*imagaro*) are defined in terms of descent, with reference to a particular founding ancestor. Persons who trace membership of their group through one or more female links at any point in the genealogy tying them to such an ancestor remain technically *imagaro* even if, say, their father or father's father belonged to the parish before them. In the Hagen case, the two contrasting terms do not refer to descent ties, but to immediate ties of parenthood or filiation. *Amb-nt-mei* means someone whose tie to their group is through their immediate mother. If they remain in the group, marry, and have children who in turn stay, these children are *wuö-nt-mei*, because they belong via their father. *Amb-nt-mei* affiliation is thus constantly being transformed into *wuö-nt-mei*. In a further projection of this kind of logic, whole sections of clans are sometimes called *wuö-nt-mei* and *amb-nt-mei*, tracing their points of affiliation to an ancestral brother and sister pair. The reason for this relatively open recruitment or acceptance of persons through female ties is in essence the strong ideological weight given to matrilateral ties generally in Hagen culture. Women who divorce or are widowed or in the past were driven away in warfare when their husbands died in fighting could, and can, always go back to their natal places, where their children are always freely accepted. Regular payments are customarily made to mother's kin for the nurture the mother gives to her children as they grow up and for her "blood," shared with her group, that enters into the body of the child. In addition, as we have already seen, marriage and the exchanges of wealth that result from it are acknowledged as major elements of social structure; and, as with the Duna, there are historically established ideas about a female spirit (the *amb kor*) who stands for the flow of women, fertility, and wealth between groups (see Stewart and Strathern 1999, 2002b; Strathern and Stewart 1999, 2000a).[8] In all of these ways, then, agnatic exclusiveness is modified. Yet, overall, the ways in which Hageners refer to and think about their groups as whole groups remain agnatic, not cognatic. The agnatic ideology simply encompasses, and glosses over, the facts of mixed affiliations in practice. Clans are conceptually *öngin-tepam*, "brothers and fathers," in a male idiom. Yet there is no stress, as there is with the Duna, on a pure agnatic line leading up to an ancestor. Agnation is thus supported as an overall ideology without being reflected strongly in practice. The Duna case is the inverse of this: Agnation is reflected strongly in notions of agnatic leadership within the parish group, but it is encompassed in another way by an overall cognatic ideology. Our comparison of these two cases shows, therefore, the "recombinant" possibilities of different configurations of structural elements, also bringing out the fundamental distinction between filiation and descent as laid down by Meyer Fortes in his book *Kinship and Social Order* (1969). These analytical and comparative distinctions map quite well onto Hagen and Duna indigenous concepts of sociality.

SELF, GROUP, AND PERSONHOOD

We have sketched ideas about clanship in Hagen; and we began our discussion in this chapter by referring to the idea of "clannishness," as implying the solidarity of sets of people and their identification with their groups. Since Hagen and Duna, like all other areas in New Guinea, are societies in which kin relations are pervasive and define major frameworks of people's lives, we could argue that self and group could be equated in such societies. In some anthropological theorizing, a further step is taken. For these theorists, there is no self apart from the group or the social network. The person is defined entirely relationally. In its extreme form, this way of thinking about the data leads to a denial that there is any concept of "the individual" as such in these societies. There are only relational persons. In particular, personhood in these societies is contrasted with the "possessive individualism" supposedly characteristic of "Western" capitalist societies. Implicitly, a contrast is thus being made between precapitalist and capitalist societies; and the New Guinea societies, in which ceremonial exchanges of "gifts" of wealth goods have historically been of prime importance, are seen as the antithesis of capitalist society, following the famous work of the French theorist Marcel Mauss, *The Gift* (1970). A good deal of this stream of writing derives from the influence exerted by M. Strathern (1988) on "the dividual" (see Stewart and Strathern 2000b) and Roy Wagner on "fractal persons," (e.g., Wagner 1991).

Disentangling the various threads of argument here is a complex exercise. What we mean by terms such as "individual," "person," and "relational" can be moot, because all these are terms taken from ordinary usage and given a particular twist by anthropologists. As we see it, pointing out that people are highly "relational" in New Guinea (or anywhere else) does not mean that the self in these societies is entirely equated with the group or the kin network nor does it preclude the possibility that people are also in a meaningful way "individuals." By individuals, here we mean people who are recognizably distinct in their ways of behaving, ideas, inclinations, and practices. (It is a different matter whether persons are indigenously defined, in general terms, as "individuals" or otherwise. In our formulations, we recognize that such definitions do vary and impact, but do not entirely determine, behavioral patterns.) In our view, this is a characteristic of people everywhere and persists regardless of social ideologies, though it may be harder to discern in some societies rather than others. Therefore to say that people are relational does not mean that they are not also individuals. Indeed to deny this is to deny to them something of their essential humanity. From our own ethnographic experience, individuals in this sense certainly exist everywhere.

Second, at a more specifically analytical level, denying individuality makes it harder for us to understand conflict, violence, and the resolution of conflict, as well as the intricacies of leadership activities. Therefore, we need the concept of individuality to deal with these domains of ethnographic enquiry. Societies in which "the gift," in Mauss's sense, is or was practiced are by no means devoid of evidence of conflict, deception, trickery, and manipulation, as well as striking acts of generosity and strategic politicizing. Therefore "gift" societies operate in individual as well as in collective terms. It is for all these reasons that we have offered the term "relational-individual" to cover the New Guinea cases, and a host of others, in which relationality is marked but so is individually expressed behavior (Stewart and Strathern 2000b; Strathern and Stewart 1998). We have argued these points exhaustively elsewhere (e.g., Strathern and Stewart 2000b). We refer to them briefly here as a part of our overall theme in this book on kinship in action. Kinship in action means both conformity and deviance, both cooperation and conflict. And both in the Hagen and the Duna societies, the constitution of society is such that plenty of scope is given to persons to make choices. A basic characteristic of cognatic groups is that a person may obtain membership in more than one group and select among alternatives. This is the case for the Duna. And in the Hagen case, in spite of—or even perhaps because of—the clear patrilineal framework of group structures, similar arenas of flexibility exist and are recognized.[9]

We would like to make another point here: All of our data need to be considered historically. While we have been able only to sketch in some historical features of our cases here, what we describe as "custom" or even "social structure" is actually a moving set of historical processes. "Affiliation" in Hagen in the 1960s was not the same as it presumably was in the 1920s prior to the arrival of the Australians; and in the 1990s, it was affected by yet another set of factors such as migration, urbanization, renewed warfare, and other results of sociopolitical change. Attempts to typologize these societies as "patrilineal" or "cognatic" must always be framed against important backgrounds of this kind. And indeed, as Meyer Fortes himself often used to say, "You don't call a whole society patrilineal," because the whole society contains many other features that are not necessarily tied in with patrilineality. Even within the kinship universe, patrilineality in Hagen has historically coexisted with flexibility of affiliation and recognition of female links; while cognation among the Duna has coexisted with a strong emphasis on the important role of agnatic descent in defining what amounts to a politico-legal structure for the group as a whole.

OTHER CASES, OTHER TYPES

Matriliny among the Tolai

Our earlier discussion has been limited both geographically and topically. It is not our purpose in this book to give typologically or geographically a complete account of the variations in kin groups. We need, however, to give at least some indication of the types of organization that often appear in anthropological accounts and are not covered by the examples given earlier.

Of these types, one of the most important and interesting is the matrilineal descent group. Many societies in different regions of the world—for example New Guinea, Africa, South and Southeast Asia, Amazonia, North America—exhibit this form. It is often described as a mirror opposite of patriliny, which in some ways, though not in all, it is. In Chapter 1, we have discussed Trobriand ideas of procreation, which amount to an extreme emphasis on maternity, but with a twist relating maternity to a kind of ancestral reincarnation. In patrilineal systems, too, there is sometimes an idea that it is "spirit" that passes down in the patriline, and Duna ideas seem just one stop away from such a notion, but we were never told that the *tini* or spirit of a person uniquely comes from the father's side. Instead, the idea is that *knowledge* of the spirit world may be especially passed down culturally through males.[10] Trobriand ideas are different: They are based on the concept of the reincarnation of spirits of matrilineal ancestors through the entry of a spirit child into the mother's womb. Not all matrilineal systems depend on such a cosmological underpinning. We will look here at another case, the Tolai people of East New Britain Province on the Gazelle Peninsula off the north coast of the mainland of Papua New Guinea. They belong to the same general cultural complex of Austronesian language areas as the Trobriands but differ from the Trobriands in terms of the balance of social relations between matrilineal kin and others. The Tolai are well-known as a vigorous, historically dominant, people in their area, who since early days of German and subsequently Australian colonial control from the last quarter of the nineteenth century onward, effectively seized on opportunities for economic and political development, especially around the town of Rabaul. In the lead-up to political independence from Australia in 1975, the Mataungan Association, based in Rabaul, was prominent, from 1963 onward, in demanding solutions to disputes over land that had arisen out of the colonial administration's actions over time. Rabaul had earlier experienced wartime occupation by Japanese forces from 1942 to 1945 and had been the object of intensive economic and political "directed change" in the 1950s postwar period of reconstruction (Epstein 1992: 44–45). So the Tolai are a people with a complex colonial and postcolonial history and have a high proportion of business people and national-level politicians, as well as academics and writers among them (see also Epstein 1999). Social organization, however, is based on a complicated interplay between maternal and paternal ties of kinship intimately connected with land rights, inheritance, and patterns of marriage. Strains in land use had emerged owing to land alienation and the introduction of cash cropping, along with growing population pressure. Kinship relations were adjusted and manipulated in efforts to deal with these pressures.

Unlike the Trobrianders, the Tolai had no overarching system of chiefship in their society. Small, independent matrilineal groups were under the direction of senior elders (*lualua*) (Epstein 1969: 14), who regulated rights to land and the arrangement of marriages. Counteracting this isolation of the small groups, marriage might often be with a more distant set of people. There was a broad division of people, both among the Tolai around Rabaul and extending to neighboring areas, of a type known in anthropological literature as "dual organization." By this arrangement, each matrilineage was linked to one of two large dispersed matrilineal moieties ("halves" of the total population included), and its members had to marry into the opposite moiety. The moieties were thus exogamous, intermarrying categories. If neighboring matrilineages were mostly of the same moiety, they would have to marry further afield. At residence, however, marriage was virilocal; so a woman from a more distant group coming in at marriage would transmit her own matrilineal membership to her children. Inevitably, therefore, the moieties would tend to become interspersed.

A. L. Epstein and T. S. Epstein worked extensively on research in the Tolai area in the early 1960s. A. L. Epstein worked primarily on the small volcanic island of Matupit near Rabaul. On Matupit in 1960–1961, there were small local units within villages, known as *gunan*. *Gunan* simply means "land portion" (like *rindi* in the Duna language or *dal* in Gaelic usage), and as such can also be applied to wider units. Epstein called the small *gunan* "hamlets" (1969: 94). These hamlets were in the precolonial past fenced off by bamboo barricades and surrounded by a space of bush growth not cleared for gardening, like little fortresses. Each was associated with members of a constituent matrilineage group *(vunatarai)*, seen as the permanent owners of the land; and this right of ownership was signaled by the practice of burying the dead of the matrilineage in their own homesteads (Epstein 1969: 94). (This is an old Austronesian practice, shared by the Trobrianders and also some indigenous Austronesian-speaking groups in the mountains of Taiwan, for example the Paiwan people.) Even though bodies were subsequently buried in village cemeteries, after administrative and Christian mission influence was exercised, the idea that land ownership is tied up with proof of burial in a particular site remained strong in 1960. Not everyone, however, in the hamlet belonged to the matrilineage. Women were in-married, and through the out-marriage of natal women, matrilineage members were often dispersed elsewhere. But only matrilineage members had permanent claims to *vunatarai* land. Epstein notes that this idea inflected contemporary attitudes, since when people wanted to build "permanent European-style houses" they were usually allowed to do so only on a location "acknowledged to vest in the *vunatarai*" in which they held membership (1969: 95). Matrilineal descent thus provided a bedrock of land tenure, while other arrangements of a flexible kind were made for residence and usufruct. (In a comparable way, *agnatic* ideas, within a wider cognatic system, ultimately define land ownership among the Duna.)

Actual hamlet composition, as we have noted, was complex. In one hamlet, during 1959–1960, Epstein reports that of 99 adult householders, either male or in some instances female, 51 residents had a genealogically direct membership in the landowning matrilineage; another 7 belonged to an allied group of the same moiety which was said to "stand together" with the owning group by virtue of a coalescence between the two groups; 25 belonged through their fathers, that is, their fathers were members of the owning group; and a small minority of 4 male householders belonged through affinal links resulting from a situation where they had settled in the place of their wives (i.e., uxorilocally in technical terms). With this last category, we should also note that the children of such a household head would belong to their hamlet by matrilineal descent. Taken all in all, these figures indicate the strength of matrilineal ties, along with a complementary tendency for residence to be traced through a paternal tie of filiation where the father was a matrilineal member of the hamlet.

How could this come about? Epstein goes on to point out that among the Tolai, the tie between a mother and her sons is very strong. (For simplicity, here we use the present tense.) Daughters continue the mother's matrilineage, but after marriage they tend to marry out and go to live at their husband's hamlet. This raises the problem of how to get the sister's children of the matrilineage back to their mother's place, and in matrilineal structures this problem is solved in various ways. Because the sons·stay with their mother in their father's place, they tend to emerge as a "matricentric family," that is, a set of brothers focused on their mother (Epstein 1969: 98). On the mother's death, this group does not necessarily disperse. One son at least will tend to stay near where he took care of the mother during her lifetime, and other sons will live nearby in different hamlets of the village. Each traces his ties back to the mother's hamlet of birth, and they continue to cooperate with one another, thus forming a "local matrilineage" dispersed in a number of hamlets (pp. 100–101). Their children in turn, as long as they remain with the father, are linked to their father's matrilineage by the tie of paternal filiation.

The balance between the two main patterns of residence (matrilineal versus paternal/patrilateral) could vary considerably. This was because in some places the pattern of virilocal/patrilocal residence was continued for "two, three, or even more generations" (Epstein 1969: 103), resulting in a cumulation of paternally linked residents in numbers of hamlets. But, as Epstein goes on to reemphasize, the "dominant jural principle that ownership of a hamlet site always vests in a matrilineage" is always maintained. The memory of this is preserved in formulae such as "my father's father was begotten" by such and such a *vunatarai* (p. 103). The begotten in question is maternal in origin, even if the person's links to his area of residence consist of steps of paternal filiation.

All this may seem very technical, but we give these details because they are evidence for two significant points of understanding. First, the Tolai system, like many others, runs on a combination of fixity and fluidity. Matrilineal descent, tied to ultimate land ownership of a particular hamlet vested in a particular *vunatarai*, provides the jural fixity. Paternal ties of filiation provide the flexibility, giving people alternatives for their residence, depending on personal relations and land availability, an issue of growing importance with population increase and land alienation. This combination enables the Tolai to navigate their way in the twisting flows of historical change. Second, it should be noted here how we have again sorted out our analysis in terms of a distinction between *filiation* and *descent* (paternal filiation and matrilineal descent). This distinction is equally vital and important for understanding the Trobriand case. It was Meyer Fortes who most clearly delineated this fundamental, cross culturally applicable distinction (Fortes 1969: 282–283). Recurrent steps of filiation do not translate into descent ties, according to this model of the kinship domain. The Tolai case illustrates this point, because steps of paternal filiation do not negate matrilineal descent. Further flexibility is provided in the Tolai case, as Epstein notes (p. 104), because land can be purchased, and purchased land can also be inherited. But such rights "do not constitute what the Tolai call the *kakalei*"—a claim of matrilineal right that remains vested in the vendor lineage, whose senior member alone is entitled to be known as "owner of the soil, *a bit na pia* or *pai na pia*" (p. 104). The relevance of this point for disputes between the Tolai and outsiders who purchased land rights from them over the years is quite plain. The complexities that can arise over the combination of matriliny and patrilocality also mean that disputes and litigation over access to land are an endemic part of the Tolai social life. To make things even more complex, certain kinds of land rights have historically been obtained by offering some shell-money at the death of an important male leader ("big-man"). The petitioner used to tie shell-money around the arm or leg of the deceased, and would in return receive a piece of land for his use during his lifetime; "but at his death the land reverts again to the relatives of the original owner" (p. 135). Epstein in fact points out that the English word "purchase" is a translation of the Tolai expression *kul*. An act of *kul*, however, does not transfer all rights; moreover, it is supposed to happen between persons who recognize mutual obligations of kinship; and the "price" is not expected to be high or to reflect market values. In "purchases" by the administration, land was, by contrast, removed from the sphere of kinship and obligation, and the potential for resentment and dispute was thus increased over time.

It was, interestingly, junior men, linked paternally to pieces of land "purchased" in this way, who vociferously objected to their elders' acts of entering into such transactions with the administration. The young men feared that they would lose their access to this land and did not feel that the administration would give them enough back for this loss over time. This concern and resentment fed into the advent of the Mataungan Association, which was a large-scale popular movement of opposition to the administration, in which a Matupit islander, John Kaputin, was prominent. The association was among the political forces that led to the accelerated political independence of Papua New Guinea from Australia in 1975. This example shows us how the intersection of kinship relations, land, and colonial development practices can result in political consequences at a higher regional or national level. Understanding of the basic processes in the domain of kinship is therefore vital to the understanding of the wider domains of politics and history. Matrilineal descent does not always have the same relationship to political processes as in the Tolai case, of course; and its effects vary in accordance with how strongly it is stressed in the overall social system by comparison with other principles such as locality, residence, and political organization, as well as paternal filiation within the sphere of kinship itself.

We chose the example of the Tolai precisely because in their case matriliny has been historically embedded in a multiplicity of other factors. The cases of matriliny that have been studied around the world include a few where more "extreme" forms of it have been practiced. Perhaps the best-known is the case of the Nayar people of South India, studied by Kathleen Gough (Gough 1961 in Schneider and Gough 1961). More recently, another case has emerged, that of the Na people in Southwest China (Cai 2001). We will discuss this point in Chapter 5, with emphasis on the Na, to illustrate what is meant by labeling them as examples of "extreme" matriliny, and also to show how these examples have to be understood in the context of history.

OTHER CASES, OTHER TYPES

Bilateral Kindreds among the Iban

It is important to recognize that descent is not a prerequisite for the formation of kinship groups. It does, however, provide a useful format for building distinct political units in what anthropologists have called "polysegmentary systems," that is, those constituted through interrelations of segments in wider groups called clans, tribes, or phratries, especially where these segments are involved in collective action such as feuding or warfare. However, solidarity for the purposes of warfare or raiding does not have to rest on shared descent. Shared locality can also provide a basis for political action.

The kinship and residence practices of the Iban people of western Borneo (primarily Sarawak) became well-known as a case of the operation of bilateral principles through the fieldwork and writings of J. D. (Derek) Freeman, dating to the 1940s and 1950s (Freeman 1960: 66). Especially significant in his ethnographic work on the Iban was Freeman's demonstration of the importance of choice of residence at marriage for the local constitution of family groups. More broadly, in his Curl Bequest Prize Essay for 1960, Freeman considerably clarified and developed the analysis of "kindreds," that is, the wider kinship circles that may be created around a particular person or set of siblings through the recognition of degrees of cousinhood.

The Iban whom Freeman studied belonged to Sarawak. They were shifting cultivators who moved into the forests of the Baleh river area, cultivating the hillsides and practicing headhunting, beginning their migration about 1880 and settling on a more permanent basis by 1922 (Freeman 1960: 68). Freeman's 1960 account was published in one chapter of a volume of studies devoted to different manifestations of bilateral structures of kinship in the general Southeast Asia region. He concentrates on "the wider cognatic social structures of the Iban" (p. 66) in this chapter. This wider structure was centered on longhouse communities made up of a number of distinct family groups. Longhouses varied in size from 4 to 50 families, with an average of 14 (p. 69). They were always built on the banks of waterways along which dugout canoes could travel. Each longhouse was an "autonomous entity not subject to the control of any other group" (p. 69) and had its own territory with recognized boundaries. Most of the families in a longhouse were related by kinship to one another, but the longhouse as such was not a corporate group holding land in common. However, each person joining a longhouse had to be incorporated into it by means of a special ritual (p. 70). Moreover, each longhouse had its own ritual expert (*tuai burong*), who conducted divinations to determine the future prosperity of the longhouse community as a whole. And it had a headman (*tuai rumah*) who administered the customary law (*adat*). These two positions of ritual expert and headman could be succeeded to by any male cognate of the previous holder within the longhouse (p. 70). Headmen were established as the intermediaries between their longhouse and the British colonial administration which ruled in Sarawak at the time of Freeman's fieldwork. In earlier times, longhouses also were combined in alliances that Freeman describes as "tribes," within which disputes could be settled and whose "members did not take one another's heads" (p. 77), recognizing one another "as *kaban*, kith or kin" (p. 77).

Freeman distinguishes between this very broad definition of *kaban* and the *kaban mandal* or "close kindred." This "close kindred" of any given person consisted of all the consanguineal kin, tracing through both females and males (Freeman 1960: 71). Such kin ties tended to be genealogically recognized only up to grandparents' siblings and their descendants, that is, to second cousins, although cousinship in a more general sense could be extended to the fourth degree of cousinship. Work groups for hunting or gathering of forest products contained a majority of such kin, although affines (in-laws) also took part in them. In Freeman's definition, affines were not, strictly speaking, included in the kindred as such. He explained and justified his definition at greater length in his 1961 Curl essay, giving examples from Welsh folk custom (Freeman 1961: 193–195) and reviewing the history of anthropological definitions of the term (pp. 195–201).

As Freeman argued, kindreds as he defined them are not groups as such. We could formulate this point by saying that they are best thought of as fields of social relationships formed by network nodes of recognized kin. Freeman further distinguished between the wider kindred as a category and kindred-based action groups including cognatic kin and also some affines and friends (Freeman 1961: 203). At this point, he reveals an important piece of ethnographic fact about the Iban: that "in traditional [i.e., pre-colonial] Iban society there was an obligation on all the able-bodied mature males in an individual's kindred to avenge his killing by the members of another tribe" (p. 203). This gives us a vital glimpse of how kindreds and tribes emerged as political units in the past. The tribe was a kind of security circle. Within it, as we have already seen, headhunting was not practiced. Between tribes, as is now clear, the taking of heads was fuelled by the necessity to avenge killings.

Freeman goes on to explain that headhunting was a central feature of Iban life in the past. Warriors celebrated the taking of trophy heads, prepared themselves for further combats, and performed elaborate rituals as a pathway to political prestige based on their prowess as headhunters. Kindreds joined together in large parties for headhunting raids on other tribes, "with fighting forces of hundreds and sometimes even thousands of men" (Freeman 1961: 231).

This observation gives us the widest extension of kinship among these Iban people and indicates that in spite of the absence of unilineal descent groups, bilateral kinship ties, combined with considerations of locality and terrain, could provide the basis for large-scale, if temporary, mobilizations of people for political purposes.

In his chapter in the volume on developmental cycles of kinship, edited by Jack Goody, Freeman concentrated further on domestic arrangements within the longhouse, centering on the *bilek* or walled family compartment, housing valuables such as large Chinese pottery jars, bronze gongs, silver jewelery, and feather headdresses. Each *bilek* family also owned a cluster of trophy heads, collected through headhunting and hung in the longhouse gallery (Freeman 1969: 19). The *bilek* was a "domestic family" (p. 20) whose members prepared food and ate together, owned tracts of land for their subsistence, and performed magic for their prosperity and rituals aimed at longevity and prestige (p. 22).

Most *bilek* families were small, with a predominant range of three to seven people. This small size was maintained through the continuous re-creation of new *bilek* units. As Freeman explains, "at least one of the children of a family, when he or she reaches maturity and marries, remains in the parents' *bilek*. All of the other children may marry out, and so become members of other units, but one always stays in the natal *bilek*" (Freeman 1969: 24). According to this account, the *bilek* is a kind of stem-family, in which succession to household headship takes place over the generations. Marriage among the Iban was, he reports, "rigorously monogamous" (p. 25), so large, compounded families did not emerge. In terms of residence, the husband might move to the wife's *bilek* or vice versa (p. 26), and in fact these two forms of residence (uxorilocal and virilocal) occurred with almost equal frequency (p. 26). In terms of filiation, each child belonged to the *bilek* it was born into and not to any other. Birthplace therefore determined social filiation, and this could be changed only through physical mobility or adoption into another family. Freeman invented the term "utrolateral filiation" to describe this situation, meaning that a child was affiliated to a *bilek* on either the father's or the mother's side, but could not belong to more than one such unit. Such a system could result in some *bileks* without children dying out. Adoption was practiced to obviate this problem, and Freeman notes (p. 28) that adoption was "widely prevalent."

Membership in a *bilek* could also be obtained through marriage (Freeman 1969: 29). Since many children of a union shifted residence at their marriage and could not maintain their natal *bilek* membership, this was a necessary feature of the system. Moreover, marriage within the *bilek* was, as might be expected, forbidden, so every marriage joined partners from two different units. Co-residence further determined inheritance rights, so that an out-marrying child lost inheritance rights in the natal *bilek* but gained them in the *bilek* of marriage (p. 32). *Bilek* membership was crucial for funeral rituals as well: Those who jointly inherited *bilek* property were expected to hold these rituals faithfully when one of their members died (p. 33). Further, one member of the *bilek* was always regarded as its *pun bilek*, the "root" person. Freeman refers to this personage as "the senior member by virtue of descent" (p. 34). Since descent in terms of unilineal descent group rules of affiliation is not operative in the Iban system, this phrase means that the oldest natal-born *bilek* member becomes the *pun bilek*. As this process is repeated, a line of succession is formed, in practice not extending more than three or four generations, but nevertheless giving a kind of jural "backbone" to the *bilek* as a corporate group over time, in the same way as lines of agnatic descent do among the Duna, as described earlier. But with the Iban the line of succession was not agnatic at all. Freeman's careful quantitative work revealed that the *pun bilek* was about as often a female as a male figure; hence the principle of utrolateral filiation which he identified operated to produce a pattern in which the *bilek's* head might be either male or female. If a senior daughter elected to stay in her natal *bilek* and her husband joined her there, she would in time become *pun bilek* after the previous holder of this position died.

The Iban case, as analyzed by Freeman, thus provides us with a combination of wide-ranging kindred ties used in the precolonial past for political purposes and small-scale domestic units based on bilateral kin ties, in which residence choices at marriage were crucial for defining *bilek* membership and positions of headship within the *bilek*. The characteristics were shrewdly summarized by Meyer Fortes in his account of Freeman's findings (Fortes 1969). Fortes described the overall Iban system as dependent on "the jural equality of men and women of homologous structural placement which is a necessary condition for equilateral cognatic systems to exist" (p. 124). In a later passage, he noted that co-filiation among siblings distributed in different *bileks* provides an ongoing context for kindred ties; but that within the *bilek* itself "it is distinctive of succession . . . that it cannot be fraternal, it must be inter-generational, which means that it follows filiation, regardless of the sex of the parties" (p. 127). Finally (p. 236), he describes the Iban system as a "widely anastomosing cognatic system," employing the image of rivulets spreading out from a main stream at its outlet to the sea. These are all pertinent ways of analytically explicating Iban kinship practices.

Conclusions

In this chapter, our primary aim has been to give instances of patrilineal, matrilineal, and cognatic principles that enter into social structure. Our descriptions have had a number of theoretical intentions. First, we have tried to give enough relevant details to situate these kinship principles in their wider contexts of embodied action, in line with the overall aims of this book. Second, we have tried to show how comparisons need to be subtle and nuanced, for example, in our Hagen–Duna comparison. Third, we have made it plain in each case how what we call kinship ties are set into, and themselves influence, wide structures of politics and broad experiences of history.

Questions to Consider

1. How do kinship ties intersect with politics?
2. What is meant by the term "mixed affiliations"? What is its significance in terms of the examples discussed in this chapter?

Notes

1. For work on the Duna, see Strathern and Stewart (2004), and Stewart and Strathern (2002). These two works examine Duna kinship, exchange, ritual, and contemporary politics in detail and should be consulted to obtain a more comprehensive view of the topics sketched here.

2. "Witches" (*tsuwake kono*) were proverbially seen as local females motivated to attack the spirits (*tini*) of people out of greed for the consumption of human flesh. Male diviners, empowered by their putative spirit wife, the *Payame Ima*, were given the task of identifying such persons. Those so identified might save themselves by confessing their supposed actions and identifying other women as witches along with themselves. Rumors and gossip in the community about women who were stingy or greedy might feed into suspicions that could have guided the prognostications of these diviners.

3. This publication contains detailed texts and translations of Duna speeches made on occasions of requesting or paying compensation in wealth items for deaths in situations of conflict. It also contains an analytical account of Duna warfare and a comparison with similar practices among the Huli and other Papua New Guinea Highlands peoples.

   The texts presented indicate the importance of "talk" as a category of action among the Duna. The Hagen leader Ongka was also fond of claiming that while many men were "big-men," or *wuö nuim*, he alone "held the talk" (*ik e na mint tep mor*). (Ongka is well known to many students of anthropology through the film *Ongka's Big Moka* and also through his biography [Strathern and Stewart 2000c]). In practice, his speeches were among many made on occasions in which decisions and viewpoints might be reached. However, Ongka and his fellow leaders were well aware that talk was not all fluid and segmentary structures were not all manipulable fantasies: fluid, yes, but existing only through talk, no: they were vital constraining elements in life processes of cooperation and conflict with others. Merlan and Rumsey (1991) were correct in arguing that references to "groups" (*talapi* in their area of Papua New Guinea, *reklaep* among the Melpa speakers of Mount Hagen) are subject to contestation and variability. This is simply because the term itself is vague. Other terms are deployed to give specificity. Speech can refer to itself, but it also refers to land, violence, peace-making, sorcery, witchcraft, marriage, in short to all the embodied processes of life of which it is a part. Ethnographers of the Hagen area prior to Merlan and Rumsey emphasized the significance of speech as a factor in sociality. None, however, claimed that it represented all of sociality or that groups did not exist other than in verbal usages. See F. Merlan and A. Rumsey (1991) and J. Weiner's (1992) review of *Ku Waru* in the journal *Man*, n.s., 27, no. 3: 679–680.

4. Linguistic classifications of the Highlands languages in Papua New Guinea have been revised from time to time since the early work of Stephen Wurm (1964). Wurm was a pioneer who made field studies collecting materials over a wide region of the Highlands well before the region was opened up to road transport and development, and his data were invaluable as a basis for later work. For an up-to-date review of issues of classification and the "Trans New Guinea hypothesis," see Pawley (2005). Pawley comments (2005: 78) on the fact that lexical items (vocabulary) shared between the Huli, Duna, and Bogaiya (variant spelling Bogaia) languages may partly reflect historical borrowings between these speakers

rather than genetic relationships over a longer period of time. In our own approach, we have simply noted that Duna usages show similarities with both Huli and Bogaiya.

Malcom Ross (2005: 35) lists Duna-Pogaia (i.e., Bogaiya) as a subgroup with the Trans New Guinea "family" of languages. His classifications are based on pronominal usages, with the argument that these are likely to reflect genetic commonalities rather than borrowings. This is an arena where linguists may not wholly agree on how to interpret their findings. In any case, if there are extensive lexical borrowings, this surely is an indication of important intercultural sharing. Genetic relations are therefore not the only significant markers of commonality. An important task would be, where possible, to move beyond the simple dichotomy of genetic relationship versus borrowing in order to trace the history of relations between languages and cultures within regions. This project would bring together perspectives from both cultural anthropology and linguistics, without privileging one over the other.

5. The term "tribe" is used here in a purely local and technical sense in accordance with a classification adopted in Strathern (2007, originally published in 1971) and Strathern (1972).

6. The *moka* and *tee* became well-known in the anthropological literature as exemplars of the dramatic and impressive organizational achievements of leaders and their helpers and supporters in the Central New Guinea Highlands region. The *moka* in particular was marked by a principle of increment by which recipients of a gift were expected to reciprocate with a larger gift after a period of time had elapsed. For a discussion of the deeper implications of *moka* activities and their connections with sacrifice, see Strathern and Stewart (2008).

7. On the ethnographic writings by the early Lutheran missionaries Georg Vicedom and Hermann Strauss, see Strathern and Stewart (2007). These two missionaries provided a unique valuable account of Hagen social patterns in the 1930s through to the 1950s prior to extensive economic and political changes brought on by colonial control. There is also an important theoretical point here: The structures that anthropologists infer from their field observations must all be seen as the products of history, as emergent and also mutable over time. Ecology, local history, and colonial and postcolonial circumstances can result in transformations of social structure over time.

8. We have explored in detail a case history from the Hagen area showing the creative improvisations and "dances around custom" in an affiliation drama involving novel patterns of sexual and interethnic relations that emerged in the 1990s (Andrew Strathern and Pamela J. Stewart, "Creating difference: A contemporary affiliation drama in the Highlands of New Guinea," *JRAI*, n.s., 6, no.1 [2000d]: 1–15).

Our remark here about a "clear patrilineal framework" in Hagen refers to the representational and ideological level, the "dogmas of descent." It echoes Evans-Pritchard's much earlier observations about the Nuer people of the Sudan in Africa (E. Evans-Pritchard, *The Nuer* [Oxford: Clarendon Press, 1940]). Evans-Pritchard's views have been much contested, but perhaps also misunderstood. He did not explain Nuer social process overall in terms of agnation but only noted that agnatic ideology, maintained notably in leading lines, enables these agnates to sponsor in nonagnates and even ethnically different people as cooperating members of residential groups whose descendants will gain a stronger hold on the shared group identity. Similar processes occur in both the Hagen (Melpa) and Duna cases. Of course, many different operational reasons occur for these incorporations, as distinct from the ideological representations that encompass them. Sharon Hutchinson provides an up-to-date recontextualization of Evans-Pritchard's findings (Sharon E. Hutchinson, *Nuer Dilemmas* [Berkeley, CA: University of California Press, 1996]).

9. Ibid.
10. Such knowledge is tied to practice, however, because it enables men to communicate with the spirit world, the *tini* of the dead, by means of sacrifices and invocations.

References

Biersack, Aletta. 1982. Ginger gardens for the ginger woman: Rites and passages in a Melanesian society. *Man*, n.s., 17: 239–258.

Cai, Hua. 2001. *A Society Without Fathers or Husbands: The Na of China*. Trans. Asti Hustvedt. New York: Zone Books.

Davies, Norman. 2000. *The Isles: A History*. Oxford: Oxford University Press.

Epstein, Arthur Leonard. 1969. *Matupit: Land, Politics, and Change Among the Tolai of New Britain*. Berkeley and Los Angeles, CA: University of California Press.

Epstein, Arthur Leonard. 1992. *In the Midst of Life: Affect and Ideation in the World of the Tolai*. Berkeley and Los Angeles, CA: University of California Press.

Epstein, Arthur Leonard. 1999. *Gunantuna: Aspects of the Person, the Self and the Individual Among the Tolai*. Bathurst, NSW: Crawford House Publishing.

Feil, Daryl K. 1984. *Ways of Exchange: The Enga tee of Papua New Guinea*. St. Lucia: University of Queensland Press.

Feil, Daryl K. 1987. *The Evolution of Highland Papua New Guinea Societies*. Cambridge: Cambridge University Press

Fortes, Meyer. 1969. *Kinship and the Social Order*. Chicago, IL: Aldine.

Fox, Robin. 1967. *Kinship and Marriage*. Harmondsworth: Penguin Books.

Freeman, J. Derek. 1960. The Iban of Western Borneo. In *Social Structure in Southeast Asia*, ed. G. P. Murdock, 61–87. New York: Wenner-Gren Foundation.

Freeman, J. Derek. 1961. On the concept of the kindred. *Journal of the Royal Anthropological Institute* 91(2): 192–220.

Freeman, J. Derek. 1969. The family system of the Iban of Borneo. In *The Developmental Cycle in Domestic Groups*, ed. J. Goody, 15–52. Cambridge: University of Cambridge Press.

Gough, Kathleen. 1961. Nayar: Central Kerala. In *Matrilineal Kinship*, ed. D. M. Schneider and K. Gough, 298–384. Berkeley, CA: University of California Press.

Keesing, Roger M. 1967. Statistical models and decisions-making models of social structure: A Kwaio case. *Ethnology* 6(1): 1–16.

Keesing, Roger M. 1968. Non-unilineal descent and contextual definitions of status. *American Anthropologist* 70: 82–84.

Magnusson, Magnus. 2000. *Scotland: The Story of a Nation*. New York: Atlantic Monthly Press.

Mauss, Marcel. 1970. *The Gift, Forms and Functions of Exchange in Archaic Societies*. Trans. Ian Cunnison, with an introduction by E. E. Evans-Pritchard. London: Cohen and West.

Merlan, Francesca, and Alan Rumsey. 1991. *Ku Waru: Language and Segmentary Politics in the Western Nebilyer Valley, Papua New Guinea*. Cambridge: Cambridge University Press.

Modjeska, Charles N. 1977. Production Among the Duna. Ph.D. dissertation, Australian National University.

Pawley, Andrew. 2005. The chequered career of the Trans New Guinea hypothesis: Recent research and its implications. In *Papuan Pasts*, ed. A. Pawley, R. Attenborough, J. Golson and R. Hide, 67–108. Canberra: RSPAS, Australian National University.

Ross, Malcolm. 2005. Pronouns as a preliminary diagnostic for grouping Papuan languages. In *Papuan Pasts*, ed. A. Pawley et al., 15–66. Canberra: The Australian National University.

Scheffler, Harold W. 1965. *Choiseul Island Social Structure*. Berkeley, CA: University of California Press.

Stewart, Pamela J., and Andrew Strathern. 1999. Female spirit cults as a window on gender relations in the highlands of Papua New Guinea. *The Journal of the Royal Anthropological Institute* 5(3): 345–360.

Stewart, Pamela J., and Andrew Strathern. 2000a. *Speaking for Life And Death: Warfare and Compensation among the Duna of Papua New Guinea*. Senri Ethnological Reports 13. Osaka, Japan: National Museum of Ethnology.

Stewart, Pamela J., and Andrew J. Strathern. 2000b. Introduction: Narratives speak. In *Identity Work: Constructing Pacific Lives*, ed. Pamela J. Stewart and Andrew Strathern, 1–26. ASAO (Association for Social Anthropology in Oceania) Monograph Series No. 18. Pittsburgh, PA: University of Pittsburgh Press.

Stewart, Pamela J., and Andrew Strathern. 2002a. *Remaking the World: Myth, Mining and Ritual Change among the Duna of Papua New Guinea*. For, Smithsonian Series in Ethnographic Inquiry. Washington, D.C.: Smithsonian Institution Press.

Stewart, Pamela J., and Andrew Strathern. 2002b. *Gender, Song, and Sensibility: Folktales and Folksongs in the Highlands of New Guinea*. Westport, CT and London: Praeger Publishers (Greenwood Publishing).

Stewart, Pamela J., and Andrew Strathern. 2004. *Witchcraft, Sorcery, Rumors, and Gossip*. For, New Departures in Anthropology Series. Cambridge: Cambridge University Press.

Strathern, Andrew. 1972. *One Father, One Blood*. Canberra, ACT: Australian National University Press.

Strathern, Andrew. 2007. *The Rope of Moka*. [1971 version reissued with a New Preface by A. Strathern and Pamela J. Stewart]. Cambridge, MA: Cambridge University Press.

Strathern, Andrew, and Pamela J. Stewart. 1998. Anthropological accounts and local concepts in Mount Hagen, Papua New Guinea. *Oceania* 68(3): 170–188.

Strathern, Andrew, and Pamela J. Stewart. 1999. *"The Spirit is Coming!" A Photographic-Textual Exposition of the Female Spirit Cult Performance in Mt. Hagen*. Ritual Studies Monograph Series, Monograph No. 1. Pittsburgh, PA: University of Pittsburgh.

Strathern, Andrew, and Pamela J. Stewart. 2000a. *The Python's Back: Pathways of Comparison between Indonesia and Melanesia*. Westport, CT and London: Bergin and Garvey, Greenwood Publishing Group.

Strathern, Andrew, and Pamela J. Stewart. 2000b. *Arrow Talk: Transaction, Transition, and Contradiction in New Guinea Highlands History*. Kent, OH: The Kent State University Press.

Strathern, Andrew, and Pamela J. Stewart. 2000c. *Collaborations and Conflicts. A Leader Through Time*. Fort Worth, TX: Harcourt Brace College Publishers.

Strathern, Andrew, and Pamela J. Stewart. 2000d. Creating Difference: A Contemporary Affiliation Drama in the Highlands of New Guinea. *The Journal of the Royal Anthropological Institute* 6(1): 1–15.

Strathern, Andrew, and Pamela J. Stewart. 2004. *Empowering the Past, Confronting the Future, the Duna People of Papua New Guinea*. For, Contemporary Anthropology of Religion Series. New York: Palgrave Macmillan.

Strathern, Andrew, and Pamela J. Stewart. 2007. Ethnographic records from the western highlands of Papua New Guinea: Missionary linguists, missionary-ethnographers. In *Anthropology's Debt to Missionaries*, ed. L. Plotnicov, P. Brown, and V. Sutlive, 151–160. Ethnology Monograph Series No. 20. Pittsburgh, PA: University of Pittsburgh.

Strathern, Andrew, and Pamela J. Stewart (eds) 2008. Exchange and sacrifice: Examples from Papua New Guinea. In *Exchange and Sacrifice*, 229–245. For, Ritual Studies Monograph Series. Durham, NC: Carolina Academic Press.

Strathern, Marilyn. 1988. *The Gender of the Gift*. Berkeley, CA: University of California Press.

Wagner, Roy. 1991. The fractal person. In *Big-men and Great-men*, ed. M. Godelier and M. Strathern, 159–173. Cambridge: Cambridge University Press.

Wurm, Stephen A. 1964. Australian New Guinea highlands languages and the distribution of their typological features. *American Anthropologist* 66(4), Pt 2: 77–97.

CHAPTER 5

Structures of Marriage

Linda Stone, in her book on kinship, has stressed the importance of gender in this regard, that is, the organization of social relationships in terms of gendered identities. Indeed, she explains that one purpose of her book is to "explore gender cross culturally through the framework of kinship" (Stone 2000: 1). She takes as her starting point for this enterprise the context of reproduction. Since humans reproduce sexually, and since such processes of reproduction are invariably governed by customary norms and rules, an examination of such rules invariably leads us into the field of kinship studies. As Stone notes, "kinship is everywhere a part of the social and cultural management of reproduction" (2000: 2). And this management varies cross culturally. Accordingly, gender relations themselves must vary, since reproduction is deeply bound up with ideas of the gendered roles of women and men.

Families of procreation are classically based on an axis of gender flowing from a conventional definition of marriage as a legally recognized sexual bond between a woman and a man (whether exclusive or not), governing the affiliation of children. It is in the family, then, that anthropologists have tended to find the heart of the gendering process, a process that goes beyond the simple fact that reproduction depends on the sexual congress of male and female. The family tends to be linked to the wider society through the kinds of social roles ascribed in general to females and males. Debates over the family and the status of women in society tend to derive from the attribution of special responsibility to females in the reproduction and socialization of children, leading to the notion that women's major task in society is to raise children within the context of the home. But women's reproductive roles do not *necessarily* lead to such a division of labor in society. In many places, women engage in major productive subsistence work in addition to rearing children. They also hold special roles of ritual, political, or economic prominence, while still carrying out their reproductive activities. Nothing, therefore, in their reproductive roles as such determines the status accorded to them in society. It is just that their reproductive role is often given as an ideological justification for restricting their other roles in society. Gender, as a social construct, is therefore based on ideology rather than simply on biology, although biology and social constraints are always at interplay.

Marriage is also not simply a matter of sexual relationships and reproduction. It is often a crucial means of setting up wider sets of relationships between the in-laws. Marriage may be a way of creating or reinforcing alliances between networks of groups of people. In some cases, such a creation of alliance goes along with specific rules or guidelines that specify who should marry whom, as either a matter of preference or a prescribed form. These forms have often been defined in kinship terms and may be signaled by talk about varieties of cousin marriage. Again, two different functions or contexts can be defined for such marriages: One is their results in terms of alliances between people, and the other is their results in terms of property and inheritance. Cousin marriages are often means of keeping together the property of two related families and/or of bringing the families close together for other purposes.

MOUNT HAGEN, PAPUA NEW GUINEA

In cases in which intergroup alliances are at stake, the marriage preference involved is likely to be stated in these terms, for example, by saying "we exchange women," where the male perspective is in focus. The phrase for this in the Melpa language of Mount Hagen in Papua New Guinea is *amb aklwa etemen*. A loose calculus is kept of the flow of marriages between the groups involved, with a view to maintaining a balance in the relationship. Intermarrying does not involve an exclusive relationship between two groups in Hagen, nor does any authority manage the flow. Nevertheless, if more women are leaving for marriages to a particular group without any coming back, the imbalance is likely to be noted. There is no kinship designation involved. Those married are not, in fact, recognized as cousins. Quite the reverse. Marriages are arranged outside of the sphere of recognized kinship, which in practice means around the degree of third cousins. Yet, there is also a residual notion that once a kin tie has become attenuated, it is a good idea to bind the families together again by a marriage. (On incest and exogamy in general, see Appendix 2.)

This brief example gives us a glimpse of the complexities involved when we look into the practical working out of marriage rules described in the ethnographic literature as preferential or prescribed. In Hagen, preference is expressed in group terms. This reflects the importance of alliance in this social context, and alliance in turn is about the exchanges of wealth goods and the acquisition of prestige. Rules of prohibition of marriage are expressed in individual kin terms. From a male viewpoint, for example, a man should not marry into his mother's clan group, extending cousin terms to all females of that group, and he should not marry with individually defined cousins of the clans into which his father's sisters have married. Marriage with parallel cousins is forbidden, whether these are on the father's or the mother's side, and in the case of patrilateral parallel cousins the prohibition is extended to the clan level, because the affiliation to the clan is often traced through the father.

To summarize this set of prohibitions, in Hagen a man may not marry into his own clan or his mother's, nor may he marry his cousins to the third degree in other groups. Clan kin are assimilated to the terminology of parents, siblings, and children in fact, and so are parallel cousins (e.g., mother's sister's daughter, abbreviated as MZD): So these kin are classified as siblings, not cousins at all. The system seems to result in a likelihood of a relatively wide spread of marriages between groups, since dense patterns of repeated intermarriage between persons who are in effect kin are prohibited. While we cannot impute any conscious design to this pattern, the effect is to ensure that marriage links extend in a number of directions. This has the further effect of maximizing opportunities to seek resources for exchange purposes. Coupled with the possibility of polygamy, it can be seen that marriage is one of the prime strategies of aspiring leaders in the prestigious *moka* exchange system.[1]

Marriage, however, comes with considerable costs. Bridewealth has to be paid, and it is considerable. In the times prior to the 1930s, when outsiders first entered the world of the Hageners, bridewealth amounts were smaller. The items offered were the same as those that were given in *moka*: primarily live pigs, pork, and valuable types of shells, as well as extras such as cassowary birds, salt packs, and long tubes of decorating oil. Shells were in short supply, traded in arduously from distant places on the coast, unknown to Hageners. Pigs took a lot of work to grow. Exotic goods were expensive to obtain. The costly character of the items reflected the importance of the transaction. When outsiders came in and brought with them an increased supply of shells, which they traded directly for work or foodstuffs, the size of bridewealth payments rose accordingly. Previously, shells could be exchanged only for other shells or for pigs, that is, within their own sphere of prestige goods. Trade with the incomers cross-cut this pattern of custom and made it possible for some people to enrich themselves in ways not previously feasible, or in all probability, even thought of. The bridewealth market, as it were, was thrown into turbulence.

By the 1950s and 1960s, with established colonial administration by Australia, and the introduction of local councils run by the people with assistance from expatriate government officers, frequent entries appear in council minutes from councilors whose constituents complain of oppressive sizes of bridewealth and ask for regulations to control this process. The complaints most often related to the shell component of payments, since an influx of shells had created an erratic flow of these, including the abandonment of other forms of shell in favor of the much prized pearl shell, with its bright yellow appearance and glossy surface. Regulations were passed, with little effect, since they could not easily be enforced. In the 1970s, shells were themselves made obsolete because of a growing preference for introduced state money that could be used also to purchase goods outside of the internal ceremonial circuits of exchange. Inflation now proceeded—and continues to proceed—in terms of the new monetary part of the payment.[2]

Here another complexity needs to be noted. Bridewealth in Hagen is not a unilateral transfer of wealth. It is an exchange. The bride's family are expected to make a sizeable return in kind for the payment they receive. They cannot just take a part of what is given and return it. They must instead raise wealth on their own side and have it ready to give back in a second round of the ceremony. Inability to do this would bring them shame. The prestige of both the groom's and the bride's people is therefore at stake. It is unsurprising that preparations for a marriage are elaborate and that an event may fail if a particular contributor does not turn up on the appointed day. What the need to exchange goods, as opposed to just receiving them, indicates is the imperative value accorded to alliances established through marriage; so that we may almost say, with some truth, that "they marry in order to exchange" rather than, or as much as, "they exchange in order to marry." (Martin Southwold made this suggestion to one of us—AJS—many years ago; see also Strathern 1980.) Looking at the matter holistically, we might rephrase this proposition by saying that marriage and exchange belong to a wider political, and ritual, cosmos in which alliance is a prime value and acts in counterpoint to hostilities.[3]

A formulation of this latter point enables us to relate the discussion of bridewealth also to issues of gender. The marriages set up by bridewealth in Hagen do two things: They establish ties between sets of people bound together

Communal phase of a bridewealth occasion in Mount Hagen, Papua New Guinea. Kinsfolk, male and female, sit down around a meal of vegetables and pork cooked in an earth oven. This phase would come after a formal display of goods for the bridewealth and intense negotiations over these between the parties.   (Photo: P.J. Stewart/A. Strathern Archive)

on either side of the transaction. They also set up a new social, economic, and reproductive node within the broad network of kin relations. In both regards, there is a gendered element at work. In terms of intergroup ties, it is precisely ties through women that act as the main conduits of alliance. Women are not just passive elements here: They are both productive and reproductive. They rear pigs, which are prime valuables and bearers of social relations as well as capital worth. They bear children, who become related to their mother's kin as well as to their father's people. These kin relations themselves become the focus of intergenerational exchanges, since there is a strong ethic of making payments to mother's kin for the successful growth of the mother's children, and these then can become another focus of *moka* exchanges over time. In this connection, *moka* can be seen as a mechanism that switches and generalizes interindividual ties into broader ties of alliance. Women's special roles as the caretakers of pigs and the custodians of children validate this expansion into alliance relations. Hageners express this in embodied terms. Ties through the mother and with the mother's kin are signaled by referring to breast milk (*aem kopong,* "grease of the breast"). Ties through the father are ties of *noimb kopong,* "grease of the penis." Gendered complementarity is evidenced here, since "grease" is a vital component in the Melpa cosmos, and both kinds of it are needed for life to continue.

In contemporary contexts, criticisms about bridewealth have emerged. These criticisms result from both changes in gender relations and misunderstandings about how bridewealth originally works in social contexts marked by a value placed on exchange. The misunderstandings arise from seeing bridewealth as a simple unilateral payment, with the total amount seen as a calculated price for the marriage, in other words as like a purchase of a commodity. Heated expressions of views took place in the pages of one of Papua New Guinea's national newspapers, the *Post-Courier,* on this topic. Some writers saw bridewealth as a degrading practice and compared it to commodity transactions, arguing that it should therefore be abolished. If we are discussing systems that retain their exchange-based rationale, this view is inadequate and indeed misleading. The aims of bridewealth in Hagen relate to a world of exchanges that establish sociality itself. However, there is another aspect of the issue, which must be addressed. The advent of state money, coupled with urbanization, has the potential to transform bridewealth into something more like the practices that became a target of criticism. In other words, if bridewealth becomes a lump sum of money, and if the reciprocal payments are truncated, it indeed becomes much closer to a commodity transaction. It also becomes highly subject to changes in the economy at large, and makes it desirable, almost inevitable, that with a growing need or demand for money the parents of a girl will demand higher amounts of payment. So the institution is transformed.[4]

It may be that the special emphasis among the Melpa on *moka* exchanges marks them out from some other cases. In an earlier publication (Strathern 1980), it was argued that a distinction made in the Africanist literature by Meyer Fortes needed to be modified in order to understand how bridewealth worked in the Papua New Guinea Highlands. Fortes made a distinction between prime and contingent prestations in bridewealth (1962: 3). The prime prestation was supposed to be related to the capital value of "the bride's sexual and pro-creative capacities" (p. 3), and the contingent prestations to the ancillary values. However, for Hagen, the whole bridewealth carries importance. There is a simple reason for this: It is assembled from a number of contributions and is distributed by the recipient family to an equally wide set of people. At a symbolic level, elements do appear in it that take on the sign of a kind of capital value. For example, the provision of a very large pig for the mother of a bride is called *mam peng kng*, "the mother's head pig," meaning the pig to recognize the importance of the bride's mother. If a large enough pig is not offered, the girl may walk away from the transaction, and people will comment that the mother "greased," that is, persuaded the daughter to do this. This is not an isolated feature. It appears also quite prominently in bridewealth negotiations among the Duna people (on whom see, e.g., Strathern and Stewart 2004; we discuss the Duna case further below). Some of the valuable pearl shells given in the past, especially fine ones, were designated as *peng pokla* shells, that is, shells to "cut off the bride's head." The meaning here is not literal, but metaphorical. "Head" stands for the person, and the person's value. Payments for killings are also said to be for "the head" of the person killed (*wuö peng etemen*). Cutting off the bride's head simply means altering her identity from unmarried to married. Her unmarried status "dies." Shells paid in this way were not reciprocated. They were said to "die" on the girl herself. Other shells could be distributed more widely. *Peng pokla* shells would be taken by the girl's parents. We see in these usages a clear parallel to Meyer Fortes's categories. On the other hand, the items given for exchange were not ancillary to the whole purpose of the marriage. They were also essential to creating the kind of alliances that only marriage established, tying exchange to contexts of procreation and the creation of ramifying kinship ties over the generations.

HUAULU, EASTERN INDONESIA

The Melpa speakers of Mount Hagen are a large, flourishing population of more than 120,000 people, affluent horticulturalists and cash croppers, much influenced by political, religious, and economic changes. The Huaulu, studied by Valerio Valeri, are different. They are a tiny population, of some 140 people, in Central Seram, the Moluccas, Eastern Indonesia. At the time they were first studied in 1972, they were holding on to their traditional customs (Hoskins 2001: xvii). The Huaulu are among a much wider set of peoples in Eastern Indonesia who are known in the literature for their "asymmetric" form of marriages, in which wife-givers (as this is conventionally formulated) are always separated from wife-takers. In the ideal-typical model of this form, it is combined with one type of cousin marriage, in which a man marries a woman classified as his mother's brother's daughter. Thus, he obtains a wife from his mother's group: The wives come from the same place. The daughter cannot be given back in this same "direction." She must be handed on to the same place as his own sister married into. A rule of this kind lends itself to a closed hierarchical connubium, with some question arising as to how boundaries can be organized at its edges. Where will those at the top and bottom of such a system get their wives, given that the system is predicated on the superiority of wife-givers over wife-takers and typically the society overall is hierarchical?

Such a situation was famously explored by Edmund Leach in his *Political Systems of Highland Burma* (Leach 1964: 101–226). Leach's answer to the conundrum of boundaries was twofold. First, the hierarchical relationships tended to break down over time and were replaced by "cousin circle path" marriage, in which a group at the end of a chain married back into the group at its beginning. Second, high-ranking Kachin families might marry into another ethnic category, the Shan, and even transform themselves into Shan (Leach 1964: 213ff.).

The tiny Huaulu population is not marked by any political hierarchy comparable to the hierarchies found among the Kachin as studied by Leach. Moreover, another practice, which Valerio Valeri explains in detail (Valeri 2001b: 139ff.), counteracts the asymmetrical or hierarchical implications of the marriage rule: The exchange of valuables at a marriage is symmetrical between the locally dominant lineages involved in any given marriage. The valuables given in marriage transactions are either porcelain pieces obtained through trade and emanating from Korea, China, or Japan or conus shell armlets. The shells are scarce and rarely added to, but other items may also be given— gongs, earrings, beads, textiles, and coins or paper money (less valued than coins) (Valeri 2001b: 139).

The next piece of information shows the connection between these valuables and the marriage rule: "armlets and women move in the one direction and plates in the opposite direction" (Valeri 2001b: 139–140). Plates thus go in the direction of bridewealth, and armlets go with women in the reciprocal direction. If someone needs a plate, they will go to the wife-takers of their lineage and ask for one in exchange for an armlet. Rates of exchange are fixed and equivalences are calculated. (This is basic, and it tends to give the lie to arguments that in cases of this kind—or the Hagen case discussed above—calculations are not made. They most emphatically are, and for good reason—to maintain parity of status, as with the Huaulu.)

Valeri goes on to point out that the plates are not directly exchanged for women. Thus, there is no bridewealth in the immediate sense. We are dealing rather with a regimen of total reciprocity, marked by "the absolutely nonreciprocal flow of women and the absolutely reciprocal flow of *arata* (valuables) in marriage" (Valeri 2001b: 141).

Although there is no payment for the woman as such, the marriage prestations do effect shifts in residence, affiliation, and social naming over time (Valeri 2001b: 142). There are three stages of prestations. The first is made when the groom goes initially to live in his father-in-law's house (uxorilocal residence). If no further payment is made, residence remains the same and any children born belong to the mother's group. A proper marriage follows the second prestation, which allows residence to become virilocal (with the husband's natal house) and the children belong to his lineage. After this, the wife and her children are tabooed from entering houses of her father's patrilineal kin. Elaborate rituals accompany this stage, and paternal affiliation confers high status, necessary for the maintenance of the status of the father's lineage (p. 148). Valeri comments that ties made through women cut across group boundaries, while those made by men create such boundaries (2001b: 145). The symmetrical and equal exchange of valuables acts as a counterweight against the hierarchy of the marriage rule itself. We suggest that such an arrangement is diagnostic of a very small social universe in which elaborate hierarchical distinctions cannot easily be maintained. The Huaulu exploit sago, hunt, gather, and fish, as well as make gardens: There is no intensive production, although there is trade for the porcelain plates (from mainland Asia) and the conus shells (obtained from West Papua) (Valeri 2001a: 155). While the Huaulu are a small population, they are divided into different lineages. These lineages are the units that enter into affinal relations. Wife-takers offer the first prestation for a marriage, which must then be reciprocated. This same temporal pattern is found in Hagen marriages, and the same analysis applies: If the initial gift looks like a payment, this is negated by the counter-prestation. The negation of the unilateral payment is also an affirmation of alliance (p. 167). Valeri stresses that in practice many complications exist. For example, "only half of one payment in antique plates (the one for the bride's mother's brother) is reciprocated by tangibles. The other half is reciprocated with something unquantifiable: blessing and fertility" (p. 169). The antique plates are considered to be the primary "price of the woman" (p. 170) (and thus roughly equal to Fortes's prime prestation). In addition, though, a number of store-bought items such as sarongs, modern plates, and red cloth are given—all as extras (Fortes's ancillary prestations). While, then, no component absolutely represents a simple purchase of a wife, certain elements do symbolically equate with interests at stake in the total transaction. Interestingly, too, the discourse of the Huaulu about reasons for exchanging valuables at the time of marriage is comparable to those Hageners supply when questioned. Asked why wife-givers also give armshells in return for plates, one man told Valeri that this was done to secure future gifts of plates (2001a: 173). At the symbolic level, Valeri also notes, the valuables given all had to do with female reproductive and life giving powers (2001a: 173). Valuables in Pacific societies also carry gendered values of a comparable kind.[5]

From this discussion, Valeri concludes that when we look at Huaulu practices, we see that a rigid distinction between "gifts" and "commodities" cannot be maintained. Actions and items carry connotations that may belong to both sides of this supposed dichotomy.[6] An ambiguity of this kind helps to explain how people involved in gift exchange transactions often enter quite easily into commodity transactions when these become available. And this in turn helps to explain how, when state money enters a local political economy, bridewealth as gift can deflect toward brideprice as market transaction—generating in turn protests from both traditionalists in the society and human rights observers outside of it.

THE BUSINESS OF MARRIAGE IN TELEFOMIN

In his Introduction to the volume *The Business of Marriage: Transformations in Oceanic Matrimony* (1993), Richard Marksbury highlights the transition from a subsistence to a partly commodity-based production as "the most significant factor acting upon traditional prescribed patterns of marriage" (1993: 11). He argues that state money and employment make it "possible for individuals to disregard kinship bonds and obligation with impunity" (p. 12). Marriage payments may come to be treated as commercial transactions (p. 12). Money received in marriage payments may be kept rather than being distributed out to kin (p. 13). Marriages are less stable, and women become more independent (p. 13), perhaps because the advent of money introduces a greater sense of a marriage market. The costs of marriage payments may cause people to be in debt for longer periods of time, but correspondingly the risks of losing one's investment are greater, we may add. Marksbury suggests that there is a shift from the collective to the private sphere, as people seek marriage for personal fulfillment (1993: 9).

Reformulating Marksbury's points here, we need to separate out the issues centering on the costs of marriage from the issue of personal versus collective aims. Wherever bridewealth is paid, the costs tend to escalate with monetization, because the overall demand for state money is greater than the demand for the locally circulating valuables such as shells or pigs. Concomitantly, the desire to hold back bridewealth money from the networks of kin may be greater. If we add to this the other element of an increasing unwillingness to make reciprocal gifts, we can easily see that with these changes the institution or custom is transformed out of all recognition. It becomes indeed brideprice, with an emphasis on the term "price," rather than bridewealth, in which the emphasis is on exchange and alliance. Urbanization and the mixing of peoples together surely add yet another transformative factor. If there is no agreed customary basis for exchanges between the parties, almost by default the transaction will take on a commoditized form, since there is a greater sense of the alienation of the bride from her kin.

This case study from the Telefomin area shows many, though not all, of the features sketched above. Telefomin is a small government station and airstrip within the circle of influence of a giant copper and gold mine at Ok Tedi, now closed, but in full operation during a part of Jorgensen's fieldwork there. In 1974, when he first went there, marriages took place within a framework of "village endogamy and sister exchange" (Jorgensen 1993: 60). This structure puts Telefomin squarely in the category of an "elementary" system, as discussed by Claude Lévi-Strauss, originally in 1949 (Lévi-Strauss 1969 [trans.]). Lévi-Strauss was drawn to the study of such elementary systems because of his interest in delineating a putative passage from nature to culture in human prehistory. He identified the primary incest taboo prohibiting marriage between siblings (or, for that matter, parents and children) as an important factor in this regard. A prohibition of this kind becomes a positive injunction when it is coupled to a rule of alliance, that is, a rule that identifies a specifically appropriate marriage partner, whether by preference or by prescription. Cousin marriage rules do this, and at the preferential level belong, for example, to the history of European society. Marrying a cross-cousin may either perpetuate an earlier alliance (the son's wife comes from where the mother originally came from), or it may constitute an exchange, as in father's sister's daughter marriage (the son's wife comes in exchange for the mother). Incidentally, it should be noted here that if we describe these transactions from the bride's viewpoint, they look a bit different. MBD marriage becomes FZS marriage, and FZD marriage becomes MBS marriage; but the structural implications remain the same, provided that we are dealing with groups in which continuity is calculated primarily in the male line.

Either type of cousin marriage, however, is less direct than sister exchange. In sister exchange, the rule that the gift of a woman can only be returned by another gift of a woman operates within the same generation, and not across generations (FZD marriage) or in a circle of intermarrying kin (MBD marriage is one realization of the potentialities). In Telefomin, as we have noted, the circle was made even tighter by the idea that marriages should take place within the village (village endogamy). Such a system is demographically vulnerable if village size is relatively small, as in the Telefomin case. It can persist in stable conditions. If any perturbation occurs, in either social or ecological terms, it is likely to change.

In Telefomin, this change occurred with the advent of the mine and opportunities for young males to work there. Already in 1974, small amounts of cash were entering bridewealth transactions (Jorgensen 1993: 60), and by 1983, when Jorgensen went back, marriages were being negotiated at a hugely inflated rate of cash payment—marriage was seen as a kind of "business" (commerce), and people were divided in their views about this new situation.

It is interesting that bridewealth was a part at all in the original sister exchange regimen. If women were exchanged in this way, why the need for bridewealth? The imperative of alliance seems to be at work. (Jorgensen does not address this point, but in comparative terms it seems rather important; compare Strathern and Stewart 2000: 30–31.) Also, the need to strengthen ties was important, so that women would not be lost to their natal group. The groom and his kin found strings of cowries (*rop tambu* in Tok Pisin, the Papua New Guinea lingua franca), and the bride's kin returned an equivalent piece of pork for each cowrie string. This return payment was made to keep the contributors to the bridewealth from making claims to any daughters of the marriage. The groom's kin shared out the pork and ate it. The bride's kin kept the shells and passed them on later when they wished to obtain a wife for one of their young men (Jorgensen 1993: 63). Thus, we may deduce that the shells passed on in one direction, always against the circulation of women, a kind of perpetual bridewealth movement. Women themselves were exchanged directly for women, but the shells were kept in limited circulation as a means of obtaining further wives. Shell strings were individual and could not be returned to their previous owner (p. 79). This fact is comparable to the rules of flow of antique plates among the Huaulu, as discussed earlier in this chapter.

Young men employed at the Ok Tedi mine site brought money back to the village and began to offer this in bridewealth in place of cowrie strings. They also used their comparatively large amounts of cash to marry girls from outside their own villages. And this in turn led to the demise of both sister exchange and the practice of returning pork to the groom's kin. While cowries were tied to the marriage circuit, cash was not. It could be used in a multitude of ways, such as building a house or buying a motorbike (Jorgensen 1993: 64).

Telefomin was affected by colonial change prior to the advent of the mine, through relations of trade with neighboring places. In the early 1960s, young men already began to earn cash, and at this stage they tried to convert the cash into shells, in order to use these in bridewealth. But by the end of the 1960s, they were no longer doing this and instead were paying increasing proportions of cash. (This would surely also have to do with relative inelasticity in the supply of shells) The young men thus controlled their own marriages.

The agency of young women was also engaged.[7] In the past, their cooperation and decision making were also involved, but their choices were within the village, or among Telefomin groups at any rate. Into the 1970s, government employees from elsewhere came to Telefomin, and girls wished to marry these outsiders, supported by the administrative officers on the station who upheld women's wishes in this regard (Jorgensen 1993: 68–69). Now payments were unilateral and in cash only. Local young men found it difficult to compete with the outsiders, who held better paying jobs. Wife-givers increasingly sought to bleed their new affines of more wealth, demanding cash on the birth of children, for example. The overall situation was clearly unstable, and the effects on internal village affairs seem unclear. What is abundantly clear is that this history represents a clear shift from bridewealth to brideprice. It is also a shift from the most elementary (in structural terms) jural form of marriage (i.e., sister exchange) to a fluid and complex combination of forms of marriage, the whole shift occasioned by major political and economic changes in the wider fields of social relations rather than by any internal kinship dynamic such as a move from sister exchange to cousin marriage. Gender relations were clearly affected, for colonial pacification opened up potential new pathways for marriages, and women seized upon those pathways. The power balance between the genders altered. But women in the new marriages may not have been happier, being subject to marital abuse and not having such clear recourse to support from their kin as they had before.

RUTH CRAIG'S EARLY ACCOUNT OF TELEFOMIN MARRIAGE

Before leaving the Telefomin case, we should consider briefly the early work by Ruth Craig on this area, based on fieldwork in the 1960s. Jorgensen used Craig's work in the course of his own exposition of Telefomin practices. Craig notes (1969: 176–177) the village-based emphasis of the Telefomin system, and how the practice of tracing group membership through both female and male links produced a dense weave of cognatic relations within the village. Village endogamy further intensified this pattern. Marriages were also expected to occur via the bestowal of the bride by her senior kin, with or without her agree-ment. If a girl unwilling to marry a chosen partner attempted to flee, her kin would suggest that the groom should abduct her. Craig notes: "many girls submit after this betrayal; others in despair commit suicide" (1969: 178). Conversely, a boy who showed an interest in a girl but was not approved of by her guardian kin "faces censure, perhaps a beating from the girl's 'brothers'" (p. 179). However, if a youth could offer a sister in exchange, the girl's family might tolerate his approaches and later act as though they were making a sim-ple bestowal of the girl upon him by their own decision. In a different context, a man who wished to marry a girl of a different parish (village) could try to abduct her, but would be likely to lose in the fight that resulted (p. 179). An unwilling bride, on the other hand, could be so uncooperative with the husband selected for her that in the end he might send her back to her kin (p. 180). Marriages with second cousins were said to be improper (p. 182), but happened in practice. If a household had an adopted girl in it, a youth of that household could be married to her, keeping all loyalties within the household (p. 184).

These telling examples from Craig's work indicate that marriage arrange-ments were underpinned where necessary by force, but worked best with will-ing participants; that young people tried to exert choice and agency, and if thwarted a girl might kill herself; that backstage manipulations took place; and that there was a great drive to contain relationships within small circles of kin.

Craig's account also reveals the seeds of change explored further by Jorgensen. She remarks early on (1969: 181) that "today the system of arranged marriage is foundering, and more self-initiated marriages are succeeding." Pacification, and the opening up of possibilities for safer travel between localities, meant that people were simply meeting more potential partners. Government authorities discouraged the use of force by kinsfolk to control the choices of young people and indeed favored the principle of free choice. Young men traveled and also earned money in wages, which they could apply to marriage payments. While certain preferences, for example, the preference for sister exchange, were still advanced, Craig's statistics showed that "only four out of eighty-five men contracted marriages where actual sisters were exchanged" (1969: 186). It seems that this situation was not necessarily a result of recent social changes as such, because the traditional system was one in which "rights of disposal are bilaterally defined and almost any close male relative may attempt to exercise a claim [over a girl] without consulting others" (p. 186). In practice, various categories of female kin might be brought into play to effect exchange marriages. This shows that while sister exchange within the village was an ideal, the broader principle involved was simply reciprocity in women. Bridewealth was not seen as a mechanism by means of which this direct reciprocity in women was no longer necessary. That situation contrasts with circumstances in larger-scale societies with exogamous clan-groups, as found among the Melpa speakers of Mount Hagen in the Western Highlands Province. There, as we have seen, prohibitions on the marriage of kin were extensive, and there was an emphasis on spreading marital ties as alliances among diverse surrounding groups, in accordance with the expansive character of the Melpa *moka* exchange system. Even so, there was also among the Melpa an idea that between friendly groups exchanges of women in virilocal marriage were desirable. Here the aim was to consolidate close political relations. But we may speculate that a further aim had to do with feelings of security on the part of women married into a particular group. Avoidance of marriage with serious military enemies clearly had such a motivation.

These Papua New Guinea Highlands systems were not ones in which divorce was prohibited. Divorce, in fact, was always a possibility, and in Hagen unhappy brides could make quite a habit of running away back to their kin. The need to repay bridewealth would always be a sticking point, of course, and most likely the bride would be sent back, but perhaps with a demand that she be better treated or compensation be paid to her kin. In the Telefomin case, Craig noted that "a wife feels secure when her protectors (father and brother) and confidants (age-mates) belong to the same local group [i.e., as her husband and his kin]" (1969: 196). Domestic relations thus depend on wider political constellations. With changes in the scale of political and economic interactions, greater possibilities of autonomy and agency emerged in Telefomin for young people. But the negative side of this was that girls, in particular, were more exposed to dangers. Such dangers would be greatly increased in urban situations in which a girl married and left the village to live in the town away from both her own natal kin and those of her husband. Then the likelihood of violence and the difficulties of settling disputes would be greatly expanded.

Finally, here, it is important to notice differences in population sizes and population densities in assessing the correlates of particular marriage arrangements. Ruth Craig set the picture firmly for Telefomin: "The 1,000 Telefomin, whose population density is three persons per square mile, live in villages on the valley floor, about 5,000 feet above sea level" (1969: 176). Their staple crop was taro, a crop that takes longer to mature and yields less at high altitudes. Relatively low productive levels and relatively sparse population, with a small overall number of people, went hand in hand with highly restricted circuits of exchange and networks of marriage ties. A system of this kind is highly vulnerable to outside forces of change, such as new forms of paid work, travel, and government control. Larger-scale systems also respond dramatically to changes, but in some ways are more robust and able ultimately to absorb such changes into their existing structures.

EXCHANGE RELATIONS AND INTERGENERATIONAL CONTINUITY: WIRU AND DUNA

What these contrasting small-scale (Huaulu, Telefomin) and large-scale (Hagen) examples do share is their concern with the distribution of exchange relations via marital alliances. This does not necessarily mean that the focus is only on a single generation. Rather, exchange ties themselves lead into the cross-generational reproduction of social relations. This happens primarily because of norms that specify ongoing obligations between kin resulting from the creation of affinal ties.

Two examples of this can be drawn from our own field research. We will cite these examples briefly. The first is from the Wiru-speaking area of Pangia in the Southern Highlands Province of Papua New Guinea, dating to the period 1967–1984. The Wiru are horticulturalists and pig rearers, with a staple crop of sweet potatoes, supplemented by taro, green vegetables, sugarcane, and bananas. Prior to Australian colonial control from the early 1960s onward, they lived in scattered settlements based on clusters of households. Maximal categories of descent units were recognized, and within these numerous smaller divisions.[8] These categories can be called phratries, and the subgroupings within them can variously be recognized as clans or lineages. The phratry, however, was not an exogamous group. Marriages took place between its component clans. In addition, local phratry segments sometimes incorporated fragments of other large phratries via marriage or friendship ties and protected them within their local territories. Individual marriages might also take place between phratries, some of whose members were on occasion military enemies. In all cases, marriages set up new obligations of alliance and dependence that mitigated the expression of hostilities between affines. In Pangia, there was no equivalent of the complex chains of intergroup exchanges known as the *moka* in the Hagen area. However, there was a very strong emphasis on payments of wealth in shell valuables and pigs to mother's kin, and ties to mother's mother's and mother's mother's mother's kin could be recognized as continuing to entail obligations to give wealth in recognition of mothering or "ancestral" mothering. The recipients of these payments were called *opianango,* "the men who gave birth" to one (thus conflating brothers and sisters). *Opianango* ties could link together people of a number of groups and of different generations.

Among the Duna, such matrilateral payments were not made, but another principle linking the generations together was operative. Here the rule was that the daughter's bridewealth should pay for that of her mother. A number of people contributed wealth items to assist a youth to marry. Years later, if a daughter of that marriage herself married, the bridewealth paid for her would have to be distributed so as to repay those who had contributed to the bridewealth for her mother a generation earlier. Such a system required long-term trust and investments in kin within a local ambit. Conflicts could arise over disputed memories of contributions made many years earlier. The main effect, nevertheless, was to bind networks of people together over time. Sometimes a man could repay the contributors to his bridewealth in advance, especially if they asked for this. Like the Wiru speakers of Pangia, the Duna had no large-scale networks of exchange such as the *moka* in Hagen. The intergenerational ties of reciprocity of marriages tended to operate within the parish, occupied, as with the Wiru, by the notional members of a maximal category of kin identified with the parish name and claiming descent from a mythical founder. The parish, however, is known by its locality name, not by the name of a line of descent associated with it. We can envisage Wiru and Duna social structure as alike in certain ways. In both cases, mechanisms of intergenerational obligations based on marriage, strengthened ties between people in the local group. The mechanisms, however, differed. In the Wiru case, matrilateral payments predominated. With the Duna, obligations of bridewealth repayment were the focus.[9]

Duna area, Papua New Guinea. Monetary notes are displayed on sticks in a showing of bridewealth for a marriage. The man with a sheaf of arrows and a hat is a local leader and famous orator, who will make a speech about the wealth later.   (Photo: P.J. Stewart/ A. Strathern Archive)

Another feature of Highlands Papua New Guinea society that anthropologists have focused on as significant in the reproduction of social relations over time is the institution of polygamy. In Hagen, this institution was linked to the emergence of leaders known as "big-men," who maximized their access to wealth and exchange partnerships by marriages to women of different groups. The prevalence of polygamy is also a mark of social and political inequality, and might be expected to correlate with a clustering of men at the lower end of the social scale who are unable to find wives, because of both their lack of wealth and an artificial shortage of women within the local context. Polygamy was less marked in Pangia among the Wiru and in the Duna area, and this feature correlates with the absence of large-scale ceremonial exchange networks among these two peoples.

Another reason why patterns of polygamy have been modified in colonial and postcolonial times is that Christian missionaries strongly discouraged the practice, on grounds that Christian marriage must be monogamous. From the 1930s onward in Hagen, older leaders with a number of wives who wished to be baptized before they died were required to take just one of their wives to be baptized with them. The others might remain *de facto*, but were not supposed to continue to have sexual relations with their husband. They were placed into a legal and social limbo. What was to happen to the children of these unions was not necessarily thought through. In practice, the situation was not fundamentally altered. The new ritual status of the baptized wife did not carry over into the legal and social spheres of life. It is a different matter altogether when couples undergo Christian forms of marriage ceremonies that then feed into a state system of registered marriages.

Missionaries also opposed the gendered spiritual separations that accompanied many of the indigenous rituals. Often they did so, not only on the grounds that these rituals were pagan in content, but also on grounds that they were demeaning to women. Missionaries saw themselves as improving the status of women. In pursuing this supposed aim, they might impose their own ethnocentric ideas of what women's roles should be, and they sometimes misunderstood the broader meanings of the rituals involved. Numerous studies in Jolly and Macintyre's book, *Family and Gender in the Pacific*, document such processes. (See especially Jolly 1989 and Clark 1989 in Jolly and Macintyre 1989.)

THE CATEGORY OF "POLYANDRY"

In the same volume, we find an unusual study of the practice of polyandry, the logical inverse of polygyny ("polygamy" most often refers to the latter). Polyandry is the marriage of one woman to a number of men, and has been studied notably in the Himalayan region. (H. R. H. Peter of Greece 1963). Nancy Levine studied fraternal polyandry among the Nyinba, a small population of people of Tibetan origin living in Nepal (Levine 1988; Stone 2001: 186–194). The Nyinba number 1,300, and live in *trongba*, corporate landholding households in which a set of brothers is married to a single woman, who is supposed to distribute sexual access and the opportunity to be declared a father of children equally among her husbands. It seems clear that this practice limits population growth and encourages the stability of the *trongba*, although other peoples in this same region have not adopted polyandry. It should be noted that structural polyandry of this type differs from a situation in which one man is the husband but may extend sexual access to other men as a means of binding them to him (cf. Keesing and Strathern 1998: 228, and see W. H. R. Rivers' early study of the Todas, Rivers 1906).

Fraternal polyandry was not the only form of marriage or sexual behavior among the Nyinba. It could be combined with polygyny, or replaced by monogamy, and sexual relations also took place outside of marriage. The patrilineal, patrilocal structure of the *trongba* basically held all these practices subordinate to the continuity of the household and its associated land.

Another comparison presents itself here. The case of the Nayar, of Kerala in South India, during the period 1300–c.1800, is also one in which continuity was vested in a small corporate group, the *karanavan*. Among the Nayar, this group was defined entirely through matrilineal ties, but authority in it was vested in males, and there was a strong tradition of military activity on the part of men of the warrior caste. Nayar marriage practices were complex, in that each commoner Nayar woman was first ritually married to a "husband" through the custom of *tali*-tying (the tying of a gold necklace around her neck by a "groom" from a linked lineage); then, when she came to sexual maturity she could entertain a number of *sambandam*, visiting husbands. Such husbands made gifts to her, and whichever one made such gifts and paid a midwife in a particular pregnancy was recognized as the father of the child that was born. The mother remained in her *karanavan*, and the children belonged to it (Gough 1961; Stone 2001: 134–147).

Comparing the Nyinba and Nayar cases, we can see that in both cases the reproduction of the basic group was paramount. Marital and procreative rights were "compressed" by this fact. Marriage was a full and complex relationship tied to the *trongba* among the Nyinba. With the Nayar marriage was "minimal." Partners did not live together, and the children were allocated wholly to the *karanavan*, although individual paternity was recognized. Among the Nyinba, a single wife was entirely incorporated into a male patrilineal household. With the Nayar, a single woman entertained many husbands, all of whom were, so to speak, "discorporated" from her matrilineage.

These two cases have become well-known *loci classici* in kinship studies. Less well-known is a case reported in the 1989 Jolly and Macintyre volume by Nicholas Thomas, dealing with the Polynesian Marquesas Islands. Thomas dates his discussion to the period around the beginning of the nineteenth century and looks for a systemic explanation rather than resorting to demographic imbalance between the sexes as a "cause" of the practices he investigates (Thomas 1989: 67–72). In the Marquesas at this time, Thomas writes, there was a distinction between chiefs and commoners. Chiefs, however, did not control all the land, since some commoners owned land, while "a significant minority" had no land and either cultivated the land of others, "paying rent in kind" (i.e., sharing the produce), or worked as servants in return for food and political support (p. 72).

Elite women (i.e., those of the chiefly category) seem to have been in a favorable position to select more than one husband. One husband was always considered the senior or principal partner, the *vahana haka'iki*, and all children born to the woman were considered to be his sons or daughters (Thomas 1989: 73). (That is, the principal partner was the *pater*, or social father, even if others were known to be the *genitor* or physical father.) Sometimes men who had been with the woman in their adolescence remained even after "she married an older and more wealthy man" (p. 73). Sometimes, also, two men together would offer themselves to the woman, who would choose one of them as the *vahana haka'iki* and the other as the *pekio*, secondary partner (p. 73). Thomas adds that this last practice may have developed after hierarchical relations in the society had begun to decline as a result of external contact with European influences (1989: 73).

Through this process, the richer households would consist of a woman and her principal husband and a number of secondary partners, plus some servants and workers. (In addition, the principal husband might have some *pekio* female partners, Thomas 1989: 73.) Importantly, *pekio* were nearly all "drawn from the *kikino*, the landless servant" category of people (p. 74). The term *pekio* appears to be related to a root *kio*, meaning "servant" (p. 75). High-status women were thus able to use their sexuality to attract and retain workers in their household. Indeed, there appears to have been competition among household workers to attain the status of such a secondary sexual partner. In no case did these men pass on their status to the children of the household. The overall situation thus differed quite radically from instances, such as among the Nyinba, in which each husband of a woman was considered to be a partner of equal status. It is notable that the Marquesas case carries no hint of fraternal polyandry. It might better be seen as an example of sexual privileges accorded to high-status women. *Pekio*, in addition, were not simply "lovers." They were subordinates, attached to the household as male workers, because of their land-less status in the society at large. The example indicates what we have learned from other cases: that relations that are from one viewpoint "domestic" are from another perspective best understood in overall politico-economic terms (see, e.g., Collier and Yanagisako 1987 for a discussion of gender in these terms).[10]

MARRIAGE, FILIATION, AND DESCENT: THE NA PEOPLE OF CHINA

"Na" is a term given to a category of people spanning Yunnan and Sichuan Provinces in South-Western China (Cai 2001: 35). Cai's field studies were made in the Yongning basin, where the population was about 12,000 people around the year 2000, cultivating a range of root and grain crops (2001: 40), and rear-ing buffalo, cows, and horses, and also chickens and pigs. Traditionally, the population was stratified into three ranked categories, *sipi*, *dzéka*, and *we* (p. 49), marked by differential rights to wear certain kinds of clothing. The *sipi* term means "chief" and consisted of the descendants of the family of the gover-nor (*zhifu*) of the prefecture established as such in the past. Cai translated *sipi* as "aristocracy" (2001: 50). The children of a married *sipi* man belonged to his lineage, and people of *sipi* status were expected to marry within that category.

Dzéka means "people" (Cai 2001: 51). These were the majority, and Cai calls them "commoners" (p. 51). Occasionally families of *zhifu* descent fell out of favor historically and were demoted to *dzéka* status. Among the commoners a form of sexual cohabitation which Cai calls "the visit" prevailed, and in these cases children were said to have belonged to the mother's line (2001: 52). The *we* were serfs and could be transferred between households or sold to another household. The *zhifu* could also demote people to the status of *we*. This category also included descendants of other ethnic groups who worked for the *zhifu* in order to survive, and debtors who could not pay off their debts (p. 53; this last is a classic example paralleled by South East Asian cases; see Strathern and Stewart 2000: 13–28). Most serfs were from families that had originally been commoners (p. 55).

The working out of relations of filiation in this hierarchical order of groups together with different forms of recognized sexual relationships produced some complex and unusual results. The rule was that daughters would follow the status of their mothers and sons the status of their fathers. Thus, if a commoner woman had a union with a serf man, her daughters were commoners but her sons were serfs (Cai 2001: 57). The operation of rules of this kind was also inflected in terms of what Cai calls the "four modalities of sexual life" (2001: 414). These modalities were: the furtive visit, the conspicuous visit, cohabitation, and marriage. Cai's study is historical, and he argues that what he calls "marriage" was not present among the Na prior to influence brought to bear on them during the time of the Qing dynasty (1644–1911) (2001: 67, 413). The Na are an ethnic minority, and different dynasties treated these minority groups incorporated into state control differently. Over time the dynasties gradually extended their direct control over the governance of minority groups, and mandated more power to the *zhifu* as hereditary governors. The *zhifu*'s power was based on land ownership and the collection of taxes as well as the employment of serfs as workers. From Cai's account it appears likely that the legalities of marriage as an institution stemmed from the growing influence of the state as it bore on the descendants of the family of the *zhifu*, ensuring a form of patrilineal and virilocal succession among the aristocrats which ran counter to the basic matrilineal principles of the indigenous Na kinship system.

This basic importance of ties through the mother is reflected in the ideology that bone (*ong*), standing for the whole body, comes from the mother (Cai 2001: 120). Na residential groupings closely resemble the Nayar *karanavan*, matrilineal corporations that maintained residential continuity over time and controlled land. The Na call this group the *lhe* (p. 121). Within each *lhe*, there is a male chief, said to be in charge of external relations, and a female one in charge of internal matters (pp. 122–123). The female succeeds to her mother as eldest daughter; the male to his mother's brother as oldest nephew (p. 124). People of the same *lhe* cannot have sexual relations (p. 125), on punishment of a painful death (p. 126), although Cai's informants had never seen any of the methods of executions cited. Brothers and sisters live together in the same household, but must observe taboos in relation to each other, and sexual partners visit them. This institution of the visiting partner parallels the Nayar *sambandam* relationship, in certain respects, but does not come so close to a legitimized relationship of "marriage." Furtive visitors, or *acia*, are best described as "lovers" or simply "sexual partners." Both sexes tend over time to have a large number of such partners (p. 209). Women may expect to be active in this domain up to the age of 50 and men up to 61 (p. 210), after which age to continue is frowned on.

In many systems, the issue of who is to be named as the physical father or *genitor* of a child is important, regardless of the issue of plurality of sexual relationships. For the Na, Cai denies that this is so, arguing that men are interested only in the children borne by their sisters (2001: 227).

The furtive visit exists alongside another modality, a public kind of visit (Cai 2001: 237). This is called *gepie sese*. Such a relationship may grow out of a furtive visiting relationship. The partners exchange belts as a mark of their more enduring feelings for each other, and the woman arranges for the man to be received at her home. When he comes, he presents gifts to the female chief, who makes offerings to the household ancestors (p. 239) and prepares a feast for him. The couple then exchange gifts of clothing. Gradually the man's new status is recognized by neighbors. The partners grant sexual privileges to each other, although the new tie does not annul the possibility of other *acia* relationships (p. 242). Jealousy may ensue (p. 244); but the new relationship is still based on voluntary consent, not compulsion. A delicate balance has to be maintained. One constraining factor is that no woman can take the initiative and visit a man's place (p. 261).

The third sexual modality is "cohabitation" (Cai 2001: 263), *ti dzi ji mao the*. In this arrangement, the couple live and work together. Residence may be at the female's place (uxorilocal), the male's (virilocal), or in a new household (neolocal) (p. 264). The choice of residence depends on circumstances. For instance, a woman may bring her cohabitant partner into her household if her brothers have left it to become monks, as can happen (p. 265). The cohabitant in that case is expected to provide for his partner's household (p. 273). It does not appear that cohabitation was a frequently taken road of choice. Cai notes that before 1956, during the time of governance by the *zhifu* chief, if a person left home to cohabit with a partner and by this choice annoyed their natal household, the *zhifu* could demote that person to a serf (2001: 288). In cases in which the relationship is approved and endures, the children belong to the *lignée* that received them (295). (Cai uses this French term to describe the small corporate household group usually structured around matrilineal descent.) If residence is uxorilocal, they are members of this group anyway. If it is virilocal, this extension of the receiving group's name to them is a courtesy, but they do not actually become full members of it (p. 295). In general, Cai argues, cohabitation is a temporary mode of conduct for a particular group that is short of either males or females. When this imbalance is rectified, the modality of the visit is resumed (2001: 300).

In addition to these modalities, there is also a practice that Cai says can be recognized as "marriage." This looks more like marriage as it is known in patrilineal cases. It is an arrangement between groups (the *lignées*).

Chiefs act as mediators. The chief of the male involved asks for a daughter of the chosen household, and brings elaborate gifts of alcohol, tea, and clothes, also rice and boned pork. The female chief of the girl's household makes an offering to the ancestors, and negotiations over a brideprice are set in hand. If the negotiations succeed, the bride will be formally transferred to her groom's home. Further feasting ensues (Cai 2001: 307), accompanied by rituals marking the importance of the transactions. An incoming wife gains full rights in her husband's *lignée* (p. 309) and can even become a female chief in it. The couple may still have "furtive visit" relations with others, says Cai. It seems likely, though, that with so much commitment and expense these would be reduced, if not curtailed. Children that are born of marriage that is virilocal belong to the husband's *lignée*, we are told (this contravenes the supposed rule of universal matriliny). Divorce can, however, occur. The choice of marriage belongs only to wealthy families and particularly to those lacking females to carry on the line of descent. Successively repeated marriages over a number of generations appear to have taken place only in the family line of the *zhifu* chief (p. 335 and sqq.), and in particular here such marriages fell upon eldest sons. The groom's sisters tend not to get along with the bride, presumably because of competition for control of resources (p. 350). A *lignée* may split over such an issue. The reason for marriage is clearly that there was primogeniture by the son who was the eldest (p. 352). At the end of his ethnographic discussion, Cai finally notes that prior to 1644, no system of marriage existed among the Na and that after this time the new Qing dynasty imposed marriage on the Na chief (p. 382).

A further chapter in this complex historical case is provided by the fact that Han officials of the People's Republic of China after 1950, attempted to reform sexual relations, partly on the grounds that Na practices caused 50 percent or more of the adults to have sexually transmitted diseases, particularly syphilis (Cai 2001: 385). The PRC officials attempted to promote monogamy and the nuclear family as against matriliny and the matrilineal residential group. In successive years, 1966 and 1971, further attempts were made to achieve this aim, and in 1974 the governor of Yunnan province instituted a further program of reform, requiring the registration of visitor relations and of the imputed genitors of children born from these relationships (p. 393). Couples were rounded up and their fingerprints taken and marriage licenses were handed to them (p. 394). Twenty-eight couples were brought together in this way (p. 395). A research group investigated the results a year later. Cai states that by August 1975, however, 16 out of the 28 couples had broken up (p. 398). The government imposed a fine in each case in which no genitor was recognized for a child. Han culture and ideology about life were taught in school textbooks (p. 402). Villagers, in response, hid their practices. It is remarkable to note here that the government's ideology followed the old idea that monogamy was considered the most advanced evolutionary stage of marriage (p. 409). Cai reports that these reforms are pursued less rigidly today, since Deng Xiaopoing brought in pragmatic reforms from 1981 onward (2001: 410).

At the end of his book, Cai launches into a general theoretical discussion of the concept of marriage, based on his study of the Na. Here, two empirical points are in order. First, this study of the Na shows that marriage in a fully recognizable sense was present among them only in the upper stratum, was a sign of wealth, and was imposed as a result of state dynastic influence only after 1644. The bulk of the population practiced modes of sexual relations that were not "marriage," although cohabitation perhaps came closest to such a situation. The affiliation of children was determined largely on maternal and matrilineal lines. Second, we have therefore been dealing with a case of "extreme matriliny." The nearest paral-lel to the Na case would appear to be the historical case of the Nayar as described by Kathleen Gough (e.g., Gough 1961). Gough saw the Nayar *sambandam* or "visiting husband" institution as a case of minimal marriage, as it were; the Na "visitor" relationship is even more minimal, since it involved no recognition of the status of genitor and was not so regulated as the *sambandam* tie was; while the *enangar* ties among the Nayar represented a ritualized way of recognizing affinal alliance relations, also absent from the Na "visitor" practices, according to Cai's account.[11]

We have relied on Cai's data and discussions in the above account. The relatively unusual features of the materials make it likely that variant versions exist or will emerge. The case study as it stands is sufficiently instructive, however, to be used in our treatment of it here.

COUSIN MARRIAGE SYSTEMS

We have mentioned earlier Claude Lévi-Strauss's fundamental comparative work, first published in French in 1949, on "The Elementary Structures of Kinship," by which he meant, primarily, systems of "cousin marriage"; and within this category he was interested in such marriage forms as operating on a classificatory basis and effecting marital alliances between significant groups in a social network (Lévi-Strauss [1949]1969). A great deal of discussion ensued from this massive study.

Systems of cousin marriage may be seen as opposites of the Nayar and Na practices in which marriage is minimal, and social continuity takes place entirely via filiation and descent. In cousin marriage systems that are in prin-ciple prescriptive, that is, spouses are categorized as cousins, the institution of marriage is pivotal to the wider structuring of society; so much so that anthro-pologists have sometimes described these societies as based on the concepts of alliance (i.e., through marriage) rather than descent. In practice, however, marriage prescriptions and forms of descent tend to work together.

Rodney Needham's classic analysis of the marriage practices of the Purum, a very small population of people who lived on the eastern border of India, can be taken as a further example of how marital connubium structured by a kin-based marriage prescription was organized. The account dates to the 1930s, and Needham drew it from the work of the ethnographer Tarak Das (1945; Needham 1960). We have in this case of the Purum an example of a small, relatively isolated population comparable to the Huaulu, discussed earlier in this chapter. An important point to note initially is that in spite of their small numbers, the Purum habitually married inside their own group. Even without a prescriptive kin-rule of marriage, this means that they inevitably would marry persons seen as kin. What the marriage rule did was to structure this situation and give it a particular form.[12].

The 303 Purum were divided into four villages, each containing a number of households. Local descent groups, based on patrilineal descent rules and belonging to five larger dispersed clans, gave a structural framework to these households (Needham 1960: 75). Each clan was exogamous. Needham wrote that the prescribed marriage was with the "mother's brother's daughter" (MBD) and marriage with the "father's sister's daughter" (FZD) was forbidden (1960: 76). He went on to explain that MBD here can refer to any woman belonging to the mother's brother's clan (p. 76). With many such prescriptive systems, a latitude of this kind tends to be built in, making it more possible for the system to survive in demographic terms. The widening of the definition also means that it is ties between the groups rather than ties between specific families that are the overall focus of continuity. A man's bride need not have any close genealogical relationship to him. Marriage was also marked by three years of brideservice, following which residence became patrilocal (p. 76). Kin terms accorded with the marriage rule. For example, the term for mother's brother (MB) was the same as that for wife's father (WF) (male speaking).

Descent groups were aligned via "ties of prescriptive alliance" (Needham 1960: 78). These were seen as traditional. Any descent group's members saw their fellow Purum as either wife-givers to their own group or wife-takers (p. 78), and kin/affinal terms were applied accordingly. Since each lineage had ties with more than one other lineage, marriage was not necessarily into the immediate mother's clan or lineage group (p. 79).

Needham suggested that, in common with other systems of matrilateral marriage prescription, wife-givers were seen as superior to wife-takers (1960: 84). (We have seen how this was the case for the Huaulu but was modified in practice by the reciprocal exchange of valuables.) Wife-takers (*maksa*) had a number of duties—or, we might also say, indispensable ritual roles—in relation to their wife-giving group. They were expected to ceremonially sacrifice oxen on behalf of their affines; to prepare the rice beer consumed on such occasions and to distribute it when a village official of the wife-giver's group is installed in office. The *maksa*, with their wives, also offered rice beer and curried pork to the ancestors at the time when a child of the wife-giver's lineage was given its first hair cutting (p. 91). When a period of bride service was over, the *maksa* brought gifts of beer and pork to the wife's father. And they performed the ritual washing of the wife's father's body at his funeral (p. 91). During bride service, the wife-taking son-in-law stayed in the left side of the house, (*ningar*) symbolically construed as inferior to the right side (*phumlil*) where the wife's father slept (p. 88). There is gender hierarchy here: Male lineage members were superior to females and those classified on the female side, such as wife-takers. Such visiting affines, as we have noted, would sleep on the female side of the house when they came to stay. As a wife-taker a man was on the female side; as a wife-giver he was on the male side. Needham notes that "male" is linked to the right side, and "female" to the left in a cultural system of symbolic equations (1960: 96). The goods offered by wife-takers to prospective wife-givers, beer and pork, are the same as those that people offer to the spirits and deities, and Needham suggests that there is an analogy here between wife-givers and spirits—both are superior entities to whom respect must be shown. A woman does take some household goods with her at marriage—all goods she will use in her marital capacity (p. 94).

Purum bride service continues for three years before the husband can take his bride to his house, so his work in helping her household is of considerable value. Needham also rightly, in our view, recognizes that the *maksa*, wife-taker in-laws, provide vital "ritual services" (1960: 95) for their wife-givers. Needham goes further and writes that the system of symbolic categories "orders both social life and the cosmos" (1960: 96). Needham was concerned throughout his book with a number of further polemical controversies surrounding the explanation of cousin marriage systems, but these need not concern us here. His explication of the Purum case as a total system ordered by classifications that comprised a cultural cosmos as well as a social structure remains useful. Rephrasing the argument of superiority/inferiority relating to wife-givers and wife-takers, we may suggest that the balanced complementarity of services between these categories fits well with a concept of "collaboration" in the reproduction of social life; and in terms of gender relations, this in turn fits with our concept of the "collaborative model" applied to New Guinea materials (e.g., Stewart and Strathern 1999.)

There is some confusion in the literature about the term "prescriptive" versus "preferential" in relation to cousin marriage. This is partly because even a prescriptive system may not be followed in practice; and a preferential system may show as high a percentage of actual cousin marriages as a prescriptive one does.

The real issue, however, is between categories of systems. Prescriptive systems prescribe total categories of marriageable partners in kin terms. Preferential systems do not. There is also an important difference between prescriptive rules that order marital alliances and preferential rules that have mainly to do with inheritance and property in societies in which there is some inequality of wealth. Cousin marriages in the latter case have usually to do with genealogically close cousins, first or second, and are in any case arrangements made between families, not descent groups.

An example of cross-cousin marriage arranged between families for reasons of inheritance is provided by work carried out in Ghana by Jack Goody and Esther Goody. Studying a number of societies with unilineal descent groups, they found that those with only one type of (corporate) unilineal descent group, that is, patrilineal groups, tended to prohibit cross-cousin marriage. However, a few societies in this region had double unilineal descent, that is, persons belonged both to a patrilineal group through their fathers and to a matrilineal group through their mothers, and in addition property of various kinds was inherited through both lines of descent (Goody and Goody 1969: 221). Some societies, also, had no unilineal descent groups, but it seems they had what are now recognized as cognatic descent groups ("descending kindreds" in the terminology of the day, p. 221). For these two categories, opposite kinds of cross-cousin marriage were stated as preferential forms. With double descent (immediate example the Lo Dagaba) the tendency was to prefer father's sister's daughter marriage (FZD). The authors explain this tendency succinctly with regard to property inheritance (p. 223).

On a man's death, a part of his property would go to his son (or perhaps sons) in his patrilineage, but another part would go to his sister's son/sons. If, however, this inheriting son marries his father's sister's daughter, the child resulting from this union will belong both to the same patriline and the same matriline as its grandfather, or MMB/FF: That is, the MMB and FF are in this case the same person.

It all sounds quite complicated, but for people living in a system of this kind such a calculation would come easily and with little mental effort, since they are living in a kinship-ordered universe, one exceptionally highly structured by the dual presence of corporate patrilines and matrilines.

In the bilateral cases examined, we may take the Gonja of Ghana as an example. With the Gonja, the mother's brother is expected to be a primary helper to his sister's son in obtaining a wife (Goody and Goody 1969: 226). Usually the mother's brother does not provide his own daughter. Instead, he will ask another family for a bride to be given to his nephew. He has claims over his classificatory sisters' daughters in this regard (p. 227), because these are also classified as his "daughters" in the kinship terminology.

In neither of the two types of cases, however, was cross-cousin marriage practiced in more than a small percentage of instances. In the Gonja example, there is a reason given for this situation: If the marital pair quarreled, their shared ancestral kin might punish them by making their children sick (Goody and Goody 1969: 229).

Cross-cousins who marry, then, have to behave exceptionally well, and there is strong pressure on them not to separate by divorce. Ghosts on the mother's side are particularly threatening and can kill a person, it is thought. A man has therefore to think carefully about marrying a woman from his own mother's kin.

This last observation is particularly interesting because it shows the power of consanguineal kinship. If you marry kin, you share dead ancestors with your spouse, and these in turn guard and protect the behavior of both of you, whereas if the spouse is not kin, this double sanction does not exist. The Gonja's mode of thinking about this matter would resonate well with New Guinea Highlanders, who are also much exercised by the thought that their dead relatives watch over them and may punish them for wrongdoing, for example, sexual transgressions.

Indeed, even if such ancestral influences are not in question, it is evident that a cousin marriage engages the interests of kinsfolk more intensively than marriage to nonkin or strangers. Imagine marrying your maternal uncle's daughter or your paternal aunt's son if you are female. Then your perhaps kind uncle is your father-in-law or your aunt is your mother-in-law. Aunt and Uncle versus mother-in-law and father-in-law: The terms have a very different ring about them, since relations of affinity are normally characterized as more distant than those of consanguinity in the "English" kin system (we speak here of ideal-typical constructions of a cultural kind, not of how these matters necessarily work out in practice).

Yet, certainly cousin marriages are sometimes contracted. Adam Kuper, in his Huxley lecture of December 2007, has reflected on this matter. He refers to some notable examples. Charles Darwin "decided to marry a daughter of his favourite uncle, his mother's brother, Jos. Wedgwood" (Kuper 2008: 3). Further, Charles' own sister, Caroline, had already married his cousin Emma's oldest brother. So, Charles' marriage to Emma completed a sister exchange marriage arrangement between the elite families involved. The example, Kuper notes, was not unique, indeed it was a part of the scene of an "intellectual aristocracy" (p. 4) in nineteenth century England, and "sustained alliances between a few families in the same ecological niche gave the members of these clans a powerful competitive advantage" (p. 4).

Interestingly, there is a further parallel with the Gonja, transposed onto a different plane. The Gonja, we have noted, were afraid of supernatural dangers associated with cousin marriage. In nineteenth-century England, the concern was that medical research "was beginning to suggest that close-kin marriage had bad consequences for the health of the children" (Kuper 2008: 4). Since the concern of the Gonja was that dead relatives might inflict harm on the children of cousin marriages, there is a fortuitous correspondence of ideas here.

Of course, Queen Victoria herself was married to her mother's brother's son (Kuper 2008: 6); and dynastic families all over Europe were in the habit of intermarrying, preserving royalty and succession to thrones within small, involute networks of power and influence. Kuper further points out that the Rothschild banking family practiced extensive cousin marriage, specifically for financial reasons. But, he adds, the Wedgwood–Darwin alliances were not contracted for material reason alone, but as a means of consolidating friendships. Finally, Kuper reveals that in his own family background his father's parents were first cousins, and his mother's parents were also first cousins. While his own background, he notes, is Lithuanian Jewish with connections to South Africa, he also notes that "Highlands Scots migrants to New Zealand were also strikingly endogamous" (p. 10). Presumably, this was a means of conserving resources and preserving social ties in a new and uncertain environment, although Kuper does not elaborate the point. Highlands Scots would be literally "clannish," of course, since they actually had clan affiliations, so further levels of detail could be pursued here.

In any case, Kuper's examples bring us firmly to patterns of European kinship practices, practices which have also been exported, and adapted, to the Americas and elsewhere around the world. We will look at some aspects of Euro-American kinship in the next chapter.

Conclusions

This chapter, like the chapter before it on groups, has been largely concerned with discussing major empirical types and practices. Descriptive detail on wedding rituals has not been included here. In theoretical terms, we have brought out some comparisons and contrasts between cases of marriage practices in the Highlands region of Papua New Guinea. In Hagen, marriage is inflected in line with an emphasis on widespread exchange networks between allied groups and persons: in short, with the *moka* system of exchange. In Pangia and among the Duna there is less emphasis of this kind, perhaps least in fact among the Duna. In the Pangia case, alliance is expressed through matrilateral ties; in Duna by the networks of support brought to bear on the payment and reception of bridewealth, with a special rule (found, incidentally, in some other places in Papua New Guinea) that a father waits until his daughter marries to repay the contributors to his own marriage a generation earlier (see Strathern and Stewart 2004: 45).

We also discussed questions of change, especially in relation to the effects of economic and political change on small-scale societies like Telefomin that practice sister-exchange, an "elementary" type of marriage.

Finally, we considered varieties of cross-cousin marriage, contrasting prescriptive connubia based on broad categories with immediate cousin marriages based on ideas of property and also family friendship and intimacy. Knowing that Charles Darwin married his cousin as a part of a sister exchange might suddenly make us aware how certain practices may turn up in any part of the world.

Questions to Consider

1. Why are marital alliances so important in many parts of the world?
2. What is meant by the term "marital connubium"? In what kind of society do you think such an arrangement is found? How are such connubia affected by historical forces impinging differently on women and men?

Notes

1. For a cross-cultural study of polygamy, see Miriam K. Zeitzen, *Polygamy: a Cross-Cultural Analysis* (Oxford: Berg, 2008).
2. For more details on these historical processes, see Andrew Strathern and Pamela J. Stewart, "Objects, relationships, and meanings: Historical switches in currencies in Mount Hagen, Papua New Guinea," in *Money and Modernity: State and Local Currencies in Melanesia*, ASAO Monographs no. 17, ed. David Akin and Joel Robbins (Pittsburgh, PA: University of Pittsburgh Press), 164–191. See also Pamela J. Stewart and Andrew Strathern 2002, "Transformations of monetary symbols in the Highlands of Papua New Guinea," *L'Homme*, special issue, *Questions de Monnaie*, 162 (2002): 137–156.
3. The uncertainties of alliances at the time of their making and the roles of ritual speech in mediating the risks involved between the parties are explored in relation to the Anakalang people of Sumba Island in Indonesia by Webb Keane in his article "Delegated voice: Ritual speech, risk, and the making of marriage alliances in Anakalang," *American Ethnologist* 18, no. 2 (1991): 311–330. In the Highlands societies of Papua New Guinea, speech makers often have to bridge disputes, which flare up over the amount of items being offered in a brideprice payment. Among the Duna, leaders act as go-betweens in this context, retailing messages from the other side back to their own kin. They are also the ones who are able to launch into formal or ritual speech comparable to the genres employed in Anakalang, when the occasion warrants this.
4. Yunxiang Yan has described a comparable, but different trajectory in the individualization of bridewealth payments in a part of China. See Yunxiang Yan, "The individual and transformation of bride wealth in rural North China," *JRAI* 11, no. 4 (2005): 637–658. For a broad comparative discussion based on Eastern

Indonesian and New Guinea materials, dealing with kinship and commoditization processes, see Andrew Strathern and Pamela J. Stewart, "Kinship and commoditization: Historical transformations," *L'Homme*, special issue on kinship 154/155 (2000): 373–380. This paper also appears as Chapter 2 in Andrew Strathern and Pamela J. Stewart, *The Python's Back: Pathways of Comparison between Indonesia and Melanesia* (Westport, CT: Bergin and Garvey [Greenwood Publications], 2000). The article deals with marriage systems akin to that of the Huaulu. See also Yan 2006 (in References to this chapter).

5. The gendering of valuables is itself a complex topic. Pearl shells in Hagen, carry some aspects of female symbolism, and were held up by dancers in the Female Spirit performances who were representing the Spirit herself. See Pamela J. Stewart and Andrew Strathern, "Female spirit cults as a window on gender relations in the Highlands of Papua New Guinea," *JRAI* 5, no. 3 (1999): 345–360.

6. In this regard, Valeri is pointing to the uncertain basis of theorizing in works that depend on the gift/commodity dichotomy (e.g., the early work by Christopher Gregory, *Gifts and Commodities* (New York: Academic Press, 1982) and the "as if" use of this distinction by Marilyn Strathern, *The Gender of the Gift* (Berkeley, CA: University of California Press, 1988). See Andrew Strathern and Pamela J. Stewart, "Ceremonial exchange," in *Handbook of Economic Anthropology*, ed. J. Carrier (Elgar Publishing: Northampton, MA and Gloucester, England, 2005), 238–245. Yunxiang Yan in his chapter in the same book, "The gift and gift economy," also comments on this dichotomy, with further references to the literature, pp. 254–255. (His whole chapter is chapter 15, pp. 246–261.)

7. This question of women's agency is generally important in the context of transformations of bridewealth and marriage. See, for example, Chris T. Fuller and Haripriya Narasimhan, "Companionate marriage in India: The changing marriage system in a middle-class Brahmin subcaste," *JRAI* 14, no. 4 (2008): 736–754. In Hagen, the *idea* of female agency was also expressed very strongly in representations of the Female Spirit, cf. note 5 above. Issues relating to agency, of either women or men, nowadays come strongly to the fore in studies of change (as we note for Telefomin). The topic is signaled in studies that refer to neoliberalism and the Internet in globalizing contexts. See, for example, Jennifer Johnson-Hanks, "Women on the market: Marriage, consumption, and the Internet in Urban Cameroon," *American Ethnologist* 34, no. 4 (2007): 642–658; and James Ellison, "Governmentality and the family: Neoliberal choices and emergent kin relations in Southern Ethiopia," *American Anthropologist* 111, no. 1 (2009): 81–92. Johnson-Hanks discusses women's agency and concepts of honor. Ellison describes how people can enter into new kin relations as a part of economic development.

8. Such descriptions, which depend on classifications like "maximal categories," as given here must be understood in two ways. First, they derive from putting together statements by people who belong to the social context involved. In other words, they are "folk models." Second, they are constructions made by the anthropologist to enable the folk models to be intelligible cross culturally, and in so doing the anthropologist makes them into observer's models. They remain models, not full accounts of the complex processual realities and historical experiences of persons and groups. They can be thought of as short-hand terms that can be explicated at greater length. However, they are not simply "fictions." What we here call the phratry or "big name" (*imbini tumbea*) was involved in fighting in the precolonial past as a maximal unit of potential solidarity in situations of conflict.

9. In both cases (Duna and Wiru), we see that payments of wealth for "bodies" (i.e., persons in relations of consanguineal kinship or affinity) are employed as the mechanism of opposing the "mystical" influences of "others," who are nevertheless by rules of exogamy essential to the reproduction of relations over time, and are therefore both "other" and "not other" (thus, anomalous). The Duna men pay bridwealth in order to gain the bodies of wives who will notionally stay on the *rindi* parish territory. Wives come in and later daughters go out: The daughter's body repays the mother's, via the mechanism of wealth in pigs and shells. There is an attempt to incorporate the new wife literally into her marital place. But her total identity does not change, since her children can claim membership in her natal parish later if they wish to do so. In the Wiru case, maternal influence is seen as so strong it has to be opposed continuously by payments of wealth, and the mother's brother is thought to have the ability to "eat" the liver of the sister's child. Affines are others; but matrilateral kinship can be inside one's body. Self and other are two co-existing principles. Rupert Stasch has produced an interesting ethnographic analysis around this point. (Rupert Stasch, *Society of Others: Kinship and Mourning in a West Papuan Village* [Berkeley, CA: University of California Press, 2009]).

10. One of the peer reviewers of this book questioned whether the Marquesas case can properly be classified as polyandry. Presumably, the meaning of this question was that (a) in the Marquesas the arrangement was not universal, and (b) it involved men in secondary arrangements, as well as a principal husband. The example, however, has the merit of indicating a custom of polyandry in a historical process of becoming. Polyandry "proper," in which the husbands have relatively equal status, is perhaps most often linked to sets of brothers married to the one woman.

11. The position of "fathers" in societies in which matrilineal descent is practiced can vary considerably and was the focus of many early studies on Africa and elsewhere; see, for example, David M. Schneider and Kathleen Gough, eds., *Matrilineal Kinship* (Berkeley, CA: University of California Press, 1961). We have earlier in this book reviewed the Trobriand case. For a recent study on New Ireland (in Papua New Guinea) see Göran Aijmer, "On making fathers in Lesu: The historical anthropology of a New Ireland Society," *Oceania* 77 (2007): 233–246. Aijmer argues that secret male initiation rituals in Lesu, in which boys were under the tutelage of social or ritual fathers who need not be their putative genitors, were an emergent means of countering matrilineal influences through the establishment of cross-group male bonds.

12. "The Purum" constitute a classic case in the scholarly literature on marriage forms, precisely because Needham used it to contest various anthropological theories regarding "structure and sentiment" at the time and to assert a *model* of a matrilateral cross-cousin marital connubium. We have earlier discussed the somewhat comparable case of the Huaulu, studied by Valerio Valeri. Our account here is necessarily schematic. The importance of ritual actions is evident in establishing relations between affines. Throughout parts of Indonesia, matrilateral marital connubia have been historically practiced, and this Purum case as analyzed by Needham can stand for this whole genre of marriage arrangements. That is why we have included it here. It is for similar reasons that we included (Ch. 4) Freeman's 1961 analysis of the Iban *bilek*: It is a classic account and reveals important structural principles. For an Eastern Indonesian case, Tanimbar, see Susan McKinnon, *From a Shattered Sun: Hierarchy, Gender, and Alliance in the Tanimbar Islands* (Madison, WI: University of Wisconsin Press, 1991).

References

Cai, Hua. 2001. *A Society Without Fathers or Husbands. The Na of China.* Trans. Asri Hustvedt. New York: Zone Books.

Clark, Jeffrey. 1989. Gods, ghosts and people: Christianity and social organization among Takuru Wiru. In *Family and Gender in the Pacific,* ed. M. Jolly and M. Macintyre, 170–192. Cambridge: Cambridge University Press.

Collier, Jane F., and Sylvia J. Yanagisuko, eds. 1987. *Gender and Kinship: Essays Toward a Unified Analysis.* Stanford, CA: Stanford University Press.

Craig, Ruth. 1969. Marriage among the Telefolmin. In *Pigs, Pearlshells, and Women: Marriage in the New Guinea Highlands,* eds. R. M. Glasse and M. J. Meggitt, 176–198. Englewood Cliffs, NJ: Prentice-Hall.

Das, Tarak Chandra. 1945. *The Purums: An Old Kuki Tribe of Manipur.* Calcutta: Calcutta University Press.

Fortes, Meyer, ed. 1962. *Marriage in Tribal Societies.* Cambridge: Cambridge University Press.

Goody, Jack, and Esther Goody. 1969. Cross-cousin marriage in Northern Ghana. In *Comparative Studies in Kinship,* ed. J. Goody, 216–234. Stanford, CA: Stanford University Press.

Gough, Kathleen. 1961. Nayar: Central Kerala. In *Matrilineal Kinship,* eds. D. M. Schneider and K. Gough, 298–384. Berkeley, CA: University of California·Press.

Hoskins, Janet. 2001. Preface. In *Fragments from Forests and Libraries,* ed. Valerio Valeri, J. Hoskins, xiii–xx. Durham, NC: Carolina Academic Press.

Jolly, Margaret. 1989. Sacred spaces: Churches, men's houses and households in South Pentecost, Vanuatu. In *Family and Gender in the Pacific,* ed. M. Jolly and M. Macintyre, 213–235. Cambridge: Cambridge University Press.

Jolly, Margaret, and Martha Macintyre, eds. 1989. *Family and Gender in the Pacific.* Cambridge: Cambridge University Press.

Jorgensen, Dan. 1993. Money and marriage in Telefolmin: From sister exchange to daughter as trade store. In *The Business of Marriage,* ed. R. Marksbury, 57–82. Pittsburgh, PA: University of Pittsburgh Press.

Keesing, R. M., and Andrew Strathern. 1998. *Cultural Anthropology: A Contemporary Perspective,* 3rd ed. Fort Worth, TX: Harcourt Brace.

Kuper, Adam. 2008. Changing the subject—about cousin marriage, among other things. *Journal of the Royal Anthropological Institute* 14(4): 717–735.

Leach, Edmund R. 1964. *Political Systems of Highland Burtna.* London: The Athlone Press.

Lévi-Strauss, Claude. 1969. *The Elementary Structures of Kinship.* Boston, MA: Beacon Press (first published in French in 1949).

Levine, Nancy. 1988. *The Dynamics of Polyandry.* Chicago, IL: University of Chicago Press.

Marksbury, Richard A. 1993. Introduction. Marriage in transition in Oceania. In *The Business of Marriage. Transformations in Oceanic Patrimony,* ed. R. Marksbury. Pittsburgh, PA: University of Pittsburgh Press.

Needham, Rodney. 1960. *Structure and Sentiment: A Test Case in Anthropology.* Chicago and London: The University of Chicago Press.

Peter, H. R. H., Prince of Greece and Denmark. 1963. *A Study of Polyandry.* The Hague: Mouton & Co.

Rivers, W. H. R. 1906. *The Todas.* London: Macmillan.

Stewart, Pamela J., and Andrew Strathern. 1999. Female spirit cults as a window on gender relations in the Highlands of Papua New Guinea. *The Journal of the Royal Anthropological Institute* 5(3): 345–360 (n.s.).

Stone, Linda. 2001. *Kinship and Gender: An Introduction*, 2nd ed. Boulder, CO: Westview Press.

Strathern, Andrew. 1980. The central and the contingent: Bridewealth among the Melpa and the Wiru. In *The Meaning of Marriage Payments*, ed. J. L. Comaroff, 49–66. London: Academic Press.

Strathern, Andrew, and Pamela J. Stewart. 2000. *The Python's Back: Pathways of Comparison between Indonesia and Melanesia*. Westport, CT: Bergin and Garvey (Greenwood Publications).

Strathern, Andrew, and Pamela J. Stewart. 2004. *Empowering the Past, Confronting the Future: The Duna of Papua New Guinea*. New York: Palgrave Macmillan.

Thomas, Nicholas. 1989. Domestic structures and polyandry in the Marquesas Islands. In *Family, and Gender in the Pacific*, ed. M. Jolly and M. MacIntyre, 65–83. Cambridge: Cambridge University Press.

Valeri, Valerio. 2001a. *Fragments from Forests and Libraries,* ed. Janet Hoskins. Durham, NC: Carolina Academic Press.

Valeri, Valerio. 2001b. Notes on the Meaning of Marriage Prestations among the Huaulu of Seram, ed. Janet Hoskins, chap. 8 in Valeri 2001a, 137–152. Durham, NC: Carolina Academic Press.

Yan, Yunxiang. 2006. Girl power: Young women and the waning of patriarchy in rural North China. *Ethnology* 54(2): 105–124.

CHAPTER 6

Euro-American Kinship: Concepts and History

"THE FAMILY"

For much of this book we have been adducing examples of kinship structures, and customary patterns of conduct associated with them, that might seem relatively remote to readers brought up in North America or parts of Europe. The Central Highlands of Papua New Guinea are indeed very distant from Essex in England, the Lowlands of Scotland, or Pennsylvania and its environs in the United States. The primary reason for studying kinship in parts of the world such as Papua New Guinea, Africa, and Southeast Asia is that extended kin relations are very prominent in them. By contrast, kin relations in industrialized nations are often said to be truncated in scope, that is, kinship is seen as no longer the basis of social structure and consequently is not of major importance as a topic. Moreover, even in places where kinship was previously the centerpiece of anthropological investigations, the emphasis for a while shifted elsewhere: to modernization and development, political identities, religious movements, and the like.

However, these viewpoints and shifts of emphasis have proved to be inadequate over time. First, no matter what changes have taken place in people's lives, a certain importance remains attached to kinship relations, whether in a metropolitan city or in the settlements of the New Guinea Highlands. People still live in immediate households, reproduce, and inherit. Second, kinship ties continue to be enmeshed in, and to influence, many other domains of life. And third, the importance of kinship is underlined by the development of new technologies to assist reproduction and to make it possible outside of the normative parameters that have operated previously. For example, in vitro fertilization makes it possible for conception to occur independently from an act of sexual intercourse, and in principle unties reproduction from its tight bond with the regulation of sexuality. Also, controversies emerge over issues such as same-sex marriages. But what controversies of this sort reveal, at a deeper level, is the ongoing significance of cultural models that give value to concepts such as marriage, reproduction, and family as social forms, and thus remain within the broad parameters of kinship relations as such.

With these points in mind, we take up a number of topics in this chapter. We make no effort at comprehensive generalizations here. To do so would be impractical. While we may reasonably hope to make generalizations about small-scale social fields, such as "the Hageners" or "the Duna" in Papua New Guinea, one cannot do the same for regions so diverse and vast such as America or Europe. Nevertheless, because of the historical diffusion of populations and practices between Europe and North America (including Canada), as well as places such as Australia and New Zealand, it is evident that certain continuities exist and certain patterns are quite pervasive, although locally variant.

If there is one concept around which such senses of continuity cluster, it is the notion of "family." In some arenas of kinship study, such as "kindred" or "descent group," "marriage," and particularly the "family," analytical advances have been made primarily by seeking precise and unequivocal definition of concepts, but often complete clarity is elusive. "Family" is an expandable term. It can apply to the smallest unit, the "nuclear family," formed around a conjugal pair and extended generationally by the addition of children born to or brought up by a conjugal pair. In its widest sense, we encounter phrases such as "the family of man," applied to the whole human species (and since putatively vast numbers of humans have descended from an original pair, a certain logic may apply to this usage). Also, there can be different levels of application of the term, as well as a number of extensions of it that might be "metaphorical," that is, carried over into another domain of relationships, as when university administrators refer to the academic community as a "family." What is being appealed to in such a usage is one side of two elements that ideally-normatively are found together: consanguinity and sentiments of solidarity or "amity," as Meyer Fortes put it (see, e.g., Fortes 1949). The side appealed to is that of amity, as an ideal. Of course, it does not always apply in practice in academia, any more than it does in actual contexts of consanguineal relationships. If one of the parts of the kinship metaphor is viewed as based on "sibling relations," it is clear that sibling solidarity is matched by sibling rivalry as a proverbial theme; and competition for resources is the locus of such rivalry, occurring between individuals and departments in academia as much as it does between brothers and sisters in immediate families.

While "family" is thus a term with a very flexible and potentially wide fan of referents in Euro-American usage, in practice there is also a very narrow and specific form of the family that is predominant: the nuclear family itself, as against the wider kindred or any notion of a descent group. The nuclear family emerges as a dominant unit owing to a combination of factors that have arisen historically. There is also a notion that this family is an economic, reproductive, and co-residential unit of both production and consumption. Correlatively, the idea is that when a couple marry, they should establish, or seek to establish as soon as possible, a separate household, within which they may begin again the whole process of reproduction. This is a crucial assumption, one which precludes the formation of three-generational extended or expanded joint families based on sibling ties. While the linkage of nuclear family households by the recognition of kin ties beyond the nuclear level is guaranteed by the application of kin terminology, the family itself, in the sense of a co-residential economic unit, is continually being kept to its minimal level of expression via the assumption that with marriage a new residential unit should be set up.

This stress on the nuclear family as a domestic group encompassing both production and consumption goes with a number of other patterns. One is the idea of the conjugal pair as a cooperative unit running their own economic affairs. In cases where both parties to such a conjugal pair also expect to inherit resources from their own parents, such a pattern of bilateral inheritance also feeds into the viability of the domestic group itself as an economic unit. The anthropologist Jack Goody has built this point into a general series of comparisons he has made between "Eurasia" and "Africa," arguing that diverging devolution, that is, the passing of similar types of property down through both males and females, strengthens the conjugal tie as against natal ties with a wider group such as a unilineal descent group (UDG). This inheritance pattern appears to depend on a rule of premortem transmission of resources, that is, it is expected to occur at marriage and therefore potentially before the death of the parents. Goody notes, "the establishment of such a fund weakens the corporate nature of the UDG (where these exist); at the same time its existence clearly establishes the conjugal unit on a footing which is at once more intimate and more solid, a fact that again tends to separate the members of the unit from relationships of a lateral kind" (1983: 38).[1]

Goody's observations are based on a broad set of comparisons. They apply well, however, to the key point we are emphasizing here, one that does not necessarily apply to all cases of diverging devolution, but does apply to the concept of the nuclear family as a potentially mobile economic unit that can be adapted to industrial conditions where people have to change their employment and move from place to place as may be necessary for them to survive economically. This latter idea operates separately from any matter of intergenerational inheritance. One theory, therefore, is that this form of the nuclear family becomes emphasized precisely as a result of industrialization and urban migration in Europe. However, it does not appear that the nuclear family as a domestic group found its origins in such a context; rather, it existed in earlier times also.[2]

HISTORICAL FACTORS: HOUSEHOLDS, PROPERTY, AND INHERITANCE

Martine Segalen has contributed prominently to the theme of the history of the family and co-residential groups, especially in France. Segalen (1986: 14ff.) discusses a number of family formations from the Middle Ages onward. The "family community" was a set of persons who lived together sharing a single cooking hearth and were able to pass on property to their descendants (p. 15). Each community had its headman and headwoman, and community goods were held in common. The preferred form of marriage was endogamous. Girls who married out were given a dowry and they relinquished their claims on natal property (p. 16).[3] These communities tended to disappear when members claimed individual shares under Roman law and seceded: "Gradually, individualism and a right to personal gain and the increasing focus of family feeling on the nuclear family induced people to reject the burden of community life" (p. 17).

Another type was the stem family, "a domestic group that gathered three generations under one roof" (Segalen 1986: 18). Such groups could be quite large when there were many children in one family. The stem family was closely connected with a house (p. 19), typically including farm buildings and land, and a plot in a local cemetery for its dead (p. 19). The aim was that the house and its property should be handed on directly from one generation to the next, and there was only one heir, usually in a patrilineal line. Hence daughters-in-law were married into the house and had to take their orders from their mothers-in-law. And children, female or male, who did not inherit would be provided with cash on marrying out or would simply stay at home as long as they were unmarried (p. 19). The eldest son was expected to be the heir and successor to authority in the household (p. 20). This pattern was by no means peculiar to France. It was widespread in landowning families in Europe and is a theme that appears in novels as a source of tension within families. Robert Louis Stevenson's novel *The Master of Ballantrae*, published in 1889, is set in the year 1745, at the time of the Jacobite rising against the Hanoverian succession of King George II and tells the story of a conflict between an elder and a younger brother over the rightful inheritance of the estate of Durrisdeer. The plot is complex and involves the obsessive rivalry between the two brothers and the younger brother's fear of his ill-intentioned elder brother's quasi-magical powers of survival, linked, we may suggest, to a feeling that, no matter what, the elder holds the prerogative of succession and is irrevocably "the Master." The two are described on a common gravestone as "fraternal enemies," a monument to sibling rivalry rather than sibling solidarity (Stevenson 1889).

Segalen and many others (see Gullestad and Segalen 1997) have pointed out that in the case of larger domestic groups in the past, they would have a structural core of relatives but might also include nonrelatives as servants or lodgers, especially if the house had agricultural land attached to it. In Scotland, a type of domestic structure centered on the land was known as the *fermtoun*, a farming settlement focused on a family but also incorporating maids and milking cows and several workmen housed in an outbuilding known as a bothy. These workers would get their meals from the shared kitchen of the farmhouse, tended by the maids. David Kerr Cameron has given a detailed portrait of farming based on the *fermtoun* pattern, with emphasis on the cyclicity of seasonal work, but without details of the kinship relationships that formed the basis of intergenerational continuity in these units (Cameron 1986, 1997). In general, the *fermtoun*, which had its heyday following agricultural improvements but prior to extensive mechanization of farming, belongs to a pattern in which a core of family members is surrounded by servants and helpers. The domestic group in this sense is bigger than the family, but the family encompasses these nonkin within the patterns of food consumption and co-residence.

The category of "domestic group" itself calls for some further clarification. Drawing on work by the English historian Peter Laslett and his collaborators, Martine Segalen notes distinctions between "simple" groups (consisting of the nuclear family); "extended" groups (nuclear family plus ascendants and collaterals); and "multiple" groups (in which several related families may live together, either under the authority of a senior couple or as fraternal sets with spouses) (Segalen 1986: 23–24). Data collected by Laslett's team indicate, Segalen says, that the average domestic group in England, based on a sample of over 100 parishes, throughout the sixteenth, seventeenth, and eighteenth centuries, consisted of parents and children (p. 22), with an average size of just under 4.75 persons—this from the time of earliest records to 1901 (p. 22). In one English parish (Ealing), 78 percent of the domestic groups were "simple" in type over the sixteenth to eighteenth centuries (p. 24). Segalen also notes that household composition varied with status: Laborers' households were smaller and simpler, while the wealthy families kept children about them longer and maintained nonkin servants (p. 29), as was probably the case with the larger and wealthier *fermtouns* in Scotland. Also, industrialization sometimes brought family members together rather than separating them. Segalen notes that the 1851 census in Britain showed that in Preston, an industrial textile-producing town, 23 percent of the domestic groups were extended or multiple in types (p. 31).

Demographics and work exigencies strongly influenced family patterns. Men tended to remarry quickly after a spouse's death, perhaps in childbirth, because the gendered character of labor required a conjugal pair to keep a farm household running (Segalen, p. 32). Men were able to remarry until the age of 60, women up to the age of 40 (p. 33). With stem family rules, younger siblings had in any case to move out (or stay on, perhaps, as bachelors or spinsters, a pattern sometimes found in Ireland).

The question of the "domestic group" is also influenced by material concerns. The whole idea of a "house," or "one roof" or "one hearth," is influenced by considerations of what kinds of social relationships are normatively accommodated within the unit; and as Segalen, following Jack Goody, notes, permanent structures, once built, place a constraint on who can live in them and how (pp. 39–40). Think here of the idea of the living room, the kitchen, the bedrooms, and who normatively should occupy and control these spaces. Think also of the expense of such structures compared to the less permanent but more easily extended or replaced structures in some tropical areas. The "housing crises" repeatedly experienced in industrialized countries result basically from the assumption that the nuclear family should have its own house, preferably detached and with a garden, and a certain kind of internal structure of rooms; and from the fact that such buildings are costly and become the focus of price-raising in the market, leading to real-estate "bubbles" that eventually burst, leaving many people unable to maintain mortgage payments and facing foreclosure. The demise of the housing bubble at the end of 2008 in the United States and Europe led to a worldwide financial crisis.[4] All this is predicated on the idea of the family as a domestic group. Who could maintain, then, with any plausibility, that family and kinship have become unimportant in industrialized societies?

David Sabean has made a detailed study of kinship and household structures in Neckarhausen, a village in Württenberg, South Germany, centered on the production of winter wheat or spelt (Sabean 1990). The Neckarhausen people had adopted a system of dividing family property in each generation among the children of a particular couple (Sabean 1990: 1). This provides a contrast with stem families or multiple families in which primogeniture has been the rule. With land plots that were smaller, methods of intensifying cultivation were adopted (p. 4). Sabean points out that at the time of his publication, few studies had concentrated on partible inheritance, while most work had been done on situations resulting from impartible inheritance rules and their aim to preserve estates (1990: 13). Impartible inheritance combined with male primogeniture leads, of course, to classic family stories of rivalry and resentments, as discussed in relation to Stevenson's *The Master of Ballantrae*. It also provided the context in which Jeanne Favret-Saada's study of the phenomenon of witchcraft in the Bocage area of Normandy was set. Here, farm households and their stock and land were all identified with the "personage" of a single owner who had inherited the farm, and illness or death of stock or other misfortunes affecting the household were all seen as an attack on the "personage" of the owner himself (Favret-Saada 1977). The example shows us that important phenomena in the spheres of ritual and belief may be closely connected with familial structures, a point that was brilliantly demonstrated by Meyer Fortes long ago in his classic studies of patrilineal structures and inheritance patterns among the Tallensi of Ghana (Fortes 1945, 1949, 1987).

Returning to Neckarhausen and David Sabean's carefully documented study of it, we find that with partible inheritance also definite social patterns ensued or were implicated. Partible inheritance kept a large number of families interested in the land and needing to make a living from it. Inheritance itself did not secure a livelihood for people and wider sets of kin relationships had to be mobilized. Land sales further complicated the picture. Sales and divisions of land by inheritance meant that there were no long-term attachments to particular pieces of land (Sabean 1990: 18). Village men undertook a number of craft and construction jobs to supplement income, and pledged their land as a guarantee for their performance (p. 19). Villagers developed new specializations as markets changed with the growth of capitalist enterprise. It seems likely that partible inheritance and the resulting population pressures on land were conducive to these innovations, as Sabean implies (1990: 21). Field crop rotation patterns were a part of these innovations. And while some families were better off than others, family relationships ran across families, linking houses together. Where convenient, marriages between kin served to keep property together.

Sabean notes that the state authorities in Württenberg were very much concerned with familial structures. Inheritance laws were set in 1555 and continuously reviewed (Sabean 1990: 26). The state was instrumental in defining what constituted a well-ordered "house" (*Haus* in German) (p. 27), one whose property inventory could be measured and taxed to produce state revenue (p. 27). Gender relations were also affected by work regimens. Women, for example, took on a great deal of hoeing and weeding work when new fodder crops were grown more intensively (p. 29) and used them to feed stock in stalls (p. 53).

In analyzing the farm household and the ideology of the house in Neckarhausen, Sabean argues that the tie between a man and his wife was crucial (1990: 98), including the changing terms of that alliance over time. Men and women sometimes viewed the processes of production and consumption linked to the house differently (certainly this is a pattern which is not confined to Neckarhausen). Households were not autarkic (self-sufficient) or permanent, but were linked together and permeable. Given all these complications, however (and the different views of scholars about the household as a social unit), the Neckarhausen villagers themselves had strongly developed notions about the *Haus* and about living in it, expressed in the verb *hausen* (p. 103). This term was closely connected with the institution of marriage and how marital partners managed to get along with each other (p. 103), including economic elements, such as saving money.

Magistrates would determine on a local basis how the process of managing relations should be worked out, especially in contexts of conflict and divorce. *Haushaltung* was a term that applied to how a spouse managed the resources of the house. A wife might accuse a husband of wasting such resources by excessive drinking and demand that his behavior be curbed, for example. In the nineteenth century, *Haushaltung* became especially the wife's arena of competence (as in "housekeeping"). The task required diligence, sobriety, and responsibility (Sabean 1990: 111) Central to this division were the proper forms of exchange of tasks between spouses. Sabean devotes a whole chapter to marital conflicts arising out of claims of bad *Haushaltung* (1990: 124–146). Women's tasks were much harder when they had to take on the stall feeding of stock, flax breaking, and hoeing, as well as cleaning and meal preparation (p. 181).

The basis of the alliance between spouses lay in the character of the "marital estate" (Sabean 1990: 183). Sabean points out that the term "partible inheritance" is itself ambiguous unless we specify more details. The Württenberg case differed strongly from some other areas, in which men controlled land and their incoming wives brought monetary dowries. In Württenberg, both sexes inherited equal amounts of property (p. 186). Whatever each partner brought, in this way, was made part of an official inventory, sometimes along with a prenuptial agreement (p. 189). Marital property consisted of what each party brought to it at the time of marriage and what was added to this during the course of the marriage. At the death of one party, their share of this property was apportioned to any children before the surviving spouse could remarry (p. 197). Wills could be made, but an obligatory portion had to go to the spouse or children (p. 202). A child could be disinherited for dishonorable conduct, such as striking a parent or "using witchcraft or poisoning a parent" (p. 202). A spouse could be disinherited for adultery, and this might also end in divorce. Roughly a third to a half of the estate could be freely disposed of. Marital partners were in any case not seen as guardians of a joint estate to be passed down in entirety, and property regularly entered the market (p. 207).

Inheritance was bound up with reciprocities between kin, and these were overseen by village officials (Sabean 1990: 418). Obligations could be extended to collaterals such as uncles, aunts, nieces, nephews (one must wonder about cousins). In line with other work, Sabean notes that sentiment was involved (p. 418) (see also Medick and Sabean 1984, a volume that discusses the juxtaposition of emotions and material interests in kin relations in different parts of the world, with an essay on the Melpa of Papua New Guinea by A. Strathern). At the same time, in accordance with the rules of inheritance, property was held by individual persons (p. 421)—albeit, we may add, individuals bound up in relationships; in other words, the "relational individuals" that we have identified from our own work in Papua New Guinea (Stewart and Strathern 2000; Strathern and Stewart 1998). These persons were also often bound in ties to the lords of estates, and in religious disciplines also to the church (p. 428). Finally, Sabean notes that all the processes he discussed were caught up in continuous aspects of historical change. Rural society was not marked by unchanging tradition; instead, customary practices were continually shifting in accordance with wider changes of power and economic influences (p. 432).

Sabean's study provides detailed information about one small area in Germany. But the patterns he uncovered seem remarkably "modern" in character and reveal the longer-term historical roots of features that are sometimes assumed to be very recent. And these patterns certainly applied in many parts beside Neckarhausen. From another perspective, it is worth noting that the pattern of farmers also working as entrepreneurs and builders is one that is found today in the UK, where farmers find it necessary to do other jobs to keep their farms and families in viable economic standing. The stress on entrepreneurship and initiative that Sabean identifies also has a resonance with early studies of entrepreneurs in the Papua New Guinea Highlands (e.g., Finney 1973). As Sabean insists, the peasants made these adaptations off their own bat, as it were, not just in response to outside pressures; and these adaptations long pre-dated the so-called times of "neoliberalism" that have subsequently been labeled as such by anthropologists studying late twentieth-century capitalism. Perhaps it is time to acknowledge that initiative and agency can emerge at any historical time and need not always be trammeled up with critical perspectives on neoliberal economics at large.

INFLUENCES OF THE CHURCH

Sabean (1990: 427) notes that his account has not dwelt at length on the influences of the Church on family life. Such an influence has been generally strong in the past in Europe, and certainly remains strong in many parts of the world today, particularly considering the Catholic Church and its policies toward family life, abortion, same-sex marriage, contraception, and the like. In the past, church interests centered more around marital fidelity, the upbringing of children, rules of incest or who could marry whom, and questions of inheritance. Jack Goody, among his numerous and wide-ranging contributions to the study of kinship, has addressed particular historical questions of church property and inheritance patterns in Europe (Goody 1983: 103–156). Gifts of land and other property were made to the Christian Church during 600–1100 C.E., often with the aim of securing the salvation of the souls of those who made these bequests (forerunners of today's philanthropic donors, we may suggest). These bequests were in addition to taxes and tithes (pp. 105, 106). Monasteries and donor lineages often maintained close connections (p. 107), partly because of remaining obligations to wider kin groups. As a result, particular kin lines became attached to monasteries (p. 108). In England, prominent families founded particular local church buildings, which also remained their effective family property through many generations although ultimately designated for the Church (p. 112). These lay interests in church property were ended by reforms instituted by Gregory VII in the eleventh century (p. 113). (Pope Gregory VII held his position from 1073 to 1084; p. 118.) Gregory put an end to practices of the laity in reclaiming church property, and he enforced rules of celibacy for priests and monks or nuns. The adoption of feudal rules went along with single-heir inheritance, namely, primogeniture (Goody 1983: 119), applied to tenancies under feudal tenure. It appears that the Church favored this rule because it kept estates together and made them easier to tax and administer. Goody notes that free tenants (not serfs), however, could practice partible inheritance among sons, as in the region of Ely, and that this gave rise to a land market in Ely in the thirteenth century (pp. 119–120): a finding that nicely fits with the data from Sabean's study of Neckarhausen. The lords in England, however, discouraged these trends and they disappeared there by 1299 (p. 120). Among both nobles and tenants, agnatic lines of succession emerged, and wider kin were cut out from shares in land.

The Church also made its own rules that militated against the maintenance of wider kin ties. Divorce was discouraged; god-kin relatives were introduced as a partial replacement for consanguinity; and cousin marriage was prohibited (Goody 1983: 49). Over time, the ban on cousin marriage was extended beyond first cousins to cousins of the second, third, or even further degrees (p. 56). Cousin marriages were assimilated to the idea of incest, and church authorities proposed that it was both socially and biologically more healthy to "marry out," beyond the ties of kinship or affinity (p. 57). The prohibitions were even extended to spiritual kin via god-parenthood (p. 59). From 393 C.E., the Church also forbade leviratic marriage (i.e., marriage with the brother of a deceased husband) and sororate marriage (marriage with the sister of a deceased wife) (p. 60).

Goody points out that these rules, however they were motivated and justified by authorities, had indirect effects that benefited the Church's property interests. Widows often survived their husbands and were in possession of property through dowries. They could protect this property and themselves by founding religious houses (Goody 1983: 65), thus segregating themselves from kin who might claim their shares in such property. The Church gave widows a special position as persons to be pitied and given protection (p. 66). Christian influences also led to the disappearance of adoption as a legal practice, a disappearance that (surprisingly) lasted in the UK until 1926 (p. 73). Given the prevalence of this custom cross culturally (see Chapter 3), this absence of formal adoption is quite remarkable. It is even harder to see what is meant by "Christian influence" in relation to its disappearance in Western Europe until recent times. Adoption was common, as Goody notes, in Roman law and practice (p. 72). The Church had godparents look after orphans rather than allowing adoption, and so children were kept within the religious circle (p. 75). In addition, Goody argues, the effect was that property could more easily go to the Church, in a case where there was no heir, since a fictional heir could not be created if adoption was disallowed. Finally, legal concubinage with rights of inheritance by the children of a concubine was forbidden in the interests of monogamous marriage, thus further narrowing the possibilities for heirship and increasing the possibility of property going to the Church (p. 77). The Church's control over the definitions of marriage and heirship made it feasible for it to deny legitimacy to customary forms of marriage such as were practiced by the Celtic Highlanders of Scotland. The chiefly Mackays were by this means placed outside of church law and their legitimate possession of their lands was threatened (pp. 216–219). This is a clear example of how the Church's rules regarding kinship and marriage worked as political strategies.

As Goody further points out (1983: 146), the marriage ceremony itself became more and more defined by the Church, between the seventh and twelfth centuries c.e. Betrothals, banns, gifts, and the like were progressively defined. The Church took over an authoritative role hitherto held by the contracting parties and their families. The Church favored marriage founded on consent and choice, however, and on the production of children in the nuclear family. The Church thus began a trend that influenced the form of the family in subsequent centuries. At times, though, people took decision making further into their own hands. Goody reports that the Lollards of the fifteenth century, partial followers of William Wycliff, declared that marriage to second cousins was valid and that consent to marry was sufficient for a valid marriage between two partners, regardless of the Church (like Quaker marriage, we may note). But Church attitudes to marriage continued into the Protestant Reformation. Luther, for example, thought that cousin marriages, while not "positively harmful," were not proper because people would marry just to keep property in the family, rather than for love, and "poor women" would remain spinsters (p. 182). We find here the ideology of love and choice being used for purposes of church policy, while the idea that marriage choices are to be kept separate from property considerations does not square with actual practices even in the sphere of putative choice and "romance."

We note here that the roots of ideas about romance and even companionate marriage, seen perhaps as "modern" patterns, lie far back in time and are connected with Church policies. The elaboration of the marriage ceremony itself was elevated to the pivotal role marital relations were given in the

Christian scheme of things. A part of this elaboration that grew up over time is the wedding cake, of which Simon Charsley has provided us with a cultural history, based partly on fieldwork in Glasgow, where he was based as a university teacher (Charsley 1992). A wedding cake is par excellence an object of conspicuous consumption, elaborately made from rich and costly ingredients, and divided out in small pieces among many guests, sometimes sent to kinsfolk who could not attend the wedding itself. Cutting the cake by the bride and groom is a central ritual moment in wedding feast occasions, captured endlessly in photographic records (cf. Charsley 1992: 115–116).[5] After a detailed discussion of the culinary aspects of the cake, Charsley makes a small foray at the end of his book into aspects of meanings. Wedding cakes came to stand for all the good things associated with weddings as a whole and the achievements involved in becoming married (and, notionally, the expenditure of resources by the bride's kin). Concomitantly, the wedding feast is preceded by the church ritual at which the bride's father "gives her away." There is great stress on the bridal dress, more so than on the groom's outfit. Bride, dress, and cake with white icing all become icons of the wedding itself. Cutting the cake becomes like the couple's "sexual inauguration" (p. 127). Regardless of the validity of this point, a custom of "cake-breaking" was a long-lasting part of the rituals of marriage, with at least one writer identifying it, if dubiously, with ancient Roman custom (pp. 29–30, 50).

Cake-breaking was always done over the head of the bride. Charsley gives some examples, drawing on the work of a folklorist writing about Strathdearn in Scotland in 1774–1783, an area some 15 miles south of Inverness. Charsley writes, "In parts of Scotland an oatcake or shortbread might be broken over the head of a bride as she entered a house after the marriage. This was often her entry into the groom's house where she would henceforth be living . . . It was distributed among the guests, who carefully preserved it, particularly the unmarried, who placed it below their pillows to dream on" (Charsley 1992, p. 105, quoting in part from W. Gregor, "Notes on the Folklore of the North-east of Scotland," London Folklore Society 1881, pp. 92–93). This part of the celebrations was called the infare and the cake in question was the "infar cake" (p. 106). "Infar" refers to the "going in" or entry of the bride across the threshold of the groom's house (cf. German *einfahren*). In any case, we see here the origins of the distribution of the wedding cake to guests. It was a form of divination to enable people to dream of whom they might in turn marry—like the throwing of the bouquet in contemporary weddings. Whoever catches it may be the next to marry.

Corroborative materials come from a novel, *Bits from Blinkbonny*, written by John Strathesk and published in 1891, dealing with village life in the 1840s at a place located 30 miles inland from Edinburgh, "the centre of a good agricultural district, with a background of moorland and hills" (Strathesk 1891: 3). Toward the end of the novel, Bell Cameron, the loyal servant of the family of the minister of the village, is married to David Tait of Blackbrae farm. The couple arrive from the marriage service at the doorway to David's farmhouse a little early, intent to avoid the somewhat unwelcome pranks of local youths. David's sister is at the door and she exclaims, "I was a lookin' for ye for an hour yet, an' it'll no dae to come into the house without gettin' the lucky cake broken o'er your heid, Bell" (p. 274). She tells the pair they will need to wait till the best-man and best-maid and young unmarried people ("wanters" and "swankies" in the Scots language, "unmarried females and nimble young men," p. 274) arrive. She adds,

> It wadna' be canny [safe], forbye [besides] it wadna be wiselike to break the infar-cake till there's some wanters and swankies to scram'le for it (p. 274).

Eventually the rest of the wedding party turns up and:

> The infar-cake was duly broken over Bell's head, and the usual dog-gerel rhyme repeated:
>
> > *Welcome to your ain fireside—*
> > *Health and wealth attend the bride!*
> > *Wanters noo your true weird make—*
> > *Joes are spaed by th' infar-cake (p. 275).*
>
> [weird = fortune; joes = sweethearts; spaed = foretold]

The occasion of a wedding was thus made into an act of divination, expressing, it would appear, the community of interest in the village and the powers unleashed in it by the magical act of marriage.

CONTEMPORARY CASES: DAVID SCHNEIDER ON AMERICAN KINSHIP

Simon Charsley expressed skepticism about anthropological studies that develop symbolic interpretations in systemic ways. He is doubtful about Mary Douglas's forays into culinary domains, including wedding cakes seen in structuralist terms as a peculiar combination of liquid and solid elements (Charsley 1992: 5). Charsley concedes that there are many manifest connections between practices, as we have just briefly explored regarding cake-breaking customs; and if this is all that is meant by system, well and good (p. 2). But he prefers to follow the position of Goody (1982) in his study of cooking, who points out that where practices have grown up piecemeal "there should be no reason to imagine that they are a whole part of or manifestation of any system" (Charsley 1992: 4). Charsley is instead concerned with "cultural creativity" and the improvisation of practical procedures (p. 5).

Most of the present work is couched in similar terms, since we are dealing with kinship in action. At a far remove, however, from this approach stands David M. Schneider's work on "American Kinship" (Schneider 1968). Schneider was also the anthropologist who launched a fundamental attack on the idea of kinship, seen as based on genealogy, as a cross culturally valid tool of analysis (see Chapter 1). Here, we will outline Schneider's views on American kinship, analyzed as a differentiated cultural system expressed as symbols and consisting of definable units. Schneider states that he is not concerned with behavior and action in social life, but only with certain cultural definitions. At the outset, we should note Schneider's own report that the materials were gathered among white, urban, and middle class subjects (p. 121), supplemented by a literature search. He admits that lower-class kinship and ethnic forms of kinship relations are different (p. 122). But he sticks to his commitment of viewing culture as a system of symbols and meanings (p. 129).

Much of what Schneider distils from the 6,000 typed pages of interviews that he says were the basis of his assertions reads in a fairly recognizable, "commonsense" way. Other parts bear the stamp of his own search for meanings. He begins by discussing the meanings of the term "relatives." Kin are relatives, by "blood" or marriage, or more specifically they are blood kin, distinguished from in-laws or affines. Relatives are referred to by basic and derivative terms. "Cousin" is a basic term. "Second" and so on may be added to it as modifiers (Schneider 1968: 22). Step-terms indicate that the relatives, though given "blood" terms, are not in fact blood kin, for example, step-mother is father's wife but not mother. Blood, Schneider says, is defined biogenetically following intercourse between a genitor and a genetrix, with 50 percent of the genetic materials coming from each parent (p. 23). We can see that this is both an "ideal" and a "dogmatic" definition. Adoptees are clearly cut out, and no weight is given to experience, shared upbringing, and so on, unless as a metaphor. Kinship is cut to the bare bones, and blood kinship is seen as something that can never be extinguished, even though the parties do not have in practice anything to do with each other. Kinship is "natural," and unalterable; by contrast marriage is a legal relationship. It can be terminated by law, just as it is brought about by law (p. 26). A mother-in-law is not a "real" mother. The "real" mother is the one who gave birth to the person (p. 27). (One immediately asks why the spouse's mother is called mother at all. Clearly there is an effort made to assimilate the distant in-law relations into the closer relationship of blood—but clearly difference is still recognized. Assimilating in-laws terminologically in this way is not common in cross-cultural terms, and the presence of this practice in American—and Euro-American—usage calls for further explanation. It is perhaps connected to the relative atrophy of relations of alliance through marriage. It goes also with the assimilation of senior collateral affines into the uncle and aunt category.) Schneider sums up his own dichotomous findings by saying that relationship by "natural substance" is distinguished from relationship as "code for conduct" (p. 29).

With regard to the category of "the family," Schneider argues that sexual intercourse is the symbol for the distinctive features of the family. Intercourse is seen as a procreative act, an act of love, and as proper only between husband and wife (Schneider 1968: 38). The Christian background to this set of points will be clear. Sexual intercourse by itself need not be regarded as a procreative act in marriage or outside of it, but Schneider is dealing with it as a symbol, not a practice. Other normative or ideological elements continue to enter the exposition. Thus the family (understood entirely as the nuclear family!) "lives together, and where it lives is 'home'" (p. 45). Work and home are separated (p. 45). (This is dated as a proposition. The distinction in not so clear nowadays. Many people spend some of their time "working at home." As academics, we do this.)

On love, Schneider distinguishes between conjugal and cognatic love, both seen as standing for unity (Schneider 1968: 52). Love can also be translated as "enduring, diffuse solidarity" (p. 52). There can be such solidarity with friends also, but while people can select their friends, they cannot pick their kin (p. 53). (This is not entirely true. There are elements of optation in kin relationships of a collateral kind; and at marriage, one picks a spouse through whom further relatives will be created.) At a later point, Schneider himself notes that personal relationships with relatives can continue even after divorce, according to some informants (p. 81). Schneider also notes some uncertainties and discrepancies. Children rapidly learn, he says, to call people "uncle" and "aunt," including the spouses of consanguineal uncles and aunts. But these spouses do not necessarily reciprocate by calling these children nephews or nieces, but may refer to them as their spouse's nephew or niece. This must be variable. We cannot corroborate this point from our own experience or observations, but it does reveal some indeterminacy about boundaries between consanguinity and affinity in a system where spouses are in many ways closely identified with each other. In discussing problems of this sort, it is notable that Schneider actually discusses instances of behavior or practice, descending from his pinnacle of "cultural system" analysis to the level of everyday life (p. 104). Insofar as he does so, his account gains in validity and subtlety. Finally, here, it is interesting that the whole analysis depends on the deployment of a folk/analytical category beloved by some anthropologists, including Claude Lévi-Strauss: the nature/culture opposition. Since these categories are blurred by biotechnology, it is clear that Schneider's analysis belongs to a historical period but does not stand for all time. Yet the normative definitions he expounded are the basis for fierce controversy today, for example, concerning proper forms of conception, same-sex marriage, and the like. When conception is assisted by culture, it is no longer a matter of "nature." If a spouse is not of the opposite sex but of the same sex, all the assumptions that Schneider lays out about the symbolism of sexual intercourse, physical procreation by the sexual act, and love are potentially disaggregated and thrown into confusion. And new technological methods of conception go with this situation. If two men or two women are joined together in marriage and they wish to have children, they must either adopt or find an inseminator (source of sperm) or a womb (surrogate) to help them out. The self-sufficiency of the nuclear family is breached. (This topic is discussed further in Chapter 8.)

With Elaine Cumming, Schneider published another study, this time of "sibling solidarity," a property of American kinship (Cumming and Schneider 1961). Out of a sample of 220 adults from Kansas City, 15 were chosen as representative and interviewed intensively about their ideas on kinship. The respondents were middle-aged or older. The research workers found that parent–child and sibling bonds were emphasized, with less emphasis on spousal ties. (This may reflect stages in the developmental cycle; earlier in the cycle spousal ties are extremely prominent.) There was some reluctance to see kinsfolk as a source of instrumental help (e.g., financial aid) and there was "an eagerness to discuss socio-emotional and ritual activities" (p. 501)—this in spite of the fact that mutual aid did occur. Within this context, "sibling solidarity stood out forcibly from all other themes," becoming stronger with the age of the respondent (p. 501). The authors suggest that this emphasis derives from a value given to autonomy and choice. Siblings express this autonomy by choosing to remain close, on the basis of their consanguineal ties but not necessarily through any compulsion of obligation. If this conclusion is correct, it is a reflection of a stress on the nuclear family, because siblings are the residue of an original family of orientation after the parents are dead. Cumming and Schneider refer to this as "horizontal solidarity" (p. 505). Interesting as these findings are, we may comment that the element of choice here can also lead to siblings having little to do with each other as their own families of procreation develop. Much depends on social and physical proximity. Without such factors, sibling solidarity may remain quite underdeveloped or nebulous, even though the "blood ties" as such are fully acknowledged. And in cases of inheritance where siblings are pitted against each other, their conflicts may be quite as bitter and as unrelenting as those between ex-spouses locked in divorce disputes and determined to ruin each other. The love of spouses or blood kin may easily enough, it seems, turn into hate in cases where the relationship breaks down.

Schneider's ideas on American kinship have frequently been reviewed. Harold Scheffler, a noted and rigorous kinship theorist, challenged the empirical basis of the categorical distinction between relatives by nature and relatives by law (Scheffler 1976). Here, we might comment in general that although Schneider suggested that the 6,000 pages of field transcripts simply supported his abstract generalizations (Schneider 1980: 123–124), it would be interesting to compare the "raw" data themselves with his formulations: no inconsistencies, lacunae, disagreements, and so on? Schneider's account sometimes reads like his own formulation, based on linguistic usages, such as "in-law." In practice, those terms supposedly defined by "nature" alone are also defined by "law," since the law of marriage determines the legitimacy of children—though expressions such as "natural child" do pick out "genitor" ties as against "pater" ones.

Another commentator on Schneider is Linda Stone. She gives a generally sympathetic and appreciative resume of Schneider's main points, and she suggests that "what Schneider had to say about consanguineal kinship as shared biogenetic substance continues to be valid today," as well as his idea about sexual intercourse, seen as "love," being a central symbolic core "of family relationship" (Stone 2000: 271). Here, we might express some skepticism about the 50 percent rule of shared substance—is it really so clear-cut? And why would the conclusions of "science" be so readily incorporated into folk ideas? And when, as Stone also asks (p. 272), did this take place, since "scientific" ideas have themselves changed over time? At the very least, Schneider's bold formulation leaves out a good deal of what can also be called "culture": for example, ideas and suggestions about how children may resemble particular relatives, not just parents but also grandparents, siblings, cousins. A cousin of one of us (AJS) in Ayrshire, Scotland, seeing him either for the first time or after a long interval, commented as we both walked through their doorway, "We can see you are a Strathern." Appropriative remarks of this kind reveal biases and aims of an interesting sort. Claiming similarity of appearance is a claim of closeness, and thus is an ideological attempt to set up relatedness, in a way that is parallel to, and separate from, naming practices. In the case mentioned above, suitably enough these were relatives on AJS's paternal side (FZDS), while from their viewpoint they were tracing themselves to a descendant of a cross-sex sibling pair in their grand-parental generation (MMBS). The operative point is that the FZ to AJS and the MM to the cousins bore the natal surname "Strathern."

A more skeptical commentary than that provided by Stone is given by Adam Kuper (1999: 122–145, followed by a further critique on Schneider's work on Yap, pp. 145–158). Kuper first takes up the question of Schneider's use of the term "symbol" as arbitrary and referring only to cultural constructs. Must all symbols be arbitrary? The use of "sexual intercourse" as an "arbitrary" symbol of conjugal love might be a test case. Plausibly, if we agree that humans are biological organisms (as well as culturally defined persons), that relationship ought not to be just arbitrary. Theorists such as Meyer Fortes, replying to critics who have argued that kinship should be reduced, for example, to "relations of production," have pointed out the likelihood that there are universal psychological and biological bases for aspects of kinship organization (see, e.g., Fortes 1969). Schneider, of course, could reply that he was talking in terms of cultural symbols, not in terms of behavior; but cultural symbols do not float into existence from nowhere. They are grounded in both embodied experience and its ideological elaboration.

Kuper's criticism of this part of Schneider's scheme is sharply worded:

Love, it seems, is at once the very substance of kinship and a sym-bol of something else. With the best will in the world, there is no way to sort out this confusion between symbol and object (p. 135).

And:

So what, finally, is love? 'Love', Schneider asserts, 'can be translated freely as enduring, diffuse solidarity'. Gentle reader, mock not (p. 135).

Kuper implies that the definition is bathetic and cannot catch the deeper or wider aspects of the term "love," with its manifold and even contradictory senses in the English language.

Going through a number of other critical points, Kuper notes that Schneider does not discuss the intersection of ideas about kinship and about religion (p. 141). This is a significant criticism. We have seen in the section on historical backgrounds in this chapter how influential Church definitions have been in the formation of kin relations in Europe, and certainly therefore also in America.

Kuper's trenchant critique can be placed alongside Stone's more charitable view that "Love *is* still what American kinship is all about" (Stone 2000: 271). The possible confusion here is that the statement exists purely at the level of ideology; yet kinship in action is a much more complicated phenomenon than this ideology would suggest. In the next chapter, we will look at a number of empirical examples of studies of kinship in both America and Europe, with a view to taking behavior into account, as well as cultural values or "symbols," arbitrary or otherwise.

Conclusions

This chapter examined Euro-American kinship from two quite different angles. One has been historical. We have looked at the development of family, marriage, property, and gender relations in Europe from medieval times. We have seen the influence of the Church in defining marriage and inheritance rules. We have also noted the early development of the nuclear family as an economic unit. The second approach has been cultural. David Schneider's much-quoted analysis of American kinship as a site of cultural symbols presents some challenging generalizations, but parts of his model now seem out of date. Nevertheless, 'the nuclear family' emerges as a salient unit, just as it does from the historical analysis.

Questions to Consider

1. What do you know of inheritance patterns in your own social milieu? How do these compare with the practices discussed in this chapter?
2. With reference to the media, fiction, and any other source, evaluate the idea that the symbols of the family revolve around ideas of what one might term "love."

Notes

1. We note in passing here that the term "intimacy," applied to household and kinship relations, has recently gained currency in the literature, perhaps in line with emphases on embodiment and experience emerging from a general processual approach to ethnographic description.
2. See Alan Macfarlane, *The Origins of English Individualism: The Family, Property, and Social Transition* (Oxford: Oxford University Press, 1978).
3. On dowry systems, see Jack Goody and S. J. Tambiah, *Bridewealth and Dowry*, Cambridge papers in Social Anthropology no. 7 (Cambridge: Cambridge University Press, 1973).
4. Of course, many other factors were involved, including the leveraging and packaging of assets and massive fraudulent activities by some financial firms. All these were ultimately built, however, on popular ideas and ideals that we can trace back to kinship and family.
5. The wedding photograph of a couple cutting the cake often forms a central part of the ornamentations of a home, surrounded by pictures of children born to the marriage over time.

References

Cameron, David Kerr. 1986. *The Cornkister Days. A Portrait of a Land and its Rituals.* Harmondsworth: Penguin Books (first published by Gollancz, 1984).

Cameron, David Kerr. 1997. *The Ballad and the Plough. A Portrait of the Life of the Old Scottish Farmtowns.* Edinburgh: Birlinn (first published by Gollancz, 1978).

Charsley, Simon R. 1992. *Wedding Cakes and Cultural History.* London and New York: Routledge.

Cumming, Elaine, and David M. Schneider. 1961. Sibling solidarity: A property of American kinship. *American Anthropologist* 63(3): 498–507.

Favret-Saada, Jeanne. 1977. *Deadly Words: Witchcraft in the Bocage.* Cambridge: Cambridge University Press.

Finney, Ben. 1973. *Big-men and Business: Entrepreneurship and Economic Growth in the New Guinea Highlands.* Honolulu, HI: University of Hawaii Press.

Fortes, Meyer. 1945. *The Dynamics of Clanship among the Tallensi.* Oxford and New York: Oxford University Press, International African Institute.

Fortes, Meyer. 1949. *The Web of Kinship among the Tallensi.* Oxford and New York: Oxford University Press, International African Institute.

Fortes, Meyer. 1969. *Kinship and the Social Order: The Legacy of Lewis Henry Morgan.* Chicago, IL: The Aldine Publishing Company.

Fortes, Meyer. 1987. *Religion, Morality, and the Person: Essays on Tallensi Religion,* ed. Jack Goody. Cambridge: Cambridge University Press.

Goody, Jack. 1982. *Cooking, Cuisine, and Class.* Cambridge: Cambridge University Press.

Goody, Jack. 1983. *The Development of the Family and Marriage in Europe.* Cambridge: Cambridge University Press.

Goody, Jack, Joan Thirsk, and E. P. Thompson, eds. 1976. *Family and Inheritance. Rural Society in Western Europe, 1200–1800.* Cambridge: Cambridge University Press.

Gullestad, Marianne, and Martine Segalen, eds. 1997. *Family and Kinship in Europe.* London and Washington: Pinter. (Translated from French.)

Kuper, Adam. 1999. *Culture. The Anthropologists' Account.* Cambridge, MA: Harvard University Press.

Laslett, Peter, with Richard Wall, ed. 1972. *Household and Family in Past Time.* Cambridge: Cambridge University Press.

Medick, Hans, and David Sabean, eds. 1984. *Emotionen und materielle interessen. sozialanthropologische und historische beiträge zur familien forschung.* Göttingen: Vandenhoeck and Ruprecht.

Sabean, David Warren. 1990. *Property, Production, and Family in Neckarhausen, 1700–1870.* Cambridge: Cambridge University Press.

Scheffler, Harold. 1976. The "meaning" of kinship in American culture: Another view. In *Meaning in Anthropology,* ed. Keith H. Basso and Henry A. Selby. Albuquerque, NM: University of New Mexico Press. (A School of American Research Book.)

Schneider, David M. 1980 (2nd ed.; 1st ed. 1968). *American Kinship: A Cultural Account.* Chicago and London: The University of Chicago Press.

Segalen, Martine. 1986. *Historical Anthropology of the Family.* Trans. J. C. Whitehouse and Sarah Matthews. Cambridge: Cambridge University Press (Editions de la Maison des Sciences de l'Homme).

Stevenson, Robert Louis. 1889. *The Master of Ballantrae.* London: Cassell.

Stewart, Pamela J., and Andrew Strathern. 2000. Introduction: Narratives Speak. In *Identity Work: Constructing Pacific Lives,* ed. P. J. Stewart and A. Strathern, 1–26. ASAO Monograph no. 18. Pittsburgh, PA: University of Pittsburgh Press.

Stone, Linda. 2000. *Kinship and Gender: An Introduction.* 2nd ed. Boulder, CO: Westview Press.

Strathern, Andrew, and Pamela J. Stewart. 1998. Seeking personhood: anthropological accounts and local concepts in Mount Hagen, Papua New Guinea. *Oceania* 68(3): 170–188.

Strathesk, John. 1891. *Bits from Blinkbonny.* Or *Bell o' the Manse. A Tale of Scottish Life Between 1841 and 1851.* Edinburgh and London: Oliphant, Anderson and Ferrier.

CHAPTER 7

Euro-American Kinship: A Diversity of Examples

APPALACHIAN VALLEY, UNITED STATES

David Schneider's account of "American Kinship," reviewed in Chapter 6, was couched at a high level of abstraction. It was also based on interviews and their transcriptions (as well as Schneider's own intuitions) drawn from a sample. Methodologically, it resembled the survey approach in sociology. George L. Hicks' study of the Little Laurel Valley in western North Carolina, southern Appalachia, represents the opposite methodological pole, often identified with classic anthropological work: It is a local study, based on intensive investigations and intimate everyday acquaintance over a period of time, "participant observation," during 1966–1967 (Hicks [1976] 1992: 2), with return visits in 1968 and 1972. Hicks also explains that his own family background and personal work experiences helped him in integrating into, and doubtless sympathizing with, these rural people into whose lives he entered with his inquiries.

Little Laurel was a valley with about 1,300 persons in 1965, surrounded by high mountains, and cut through by a north running river (Hicks 1976: 7). Hicks reports that there were 10 settlements, each named, within a township of Kent county. The introduction of a highway since the 1930s had opened up the area considerably, with an influx of summer tourists since the 1950s (1976: 11) and the arrival of retired persons who had taken up residence there. Textile mills, constructed since 1945, produced new industrial employment (p. 12). Smaller schools were consolidated into one (p. 14). Old values were shaken (p. 15). The early settlers in the area were mostly of Irish or Scottish descent and they came on pathways from Pennsylvania and Virginia (p. 16). They were farmers, who found opportunities there to raise stock, and grow grain and grass, fruits and vegetables, wheat, oats, and barley (p. 19). They also collected forest ginseng, and later galax used by florists for bouquets (p. 20). There was some logging and mining for mica (p. 23). An enduring set of values combined ideas of "personal independence" with "personal and family honor" (p. 30). Mutual aid between kin and neighbors was important. The connection with frontier conditions of isolation is clear (p. 34).

A concomitant of this prevailing set of attitudes was that kinship relations were important in all practical ways, and a network of kin ties spread from household to household (Hicks 1976: 35). People had extensive knowledge of genealogies and marriages, including cousin marriages that were technically illegal, according to Hicks (1976: 35). People judged each other at least partly in terms of their kin ties (p. 35).[1]

Households were composed largely of nuclear families, but other kin might be present owing to family changes over time including divorce and remarriage, and death or temporary migration of a husband away from the valley, when a kinsman might move in to help or protect the wife at home. "Stick up for your kin before anybody else" was one maxim (Hicks 1976: 36).[2] This would include shopping at their store rather than someone else's, not cheating them, and not competing with them in business or politics, if possible (p. 37). By the same token, if conflicts did arise, they could cause lasting divisions among kin (a pattern certainly found elsewhere). In some cases, conflicts could arise between obligations to kin and rules of political office. Elected officials were expected to give jobs to kin, but could not favor them unduly (p. 40). Tax listers helped local people to declare their property for tax purposes, and children often undertook to list property of parents as theirs or vice versa so as to ensure as low a tax ruling as possible for family members (p. 41).

Gender roles intersected with those of kinship. Women were expected to look after the household. Hunting and fishing in the forest and heavy manual work were mostly men's jobs (Hicks 1976: 42). Both women and men gardened, but women tended vegetables and flowers, while men saw to trees and shrubbery. In the household, women had a good deal of authority, and they were also the primary churchgoers and protectors of moral values (p. 43). Kent county was supposed to be legally "dry," and liquor was not supposed to be kept in the home. Men secretly drank whiskey and beer in the woods, Hicks writes, away from women (1976: 43). In poorer families, women did more outdoor tasks; in families with college education, gender separations were less extreme (p. 44). Children were expected to take part in work (as is often the case in agricultural communities around the world, including on farms in Scotland). There was gender separation in church services and in leisure practices. Men and women generally sat separately in church, and men usually would not discuss business or politics when women were present (p. 47). Because of the importance of ramifying kin ties established through marriage, relations with in-laws were important and people did not make jokes about mothers-in-law (p. 48). There was also a strong bilateral tendency. Thus, children of both genders were expected to inherit property interests; and concomitantly, there was a notion that the parents of either spouse in a marriage should have "equal claims to aid and affection" (p. 49). All in all, there was "deep personal involvement with kinsmen" (p. 49).

In Hicks' book, a separate chapter on "land as place and property" follows through along these lines. In accordance with bilateral inheritance, nonresident kinsfolk shared in the ownership of small landholdings. Two-thirds of the valley's land was in the hands of locals linked to the land by kinship. Outsiders who bought land and came to stay in the summertime were resented for their habits of living and of fencing off areas. There were many terms indicating locations in the valley, and people born and brought up in it were thought to "belong" there (Hicks 1976: 54). People who left the valley and went elsewhere usually made frequent visits back (p. 55). More particularly, it was an aim of people to keep possession of the house in which their own parents were brought up, even if no one lived in it any more. If a man's family had enough land, they would offer to provide a site for his home near to that of his parents, otherwise the wife's parents would make the same provision (p. 63). Kin ties extended into death: People tended to be buried near kin (p. 63). Occupations, moral reputations, and settlements were all associated with particular surnames of families (p. 64). On "Decoration Day," a Sunday in June or July, families would also show respect for the dead by cleaning cemeteries and running services in church to mark the occasion (p. 69).

In line with the density of kin networks, gossip tended to move quickly from family to family, sometimes passed on in stories; and because families were tied together in multiple ways, there was a strong tendency to remain neutral in disputes if one was not immediately involved. Yet there were long-term grudges that engaged family loyalties (Hicks 1976: 92).

At the time of his fieldwork, Hicks recognized that social changes were proceeding apace and the valley was becoming less isolated and less integrated as a "place." But his account stands as a typification of rural life in the Appalachians at that time, in which kinship, far from being differentiated from the other aspects of social life, was deeply implicated in them, and they, conversely, in it.

NEWCASTLE, AUSTRALIA

Allon Uhlmann's (2006) study of family and kinship arrangements in the city of Newcastle in New South Wales, Australia, was conducted during a time of supposed crisis in the Australian suburban family and of fears regarding the breakdown of the nuclear family unit as an important factor in social reproduction. Part of the reason for these fears has been the emergence of alternative households, including preferences for people to live alone or with others of the same sex (Uhlmann 2006: 26). Uhlmann, however, makes good use of an established approach in kinship studies, the developmental cycle approach (2006: 27), pioneered by Meyer Fortes and Jack Goody (Goody 1958). This approach is a processual one. Instead of seeing social patterns as holding outside of time, they are viewed as processes in time and space, in which the pattern at any given time is a part of larger unfolding patterns of fission and fusion of units. Sole households, for example, may be seen as constituted by persons before, between, and after marriages (Uhlmann 2006: 28). Single-parent families formed 12.8 percent of Uhlmann's sample, while sole-person households were 21.9 percent. Uhlmann attributes these numbers to increases in divorce rates and also (presumably independently) increases in life expectancy (2006: 28). Uhlmann further observes that in times of economic difficulty, such as in the 1970s in Australia, "marriage rates drop and divorce rates rise" (p. 29). With expansions in the labor markets, the age of marriage tends to increase, attributable to greater use of contraception, higher costs of housing for newly weds and the difficulties of obtaining adequate employment. The underlying assumption here is one that we have met earlier as an old established pattern in the history of the family in Europe: the ideal that at marriage a new household is set up. Uhlmann points out that "suburbia was born in the 1920s when the dominant view of society saw the nuclear family in the family home as the cornerstone of society" (2006: 33). Detached houses are the ideal type of residence (p. 34), and home ownership is valued.

In expounding his theme, Uhlmann makes use of the concepts of the sociologist and theorist Pierre Bourdieu. In these terms, the nuclear family is the "doxic family," that is, the version of the family "that functions as the standard against which all other variants are compared" (Uhlmann 2006: 45). Other versions of family are valued in so far as they resemble this prototypical form (p. 45). Bourdieu further calls this prototype of the family a "realized category," that is, it has a reality beyond being just a cultural value or a mental construct (here, we observe a step beyond David Schneider's position of articulating kinship in American contexts only in terms of cultural constructs) (Uhlmann 2006: 46, referring to Bourdieu 1996). A realized category belongs to what Bourdieu calls "habitus," ingrained implicit social dispositions that carry affective meanings, and importantly, organize aspects of life on a wide number of fronts. Uhlmann also calls this a "gestalt" that incorporates different cognitive models into itself. These are important points because they bridge over between cultural abstractions and lived realities. Normalcy of this kind is what Bourdieu calls "doxic," that is, it generally passes unnoticed because it is tacitly accepted without question (p. 47). Of course, when an element of such a prototype is challenged, it is no longer doxic in a simple way. Instead, it enters into a sphere of arguments about orthodoxy and heterodoxy. Normalcy represents "symbolic capital," another concept of Bourdieu's. Anything else has to struggle to establish its legitimacy.

"Family" also becomes something that transcends its individual members and is seen as continuing over time. (The clearest example, of course, of this is when local descent groups are involved.) "The family" also falls into those categories that are subject to the "container schema" (Uhlmann 2006: 50). That is, boundaries are placed around it. For example, a boundary is placed around a married couple in terms of sexual relations. Extramarital affairs are a cause for dispute and perhaps divorce. Analogously, only parents should discipline their children (Uhlmann 2006: 52)—but, of course, the state may also intervene, so that this boundary is not absolute. Uhlmann recognizes that in other respects also, the boundaries are permeable. Young grown-ups may find themselves in liminal circumstances (2006: 58). We may add here that the proverbial interchange "Where are you going?" Answer, "Out" reflects this liminal transitional phase.

The use of these theoretical concepts and observations enables Uhlmann to argue that it is the demands made by advocates for the legitimizing recognition of, for example, same-sex partnerships, rather than the acceptance that these relationships in practice exist that causes trouble. What is at stake, in other words, is normalcy itself, and the demands made by "alternative" categories of people to have their relationship made part of normalcy. We can see, however, in theoretical terms, that it is not easy for this to come about. The first step in the struggle is often for legal recognition. Social and cultural recognition may take longer. It is the same here as with other issues variously labeled ones of class, ethnicity, and gender; and ideas of normalcy in gender terms are often invoked in struggles over same-sex partnerships. Interestingly, at an abstract level, categories remain constant. Same-sex couples want to be recognized as normal and to create families. Uhlmann brings out these kinds of points succinctly in his discussion, although the presentation here is our own. Again, with single-parent families, usually these are not forms that have been intentionally created, Uhlmann says, "It was rather that something went wrong on the way to the nuclear family" (2006: 71).

Uhlmann further notes that whereas a first marriage with a wedding ceremony was seen as a special rite of passage, particularly for women, subsequent marriages were not perceived in quite the same way. Correspondingly, de facto marriages arose and persisted (2006: 73). Such a de facto arrangement does not challenge "normalcy" as much as other practices, for example, same-sex relationships. But within these also, it is important to remind ourselves that while some cherished cultural principles are challenged, others are not: for example, the idea of a long-term stable relationship, or the idea, expressed by one of Uhlmann's interlocutors that "if you produce a child, you have a responsibility you cannot ignore" (2006: 76).

Another theme that Uhlmann takes up here has its roots in feminist debate, which historically has seen the gendered division of labor in the family, with men as "breadwinners" and women as "home-makers" as a source of women's oppression and exploitation. The proposed solution, then, is access for women to "the paid labour market" (Uhlmann 2006: 79). This problem, Uhlmann suggests, is specific to the professional classes. Working-class women are more likely to argue that their gendered home-making labor should be valued more highly than it is, not just in monetary terms but rather in social terms. The two strategies of claiming social worth may come into conflict, so that "home-makers" may criticize "feminists" for devaluing what is significant to them as a form of virtue.

Overall, Uhlmann finds, the ideal and normalcy of the conventional nuclear family was upheld and protected by various bracketing and classifying devices. Other arrangements were either seen as temporary or as second-best, or as acceptable if enclaved in a particular group or category set apart from others, such as the category of same-sex partnerships.

Uhlmann also uses the distinction between filiation and descent, stemming notably from the work of Meyer Fortes (e.g., Fortes 1969), to make some observations about his materials. Unambiguously, he notes, "descent does not appear to be a meaningful principle of ordering the world in Newcastle. Rather, filiation is the essence of relatedness" (p. 89). We may add here that successive links of filiation in different directions provide a sufficient rationale for recognizing kin relationships beyond the nuclear family. Such extended relations are projected upward and outward along what Meyer Fortes called steps of filiation; but when looked at from the perspective of the past and in terms of the descent of surnames, it is clear that kinship ties are also representing the intertwining of surname groups over time. Also, if one takes all the descendants through surname lines of a given ancestral pair, we have in effect what could be called a descending kindred or a cognatic descent category; and although this may not have any cognitive significance, it is a potentiality available to be realized. Furthermore, the existence of agnatically descending surnames together with different gendered ideas tends to produce a supposition that there is some set of qualities or character traits that go with the surname. This kind of supposition is founded on ideas of "blood," but since kinship ties of "blood" are reckoned bilaterally, an extra factor has to be attached to surnames, and we may surmise it is the mystique of the surname itself. Since it is the only element that continues in succession over the generations, it calls for some "substantivization," or underpinning with social meaning. From another viewpoint, we may contemplate the historical significance of rank. Patronymics are principally associated with the ranked status of aristocratic, landowning families. People sometimes like to trace themselves either agnatically or by other means to famous ancestral persons, identified by their surnames. This kind of thinking is also salient in Scotland where there are often strong ideas of the association of surnames with localities and with historical patterns of landowning. Tied to this is the notion that some sections of a family get cut out of inheritance over time, while others are privileged. We can see here the embryonic pattern of kinship versus class relations. Kinship connects, class divides. And if junior or cadet lines are denied inheritance claims, agnatic lines of succession emerge that coincide with what in effect become class privileges.

Not much of this longer-term historical background of cognition in relation to kinship is found in Uhlmann's study, probably because it is set in a contemporary Australian suburban context. We would have to relocate our study to the United Kingdom and to rural contexts to uncover traces of the phenomena we have mentioned here. Uhlmann describes the population he worked with as "Anglo-Celtic," referring to "the dominant cultural tradition in Australia that has its roots in the British Isles" (2006: 8). The "Anglo" part of all this is clear, and clearly connects with materials on "American" practices that we have earlier discussed. The "Celtic" part seems less clear, since on the Celtic side relations of descent are significant and this is shown in the term "clan" itself. We now turn to a classic study of a people "of the Celtic fringe" in the "British Isles," Robin Fox's study of the Tory Islanders (see also Segalen 1986: 67–69).

TORY ISLAND, IRELAND

Tory Island is a small island comprising 785 acres of land in all off the north-west coast of County Donegal in the Republic of Ireland. Robin Fox visited the island several times in 1960–1965. About 250 acres were used at that time for livestock and growing crops. The rest was treeless bog, scrub, and water. Strips of arable land were used to grow oats, potatoes, and barley (Fox 1978: 17). Overuse of peat for burning kelp and processing barley crops to produce poteen, plus overgrazing by sheep, had reduced the amounts of usable land (p. 17). The island had suffered population decline since the first part of the nineteenth century when supposedly there were 600 people living there (p. 18). Four surnames predominated in 1961–1965, one, the Duggans apparently having been there since the fifth or sixth century C.E. (p. 21). The indigenous language of the islanders is Northern Irish Gaelic, close to Scots Gaelic, infused with words adapted from English, which is also widely spoken (p. 22). Fishing was important as a means of survival in the past; by the time of Fox's work there, subsidies had become significant as a means of keeping people on the island (p. 23). Young people often migrated to find work elsewhere.

In tracing degrees of relatedness among people, the islanders preferred to start from a particular ancestor and trace the descendants down to a set or sets of living kin, thus displaying the degrees of cousin ties involved (Fox 1978: 33). Spouses of ancestors cited in this way might be included on request by the anthropologist. Only a "few old men" were recognized as knowledgeable genealogists (p. 35). Primary ancestors were those who probably lived around the end of the eighteenth century (p. 35).

The genealogies related to "clann" names of which four were seen as the most salient and ones to which most of the rest were related: Eoin, Neili, Fheilimi, and Sheamuis Mhic-Fhlaithbheartaigh (Duggans, Doohans, Rodgerses, and McClaffertys) (Fox 1978: 35). Altogether, 23 such ancestral names were recognized. Citation of the descendants involved great overlaps. The ancestors did not define exclusive groups. The verbal performance of tracing *seanchas* (p. 15), or genealogies, was a special art (like the telling of *malu* among the Duna [see Strathern and Stewart 2004]). The term "dream" or "fine" was applied to a surname group traced by genealogy (p. 68). *Teaglach* meant both "family" and "household" (equating the two terms). Fox points out that this did not mean "nuclear family." In diametrical distinction from the usages we have found as definitive in other "Euro-American" contexts, "the nuclear family . . . does not merit a separate concept" (p. 69). *Clann* itself means offspring, in the sense of "descendants" (p. 69). Since the genealogies overlap, everyone belongs to more than one *clann*, and "the descent is through both males and females equally" (p. 70). Thus the *clann* is a cognatic descent category or group, strictly comparable to the Duna reckonings of descent that we have explored earlier (see also, Strathern and Stewart 2004: 2, 30).

In reckoning cousinship degrees, the islanders referred to grandparental or more distant ties, spelling these out if appropriate. First cousins were thus "in our first grandchildship," that is, the descendants of a shared grandparent. Second cousins were "in second grandchildship" or "my mother and her father were the offspring of two brothers" (Fox 1978: 71). (We have found comparable ways of explaining kin ties among non-Gaelic speakers in rural Ayrshire in Lowland Scotland.) Third cousins were "fair" or "light-skinned" cousins; and fourth cousins were "dark" cousins, a usage that is not easy to interpret, Fox says, but ties in with a love of making distinctions of this kind. Fox thinks that these ways of reckoning cousins may have been particular to Donegal as ancient forms.

Fox notes (1978: 73) that in spite of the density of kin ties, kin terms as such were not used much except in the "immediate family." Instead, personal names were deployed to help indicate kinship status. This was tied in with the fact that traditionally children were named after grandparents (for details see Fox p. 75). (This again is not confined to Gaelic areas. It is again found in Lowland Scotland. In the family of one of the authors of this book, AJS, his elder brother was named for his father and the father's father, while the name "Andrew" is from his mother's father. The firstborn of the family, Margaret, was named after her father's mother, who had died before her son became adult and married.)

Fox notes that on Tory Island it was customary in address to add a parent's name to that of the child, thus "John-Tom," that is, son of Tom. Longer genea-logical strings could be mentioned. New names arose out of genitive usages. Seamus (James) becomes Sheamuis in the genitive and gives rise to Hamish in its Scottish form (Fox 1978: 75). Nicknames or epithets could be added. The names were actually "filiative strings" tied in with *clann* descent lines (p. 76).[3]

Genealogies were tied to the land. We find here a parallel again with the Duna, among whom *malu* pedigrees were always legitimizing ways of identifying sets of people with land areas known as *rindi*, attached to male agnatic lines of descendants from a mythical founder of the units we have called "parishes," since among the Duna they traditionally, and still today, carry ritual significance (Stewart and Strathern 2002: 69–70).

On Tory Island, Fox notes, with less land cultivated over time many owners had very small holdings (1978: 82). In 1961, there were only 160 acres in holdings and only 26 cultivated with about 34 acres in pasturage (p. 83). Land had ceased to be a prime source of subsistence in fact. Yet, Fox also argues that for persons to have no land claims was disastrous (1978: 85). Without land, a person has no real claim to belong to the Island. Concomitantly, every little piece of land is named (just as people are). Methods of farming in 1961–1965 seem to have been simple. People made their own tools, used donkeys to pull them, and cut crops by sickle and scythe (p. 90).

In terms of use and inheritance, the *clachan* system held, with apparently open fields and common ownership of them (Fox 1978: 91). These fields had been divided into strips that contained land of different qualities, but bits of land could also be sold, swapped, or abandoned. According to the islanders themselves, all children of landowners had rights to a piece of their land (p. 99). (We may remember that this pattern, too, is not unique: It held in Neckarhausen as explained by David Sabean (see Chapter 6), although in Neckarhausen this practice was tied in with a strong emphasis on the nuclear family household, specifically not found in Tory Island.)

Fox points out that this pattern contradicted the system found elsewhere in Ireland whereby only one son inherited the farm, others left, and daughters were given dowries (1978: 99). On Tory Island, both men and women in practice did inherit, although women relinquished ties more often (presumably at marriage?) (p. 100). One person might be picked out as the "owner," with the expectation that this person would pay the local rates or taxes on it, but in practice it would be shared among kin. A person might get rights to land through inheritance from parents or also via marriage. If everyone demanded a share of land by inheritance, claims would become too fragmented. Also, if one family member married someone with sufficient land, they would yield their natal claims to other siblings. A married pair required land, and this requirement might be satisfied via either one of them (p. 106).

From the point of view of the islanders, a person whose name was recorded as the owner of a piece of land was really a holder of it on behalf of others as well as himself or herself. The others involved were co-descendants of a named ancestor who originally held that land portion (Fox 1978: 122). Thus, land could revert to known descendants of this ancestor in the absence of immediate heirs as claimants of it. A widow could keep her husband's land until her death, when it would revert to the husband's co-descendant relatives (p. 122). This is all made more complex by the fact that the *clann* groups overlap in membership, so that a person may have claims in more than one *clann*. Fragmentation was controlled by putting together parcels of land for each married pair. Also, there was an idea that the net result of land dispositions should be that people had equal shares overall. Marriages were often between neighbors, so land claims could be brought together (p. 125).

Given the small population and a continuing preference for in-marriage, it is evident that cousin marriages would occur. First cousins were prohibited from marrying, but it appears that their children could marry each other, so that land claims that would otherwise be divided would be brought together again (Fox 1978: 191).

Fox notes in his concluding remarks to his book that all these ways of life were imperiled by out-migration and state welfare. Guidebooks for tourists indicate that nowadays there are more immigrants, and Tory Island has become popular with artists who produce "primitivist" paintings of rural scenes that are sold in galleries in mainland County Donegal.

From the point of view of our theme of kinship in action, it is clear that the *clann* and naming practices together defined both a collectivity and the individuation of persons within the collectivity. Deriving from times when the island was isolated and populated by a few intermarrying *clann* groups whose members depended on the land and the sea for their livelihood, the system of land inheritance had survived, in Fox's times, as a way of defining membership of Tory Island proper as against nonkin outsiders. In-marrying and in-migrant people were absorbed into the "web of kinship," as Meyer Fortes would have perhaps put it. But precedence—as with the Duna of Papua New Guinea (Strathern and Stewart 2004: 26–30)—continued to belong to those *clann* that had been there the longest time. Throughout, people were able to navigate individual claims in practical action by selecting from their genealogical network (Cohen 1994: 109–114).

THE SARAKATSANI, GREECE

John Campbell studied the Sarakatsani shepherds of continental Greece in 1954–1955, who numbered at the time about 80,000, and moved in seasonal transhumance between coastal plains and high mountains (Campbell 1964: 1–2). The particular community he worked with numbered about 4,000, with their mountain home in the Pindus Mountains within the province of Epirus. In winter, they spread widely beyond this home with their flocks in search of pastures among the plains areas.

Families, nuclear or extended, were the basic units, banded together by marriage ties into "stani" or "companies" containing at least four adult males (Campbell 1964: 8). The Sarakatsani, says Campbell, saw the interests of families not related by kinship as opposed and potentially hostile (1964: 9). Each family sought to maintain its "honor" vis-à-vis other families in the wider living space (p. 9). The mountains produced fine grass and watering places for the sheep in summer. Snow came by November and winter lasted until March, so that in winter the flocks and their shepherds had to descend and fan out into the plains.

Sarakatsani society, according to Campbell, was marked by ideological gender divisions, in which male shepherds were regarded as "pure" along with their sheep, and their women were associated with "sensuality" and the powers of the Devil (1964: 26). Male shepherds were in charge of the milking ewes, helped by fierce dogs to protect them against wolves and thieves (p. 27).[4] Shepherds needed much strength to fulfill their year-round tasks, especially in the difficult winter months.

Women cared for the goats, which were expected to be fewer in the flocks than the sheep and were valued less highly. Women had to observe special spatial rules in relation to the sheep. They maintained gardens and sold chickens and eggs (Campbell 1964: 33). Obviously, they played an important part in the total way of life. Campbell comments that for the Sarakatsani "life is sheep, children, and honour . . . the family is the form in which these three elements are fused" (1964: 35). He goes further and says, "The family and flock are both forms divinely confirmed, the earthly family being a refraction of the Holy archetype family, while the sheep is a sacred animal blessed by God" (p. 35). (Interestingly, of course, we may observe, the Holy family is not exactly like the archetype of the earthly family; but the idea that the soul comes from God helps to make the analogy closer.)

The Sarakatsani recognized a group which they called *to soi* (Campbell 1964: 36) and Campbell translates as the "kindred," in which relatives were recognized as far as second cousins. From the point of view of males, a man recognized as his kindred all persons descended from his four grandparents and their siblings of either sex down to his own generation. The children of his second cousins fell outside of his kindred group as did the grandchildren of his first cousins. Thus, there were cut-off points that narrowed, rather than broadening kin ties in succeeding generations. From the point of view of kinship theory, this group was cognatic, but it was not a cognatic descent group in the sense that we have used this term for the Duna people of Papua

New Guinea (Strathern and Stewart 2004: 26–30), that is, a set of widening cognatic descendants from a single putative founding ancestor or ancestral spousal pair.

Within this kindred, or set of kin, the immediate family was a corporate group owning property, and also a religious group with its own sacred icons. Its leader was responsible for maintaining family honor and autonomy (Campbell 1964: 37). The icons were supposed to provide the family members with grace to achieve their ideal goals of wisdom, compassion, courage, and purity, and so to resist the powers of the Devil. Others outside of the family were divided into *dikoi*, one's own people, *sumpetheroi,* affines, and *xenoi*, strangers (p. 38). Within the family, people pursued shared obligations. Outside of it they pursued self interest (p. 38). This formulation allows us to see how personhood was distributed differently in different realms of sociality. Certainly, similar considerations can be applied to the Papua New Guinea Highlands accounts, in which we see a strong emphasis on in-group relations, coupled with a more fluid application of individual networking ties outside of in-group contexts, mediated through intermarriage ties. The greater stress on clanship in New Guinea, however, meant that "in-group" relations covered a much larger number of people, among whom there could also be competition. But the intensity of consultation between kinsfolk on life-cycle issues such as marriages, and particularly in regard to conflict and violence, is a highly reminiscent feature. The anthropologist Peter Lawrence's concept of security circle, applied to his study of the Garia people in Madang Province, Papua New Guinea, also applies to the Sarakatsani case (Lawrence 1984). "A man cooperates with his kinsfolk because he trusts them," Campbell notes (1964: 41). But this is not simply based on generalized reciprocity. Money borrowed from kin had to be repaid. And if blood vengeance was required for reasons of honor, kinsfolk outside of the immediate family would not act on behalf of one another as the takers of revenge (pp. 41–42). Campbell writes, "When honour demands a vengeance killing, kinsmen outside the family will lend moral support, but none of them is obliged to pull the trigger or thrust home the knife" (1964: 41).

Campbell insists on the bilateral character of egocentric kinship ties among the Sarakatsani. He is also careful to distinguish between "the kindred" as he employs the term, and "bilateral descent," that is, what we have identified as cognatic descent among the Duna people of Papua New Guinea. The Sarakatsani kindred is ego-focused and depends on ties of filiation, not descent. It is also defined in terms of a rule that marriage cannot take place within a person's kindred, so that the kindred extends further than it would do if marriage within it were permitted. In a marriage, the bride's family are treated as outsiders, and each marriage in a sense does create a new elementary family. A part of this process of creation of a new unit is accomplished by the separation of the bride from the family of her birth, and the transfer of protection of her honor from her brothers to her husband (Campbell 1964: 53). The practice of virilocal marriage, moreover, goes with an informal stress on relations between males within a patriline. When a new bride is brought in to her husband's, and his father's, residential group, she is required to be subservient (p. 62). She must use a distaff for spinning wool provided by her husband, she must not bring one in to her home as a gift from anyone else, because it was an object with magically protective powers that could keep her children safe (p. 65). She cannot address her husband in front of others of his family, and the husband, in early phases of the marriage, was not supposed to be seen as taking her side against her female in-laws. Each morning the bride had to arise early and make the fire up. Intercourse between the couple was conducted in a silent and clandestine manner (p. 67).

After the birth of a first child, however, the bride was said to be identified more with her new family (Campbell 1964: 69). And at this time the husband could talk to her more openly. She could also stop calling his siblings by terms of respect and call them by their Christian names (p. 70). She herself would now be called by the name of her husband plus -*ina*, a feminine suffix, a usage comparable to teknonyms but applied to the marital tie. Brothers would separate their households at this time. This the Sarakatsani men "explained" by saying that brothers would live together throughout their lives if their wives did not quarrel (p. 71). Also, they said that women both created the household and destroyed it (p. 71). Both statements refer to the hiving off of the new elementary family from the extended household. In practice, and in the longer run, this has in fact to do with the division of property through inheritance and a father's wish to provide for his own children in view of his death (p. 73). We also see here the significance of property stressed by Jack Goody throughout his work on "Eurasian" kinship, and the pervasive tendency for the nuclear family to emerge against the background of wider units of action (Goody 1983). Cousins, however, remained important as a source of support in conflicts. It was only among cousins that young people of the opposite sex could meet and hold conversations (Campbell 1964: 101). Cross-cousins, the offspring of a brother and sister pair, tended to have the most sympathetic relationship, since the brother in question was the uncle to his sister's children, and as mother's brother he took a particular interest in them, which continued with his own son. Like others who have written about the kindred elsewhere (e.g., Leach 1961 on the *pavula* in Pul Eliya in Sri Lanka), Campbell points out that a person's "effective kindred" may vary in size and composition, largely because kinsfolk may withdraw support if they are opposed on some issue or a kinsman does wrong. The same is surely true, *a fortiori*, with general relations of cousinhood throughout Euro-American society. Whether cousins cooperate, or even see one another much, depends greatly on whether they remain co-resident or nearby to each other. Yet a kind of dormant or potential relationship can remain and can be activated after many years of latency. The Sarakatsani case not only shows us how kindred relationships are activated in practice because of proximity and the need for support in disputes. It also shows how, when property is tied to lineal inheritance, the solidarity of the wider kindred is weakened. On the fringes of Greek mainstream society, the Sarakatsani nevertheless show the tendency to the fragmentation of kin ties that is demonstrated much more clearly elsewhere. On the other hand, we have seen how on Tory Island wider kin relations were maintained via an ideology of cognatic descent tied in to land claims. Ecology is important here. Life on a small, isolated island is different from the great transhumant sweep of life from the mountains to the plains and back which regulates the flow of Sarakatsani kinship.

Our case studies in this chapter have been quite diverse, and we have avoided typifications. Detailed ethnographies show us regularities and variations. While "the family" is an important category in each of the four cases we have examined, its precise shape in practice has depended greatly on ecology and history as well as cultural traditions. Yet in every case, kinship does emerge as important in practical social life.

In the following, and concluding, chapter, we will examine again some leading issues in the analysis of kinship and point to its universal significance as well as its plastic variability.

Conclusions

Four diverse examples of the workings of kinship have been given in this chapter. One was drawn from rural North Carolina in the United States studied in the 1960s. The second was a contemporary study of urban Australian families in Newcastle, New South Wales. The last was a classic study by John Campbell of the Sarakatsani pastoralists in northern Greece. Family and kinship were seen to be important in all three cases, but in very different ways, while in each instance kinship practices made sense in their local ecology and environment. The diversity displayed here must act as a caution against generalizations about "the family" in Euro-American contexts. We were able, however, in passing, to make reference to elements of comparison, for example, elements relating to bilateral inheritance of land. Robin Fox's study of Tory Island kinship took us into another distinct world, one closely related to the context of Highlands Scottish clan kinship and at the same time exhibiting parallels with cognatic descent among the Duna people of Papua New Guinea. Three of the studies were on "peripheral" categories of rural people, and here the greatest diversity was found. Uhlmann's study of kinship patterns in urban Australia more clearly indicated parallels with the changing contexts of kin relations today in the United States while also showing the continued salience of the nuclear family as a concept.

Questions to Consider

1. "Always stick up for your own kin". How strongly do you think this principle is held in areas other than the "Appalachian Valley" in the 1960s studied by Hicks?
2. Does Uhlmann's argument that the nuclear family is the primary recognized form in Newcastle also hold in areas you know from your own experience?

Notes

1. Cousin marriage laws and incest rules have varied historically among the different states in the United States. Karl Heider has discussed this in his article "Anthropological models of incest laws in the United States," *American Anthropologist* 71, no. 4 (1969): 693–701. Heider notes (Table 1, p. 694) that in North Carolina double first cousin marriage was prohibited but first cousin marriage as such was not. Double first cousins would be those resulting from a sister-exchange pair of marriages in the preceding generation. Such marriages were sometimes contracted in Ayrshire, Scotland, among farming families seeking alliances, as we have noted from our fieldwork in that area.

2. This aphorism certainly corresponds to the dictum David Schneider was fond of mentioning as characteristic of "American Kinship," that is, "blood is thicker than water." Schneider also expressed doubt about whether this aphorism held cross-culturally. There is a difference, however, between a symbol and what it stands for, as Schneider himself would surely recognize. The formulation here by the Appalachian people is couched in terms of action, not an ideology of "blood" as such: "stick up for your kin"—an observation that we might expect from a small place where people were densely interrelated and depended on one another for all kinds of help (i.e., in multiplex relationships). We could reformulate: "Multiplex relationships are thicker than uniplex ones."

3. On the use of names in the Irish-speaking Gaeltacht areas of Ireland, see Veerendra Lele, "It's not really a nickname, it's a method: Local names, state intimates, and kinship register in the Irish Gaeltacht," *Journal of Linguistic Anthropology* 19, no. 1 (2009): 101–116. Lele argues that local names tie in with kinship relations to "invoke a strong sense of kinship closeness . . . standing as an intimate register opposed to the more socially distant register represented by official names" (p. 102). Terms of address in kin terminologies as opposed to terms of reference tend to do the same in other systems.

   The situation on Tory Island was probably paralleled in part, at least, on other islands in Donegal. See Margaret Duffy 2004, *Innisfree: A Tribute to a Donegal Island and Its People*. Published by M. M. Duffy and printed by Browne Printers, Letterkenny, Ireland. (Thanks to Liz and Ralph Sheppard for this reference.)

4. Compare here Bryan Cummins, *Bear Country* (Durham, NC: Carolina Academic Press, European Anthropology Series, 2008).

References

Bourdieu, Pierre. 1996. On the family as a realized category. *Theory, Culture, and Society* 13(3): 19–26.

Campbell, John K. 1964. *Honour, Family, and Patronage. A Study of Institutions and Moral Values in a Greek Mountain Community*. Oxford: Clarendon Press.

Cohen, Anthony. 1994. *Self Consciousness: An Alternative Anthropology of Identity*. London: Routledge.

Fortes, Meyer. 1969. *Kinship and the Social Order. The Legacy of Henry Morgan*. Chicago, IL: Aldine.

Fox, Robin. 1978. *The Tory Islanders: A People of the Celtic Fringe*. Cambridge: Cambridge University Press.

Goody, Jack, ed. 1958. *The Developmental Cycle in Domestic Groups*. Cambridge Papers in Social Anthropology 1. Cambridge: Cambridge University Press (reprinted 1971).

Goody, Jack. 1983. *The Development of the Family and Marriage in Europe*. Cambridge: Cambridge University Press.

Hicks, George L. 1976. *Appalachian Valley*. Prospect Heights, IL: Waveland Press, Inc.

Lawrence, Peter. 1984. *The Garia. An Ethnography of a Traditional Cosmic System in Papua New Guinea*. Melbourne: Melbourne University Press.

Leach, Edmund Ronald. 1961. *Pul Eliya, A Village in Ceylon: A Study of Land Tenure and Kinship*. Cambridge: Cambridge University Press.

Segalen, Martine. 1986. *Historical Anthropology of the Family*. Cambridge: Cambridge University Press.

Stewart, Pamela J., and Andrew Strathern. 2002. *Remaking the World*. Washington, D.C.: Smithsonian Institution Press.

Strathern, Andrew, and Pamela J. Stewart. 2004. *Empowering the Past, Confronting the Future*. New York: Palgrave Macmillan.

Uhlmann, Allon J. 2006. *Family, Gender, and Kinship in Australia. The Social and Cultural Logic of Practice and Subjectivity*. Aldershot: Ashgate.

CHAPTER 8

Conclusions: Issues of Change and Continuity

Throughout this book, we have provided ethnographic accounts from many different parts of the world. Our aim was not to be encyclopedic, but to be comparative whenever appropriate. There are many different approaches in the study of kinship, from David Schneider's culturalist and deconstructive mode of analysis to correlational studies of patterns of custom (see, e.g., Pasternak, Ember, and Ember 1997), to studies of historical change and continuity (e.g., Cohen 2005 on China), or studies of gender, social change, and legal issues (e.g., Griffiths 1997 on divorce in Botswana, or Simpson 1998 on "unclear families" (e.g., p. 24) resulting from divorce and separation), to the secondary study of overall "styles" in the study of kinship by anthropologists (exemplified by Barnes 1971 on the writings of George Peter Murdock, Claude Lévi-Strauss, and Meyer Fortes). Our own overall approach in the present volume bears a resemblance to that found in Fox (1967), Keesing (1975), Holy (1996), and Stone (2000), although in our choice of examples we have drawn on our own fieldwork-based knowledge as well as our own general regional interests and analytical concerns. Our analytical orientation has been toward the study of processes in social life rather than simply the elucidation of structural forms. At the same time, processes always take place within certain guiding constraints. Good earlier work was done in this vein by the Manchester school of anthropologists, whose research was mainly carried out in Africa. Van Velsen, for example, studying the lakeside Tonga of Malawi, discussed in great detail the topic of the "social manipulation" of kin relations; but he related these manipulations to certain ethnographic anchorings, for example, in a social context

A large pearl shell, decorated with bright red tradestore paint and set on a backing of forest leaves including ferns, Tambul area south of Mount Hagen, Papua New Guinea. The shell is prepared to be worn in a dance. Beside it there are a bunch of forest plants and two King of Saxony bird-of-paradise plumes placed in a hollow stalk. The items are hung on a plaited house wall made of split hollow tubes of cane (an introduced technique). Pearl shells, traded in from the outside, complemented shells as major wealth items in the New Guinea Highlands. Like pigs, they were prime vehicles of social life and relations between kin.   (Photo: P. J. Stewart/A. Strathern Archive)

where matrilineal descent was practiced, "the hopeful expectation on the part of every Tonga [man] that perhaps one day he will be the founder and leader of an independent dominant lineage with its own village" (1964: 148). Van Velsen relates the conflicts that impede such an aim "to the inherent contradictions of virilocal marriage and matrilineal descent as the accepted principle of organization" (1964: 181). His formulation here exactly parallels that of Victor Turner on the Ndembu of Zambia, which Turner further parlayed into his notable analyses of sickness and redressive rituals among the Ndembu (Turner 1957, 1967). These classic studies stressed the interplay of process and structure in local contexts and their emergence as historical trajectories of change. We have found a similar approach useful in considering Euro-American patterns of kinship: for example, the interplay between partible inheritance, the idea of the household and family, and economic change in Neckarhausen as studied by David Sabean (1990).

In this final chapter, we review some further studies relating to two of our major concerns. One set of studies has to do with issues of change and continuity: We pick two such studies, springing from very different theoretical approaches. One is Robin Fox's *Reproduction and Succession* (1997), which relates to a burgeoning literature on assisted conception and how its related technology has altered the parameters of the definitions of kinship in Euro-American society (see also our earlier discussion, Chapter 3). The other is A. F. Robertson's *Beyond the Family: The Social Organization of Human Reproduction* (1991), in which Robertson seeks to show the influence of macrosocietal features on the family and the reciprocal influences of the family on these features. In effect, we will argue, both studies come down to fundamental issues of definition. In our other set of studies, we will return to these issues, looking at the works of a number of writers, including some recent theorists of Oceanic societies, and we will see the effects of broad versus narrow definitions of what kinship is and what it is about.

Theories of embodiment and personhood enter crucially into many of the contemporary discussions about kinship relations, and we will review again the issues in this regard also, referring to some of our earlier publications where related topics have been explored. Often arguments have revolved around questions of whether the individual and individuality have been recognized as cultural or social categories in the societies studied. In our view, "the individual" is indeed a universally recognized category, but emphases placed on it and its cognitive or practical salience may vary greatly. The ways in which ideas of self, individual, and personhood mediate relationships between people in kin networks and groups are at the heart of our topic of "kinship in action," so these issues are appropriate to address further in this final chapter of our book.

ROBIN FOX: REPRODUCTION AND SUCCESSION

There are two separate, but interrelated contexts associated with assisted conception. One is the context of a heterosexual married couple who have difficulties in achieving the conception or birthing of a child through their acts of sexual intercourse. In vitro conception/fertilization enables a sperm and egg to be brought together outside of the bodies that have produced them. However, we should note that this technological procedure belongs to the same cosmological scheme as conception within a female body. "Kinship" as such is not fundamentally altered, only the means whereby reproduction is achieved. However, the technology also enables other things to happen. Eggs and resulting embryos, for example, can be stored. Another person's egg or sperm might be introduced as substitute. Of course, a sperm or egg donor can be involved. The resultant child may be claimed by the couple who have instituted the procedure. With in vitro procedures, classically it is the egg and sperm of the couple themselves that is used, so that the child born in this way is "theirs" in the biological as well as the cultural sense, and parenthood is not split or fragmented. If the female producer of the now fertilized egg carries the resulting embryo or embryos in her womb and brings it or these to successful parturition, the process is completed.

Much more controversial and complex has been the development of surrogate motherhood, in which the fertilized egg of a woman is placed into the womb of another woman, who carries the child to term. Surrogate motherhood splits the concept of motherhood, dividing genetrix from mater (biological from social mother) in a new way, at least within the normative frameworks of

Euro-American ideas about kinship. It is worth noting, however, before expanding on this point, that a distinction between genetrix and mater certainly existed prior to this technological change. For example, in the Melpa-speaking area of Mount Hagen, a child might be "carried (born) and given" by its genetrix to an (adoptive) mother, that is, a mater. (The Melpa phrase is *mek ngorong*, "they carried and they gave"; see Strathern and Stewart 1999: 153–170 on fertility practices and adoption.) This "giving" did not expunge the social ties with the genetrix, who indeed might also remain a mater with whom the child retained both a normative and a personal relationship. Such complexities of shared parenthood transcend the simple dichotomy implied by the terms "mater" and "genetrix." How these complexities work out depends on the wider legal culture into which they are set. The problems of surrogate motherhood differ from this Melpa case because physical motherhood is split up in a new way. One female provides the egg, another the womb. There is a sense of a physical bond of substance on the part of both, but the recognition of "maternity" cannot be on an equal footing in the legal culture involved. Legal claims to the child are reserved for the woman who produced the fertilized egg and her male partner. However, sentiment may also be favorable to the woman who carried the child in her womb because of the long and intimate relationship with the child that this entails and the fact that the woman must also undergo the pangs of parturition. The cycle of parturition and breast-feeding, with its implications of mother–child bonding, is also involved here. (It is interesting, in passing, to note that the custom of employing wet nurses to breast-feed the children of elite families in the past was by itself never thought to rupture motherhood in the same way, because parturition as well as carrying the child remained with the "legal mother." Context is all.)

The specific case that Robin Fox discusses shows a further variation from the above scenarios. In this case, a married woman, who already had two children with her husband, entered into a contract with another married couple whereby she was artificially inseminated with the sperm of the male partner in the other marital pair to bear a child which would then be handed over to this other couple as theirs, under the terms of a privately drawn up contract arranged by a lawyer for a fee of US$7,500 (Fox 1997: 53). The surrogate mother was to receive US$10,000 for her service, and the payment was to end her claims on the resulting child. The agreement also stated that the surrogate mother was not to try to form a parent–child relationship with the child that might be born of the insemination. The impetus behind the arrangement seems to have been threefold.

1. The surrogate mother-to-be needed money.
2. The intended mater was for medical reasons unable to carry a child in her womb.
3. Her partner had lost all his kin in the Holocaust and wanted to have a child biologically related to him, to be a kind of replacement for the kinsfolk who had died (p. 54). The contract favored the contracting couple, because the surrogate mother was to bear all the risks of carrying the child and if the child was not healthy it would simply remain hers, and the contract would be void (p. 57).

When the child was born, the surrogate mother found that she was unable to give it up voluntarily, and she breast-fed it for over a month, and refused to accept the contracted payment. She and her husband fled to a different state with the baby (Fox 1997: 58). They were pursued and the baby was forcibly removed from her. Eventually the matter came before a court (p. 59).

One question that was brought up in court was the issue of "specific performance" of a private contract of this sort. Should the court order that the child be handed over or could it order that an indemnity be paid in lieu of this? Further, there was the question of whether the contract was enforceable, since the plan was to adopt the surrogate mother's child, and adoption law in the United States at the time, other than Wyoming, specified, according to Fox (1997: 63), that the consent to adoption has to be reaffirmed or ratified after birth. Of course, in this case, there was also the interest of the genetic father, the sperm source, whose wishes and intentions were central to the whole matter of the contract having been drawn up.

Fox discusses at length biological evidence regarding the bonding effects of pregnancy, parturition, and breast-feeding of infants. He writes in accordance with John Bowlby's (1969, 1973, 1980) work and suggests that infants are genetically programmed to seek objects in their world with which they can bond (p. 82). He adds that this may not necessarily be a biological mother-figure, although it nearly always is (p. 82). Fox also tries to assess the weight to be given in biological/psychological terms to the genetic father, saying that if the father did not know the child "he can only have bonded in imagination with the child" (p. 89). However, this assessment does not take into account just how powerful such an imagination can be (and imagination as a theoretical focus of analysis has recently become significant in anthropological writings).

Fox was himself involved in this case as a "friend of the court" (*amicus curiae*, Fox 1997: 69). Eventually the New Jersey Supreme Court ruled on February 3, 1988, that the surrogate mother's parental rights should be restored, but gave custody of the baby to the genetic father and charged a lower court to determine the genetrix's visitation rights (p. 115). The court also declared the original contract between the parties invalid and not in accordance with New Jersey law (p. 115).

Fox goes on to point out how the new technological splitting up of the components of reproduction immensely complicates notions of kinship that are based on the combination of these elements (1997: 119–121). Nevertheless, legal judgments that are in line with certain cultural and social predispositions tend still to be given. In this case, the law finally recognized the biological claims of the genetrix and of the genitor. The fact that these two were not a married couple was disregarded. The child was therefore split between two separate marital units between which a contract of convenience had been drawn up, bringing together the fertility of the male of one unit and the female of the other. The court did not recognize this contract as legitimate. It did reaffirm the basic idea of "kinship" as per Euro-American ideas, as genetically or biologically based.

Since Fox wrote his challenging study, a great deal of work has followed on the general theme of assisted conception and changing ideas of kinship and "the family." Monica M. E. Bonaccorso, for example, has written a full-length study of such topics in Southern Europe, citing much of the recent literature (e.g., Edwards 2000 on England and Franklin and McKinnon 2003 with references cited on how new technology is involved in reconfiguring kinship as a concept and a practice). Bonaccorso takes up the discussion of how same-sex couples can use technology to become parents in families (Bonaccorso 2009: 84–106). Susan Markens has written a monograph devoted to surrogate motherhood, including extensive reference to the case discussed above (Markens 2007).

A CONTINUUM OF THEMES: FROM REPRODUCTIVE TECHNOLOGY TO LESBIAN MOTHERHOOD

David Schneider's deconstructive formulations attempting to demolish any idea of universal biological-cultural foundations attached to the word "kinship," and to insert an extreme culturalist form of theorizing into the heart of kinship studies, have resulted in a number of further developments which Schneider himself probably would not have anticipated. These developments in kinship studies stem from two sources: (1) the alterations in reproductive technology that have enabled a disaggregation of the physical components of parenthood beyond the domain of a sexually procreative heterosexual pair; (2) the move toward gay and lesbian rights, including rights to marry and, flowing from this, rights to socially recognized parenthood.

While both these changes are relatively new, the situations they have produced are in some ways similar to older, established features of kinship relations. At the most elementary and obvious empirical level, corresponding to personal experience, putative biological "relatedness" does not automatically result in a close "relationship."[1] Kinship in action may involve denial of relationship as much as an assertion of relatedness. The old distinctions between genetrix and mater and genitor and pater also contain the distinction between a putative procreative role and a social role of "parenting," with the underlying theme of a distinction between biologically imputed relatedness and socially established relationship. Schneider's distinction between kinship in American culture seen as "shared biogenetic substance" (with emphasis on the "biogenetic part") and as "code for conduct" falls into line here.

All of the above distinctions set up a difference between biological and social kinship. In many systems, the two domains are normatively linked. However, in *all* systems, seen as systems of action, the distinction between relatedness and relationship emerges; and in many systems, there are arrangements whereby the "social" can supersede the "biological" domain, for example, in adoption and fosterage; in Nuer ghost marriage whereby a woman was married to a dead husband in order to raise children to his name, or woman to woman marriage in which a barren divorced woman was regarded as a man by her patrilineal kin and was remarried to a woman who would bear children for her by a "surrogate genitor" (Evans-Pritchard 1951; Stone 2010: 91–92); and in "ritual kinship" arrangements such as blood-brotherhood whereby a ritual act establishes a relationship modeled terminologically on consanguinity.[2] Human ingenuity and creativity show themselves at work here. Even if we take a different example, Lévi-Strauss's famous demonstration of the importance of the mother's brother, we see a shared principle at work: All these examples show a dependency in reproduction on more than a heterosexual pair or dispensing with a heterosexual pair. Reproductive technology involving artificial insemination or a surrogate womb sets up "transactions in parenthood" that may involve a number of people.

Possibilities engendered in this way are taken to a further level in gay/lesbian claims to be able to marry and furthermore to set up families in which the partners act as parents: in other words, follow a parenting "code for conduct" by other than heterosexual procreative means. In a lesbian pair, one may be inseminated with sperm from a male donor source by her partner and may bear a child to which both will be parents. In a gay pair, they may hire a surrogate mother to bear a child for them to care for jointly as parents. Owing to the gendered character of kin terms, a problem of terminology is bound to arise, that is, whether both parents are "mothers" in the lesbian case or both "fathers" in the gay case. In these relationships, sometimes gendered differences may be simulated, but to express this in terminology, in a culture where gender is naturalized as biological, will still create problems. With the advent of practices of this sort in the Euro-American context and elsewhere, such problems become more obvious. A new array of studies in this field of "created kinship" has emerged, with an early landmark contribution by Kath Weston, *Families We Choose*, published in 1991. Weston herself cites Schneider as a (perhaps involuntary) founding figure in this field, because of his proposition that ideas of kinship are simply cultural constructs and that "significant doubt exists as to whether non-Western cultures recognize kinship as a unified construct or domain" (Weston 1991: 34); and she goes on, "Denaturalizing the genealogical grid would require that procreation no longer be postulated as kinship's base, ground, or centerpiece" (p. 34). From these quotations, it is clear that Weston sees Schneider's work as the origin of her own studies, as a kind of founding ancestor, what the Duna people would call a *malu*, not just an origin story but a legitimizing narrative of origins (Strathern and Stewart 2004). (Of course, we have earlier discussed the pros and cons of Schneider's arguments—here we are simply tracing their rhetorical spin-offs.)

Corinne P. Hayden has written a useful discussion of how themes of biology versus culture play out in "lesbian kinship," primarily with reference to motherhood (Hayden 2004). Hayden situates her discussion in relation to American kinship and notes that lesbian and gay people have problematized Schneider's characterization of American kinship, in which heterosexual intercourse is symbolized as "love" (Hayden 2004: 379). The symbolic importance of family and kinship to the "nation" is brought out by the fact that denying family to gays and lesbians is tantamount to denying them "cultural citizenship" (p. 381).—or at least presumably this is what they themselves claim. If so, it is an important point because it helps to explain why gay and lesbian ("same-sex") marriage and, by implication, parenthood have become such fraught issues at the political and religious levels in American society.

Lesbian motherhood, for example, challenges not only the norm of heterosexuality but also the gendered roles within the family through "the existence," Hayden argues, "of a second female parent who is neither down-played nor degendered" (2004: 382). She also reports that some lesbians argue that "heterosexuality contains built-in power inequities; by contrast, lesbian mothers claim to offer gender equality" (p. 382). One might wonder here whether gay parents also seek to offer equality in this way, and how such things may work out in practice. Clearly, there is an extended arena for empirical ethnographic work here.

Hayden goes on to point out that when one lesbian partner bears a child, the other partner, as a "co-mother," has a less validated role, and thus an asymmetry, which may be a power asymmetry, is set up (2004: 382). This is because of the continuing primacy of biology in the definition of motherhood in American culture, she says (p. 382). Proponents of lesbian or gay partner-ships in turn argue that what is important is that the couple plan their parent-hood jointly as heterosexual couples are supposed to do (2004: 385), with the difference that the male sperm source has to be erased from the picture. Various strategies may be employed here to overcome these problems. A brother of the co-mother may be enlisted to provide the sperm, so that both mothers are genetically related to their child (with the third figure in the background). Or both partners may bear a child, using sperm of the same donor (the genetic situation here would be the same as in polygyny, but here again the male's social role is absent or suppressed) (p. 386). Or the sperm donor might even be incorporated as a third co-parent (p. 387). Or the women may adopt each other's biological children.

These strategic permutations of creative cultural improvisation are reminis-cent in their ethos of Nuer ghost marriage and woman to woman marriage. Gender roles are bent, identities are switched, dominant models become muted, and vice versa. In the Nuer case of woman to woman marriage, a divorced barren woman is transformed into a married male agnate with a wife and children, all within the project of patriliny and utilizing the category of submerged genitor, which is already at least in part available in the Nuer cultural repertoire. In lesbian motherhood in the United States, two females are partners and each can achieve a project of motherhood through the issue of a submerged third male party acting as genitor, all within an anti-patrilineal or anti-patriarchal project. The projects are different, but the degree of ingenuity in both subverting and conforming to cultural ideals is similar in all of these examples where biological ties are achieved within alternative sets of sexual relationships.

There is a large and growing literature on matters of this kind. See, for example, Browne (2007) on changing ideas of gender; Michael Peletz (2009) on gender pluralism in Southeast Asia; Lustig, Brody, and McKenny (2008) on biotechnology and public policy; and Roisin Ryan-Flood (2009) on lesbian motherhood.

A. F. ROBERTSON: BEYOND THE FAMILY

In many ways, assisted procreation reemphasizes kinship's foundations in the nuclear family and its biological bases. Robertson is concerned with the opposite perspective: how kinship is a part of a wider social structure. He writes early on, "Sex may be secretive, and even a pregnancy may be concealed, but reproducing people is inescapably public" (Robertson 1991: 1). He adds, "It is, after all, the process by which society itself is recreated" (p. 1). While Robertson is highly critical of what he calls conventional studies of "the family," he recognizes that the family is "identifiable by what its members do rather than what they think" (1991: 8), and he stresses the multiplicity of functions and activities that may be tied in with this category. He also identifies a basic contradiction in contemporary ideology: "while on the one hand politicians assure us passionately that "the family" is the bedrock of our modern nations, they also insist on the right of individuals to define themselves and make their own way in society" (p. 43).

This is an interesting assertion, worth commenting on further. If "politicians" use rhetoric regarding the family, we can infer that the family is actually important both as a practical and an ideological category in American cultural and social contexts: And, in broad alignment with Robertson's own arguments, we can further suggest that "the family" is important as an ideological source of motivation in the contemporary economy. This is also clearly and obviously true, because the family is a major source point of consumer spending and of a host of industries that enable this pattern of spending. The primary locus of such spending is the house and the household within it, with the associated costs of running it. Because households with children are, in turn, the major targets for spending, children in families are indeed an important aspect of social, not just physical, reproduction in the sense of Robertson's assertion. So much is obvious from a moment's reflection, and the ramifications of this point are immense. A further obvious point is that the family is also the locus from which persons are produced as workers in the wider economic and political spheres of life. Marxist anthropologists, notably Claude Meillassoux (1981), writing in an anticolonial vein in the 1970s and 1980s, pointed out that the costs of reproducing labor in places such as Southern Africa, where migrant laborers came in from different places to work in mining enterprises, were borne not by the companies but by the rural areas from which the migrant laborers came (see, e.g., Ferguson 1999 on the Copperbelt region in Zambia). Robertson (1991: 49) draws attention to this process, referring it to the appropriation of female reproductive capacity. More broadly, however, it comes down to the rural families and in turn their roles in the overall local structures in the places where these laborers came from. The point has been stressed in the African colonial context. But it also applies in principle everywhere. The family tends to remain the major locus in which persons are produced and socialized, harnessed to an educational system, often through parental expenditures, and released into the workforce. Yet this formulation also does not end the matter, because the family is not only the source of labor, it is also the ideal form of social living and is therefore the aim of the production of people. People come from families and work so that they can make new families. The proliferation of families means the proliferation of demands for houses, mortgages, insurance policies, cars, and so on: all those things that "the economy" runs on, and when expenditure on them halts or declines, "the economy" is in trouble and the people with it. The notion of the economy as something objective and impersonal is in fact a myth. The economy is the net result of people working or being put out of work, spending or not spending, socially reproducing or not reproducing patterns of lifeways.

Robertson explores many issues and contexts related to our own earlier observations, notably in the context of the development of industrial capitalism. He concludes, "Families matter both individually and collectively not because they are 'natural', stable, dependent social bedrock—which they are not. They matter because they are dynamic, and this animation enables us to *live*, continually remaking society, and providing a vital impetus for the making of human history" (1991: 167). This is well said, and in line with our own theme of "kinship in action." However, there is no need to deny a natural—in the sense of biological—basis to the family, as well as highlighting its variability in form and function and therefore its dynamic potentialities in shaping, as well as being shaped by, history.

In general, the argument as to whether the family is natural or not, stable or not, depends as much on one's definitions and perspectives as on any essential realities. Yet, because of the fascination with attempts to define "humanity" in terms of universal characteristics, and the fact that "kinship" is one of the terms in play in these debates, matters of definition continue to exercise theorists. We will revisit these matters of definition now.

REISSUING AND REFRAMING DEFINITIONS: IDEOLOGY AND PRACTICE

Richard Feinberg has co-edited a thoughtful set of studies that refer to David Schneider's work on "kinship" (Feinberg and Ottenheimer 2001). An earlier, and sharply critical, assessment of Schneider's pronouncements on American kinship was provided by the kinship specialist Harold Scheffler (1976), who took issue with Schneider's antigenealogical stance and also debated the "native" meanings of the term "relative" in American culture. One theme addressed by contributors to Feinberg's volume is the issue of relativism (see also Bamford and Leach 2009). Schneider's viewpoint stressed relativism, denying universality to any concept of kinship based on genealogical reckoning of blood and so on. Contributors evaluate Schneider's work negatively if they lean toward seeing kinship as in some way the locus of universals, positively if they also espouse general relativism. Dwight Read takes his stand for universalism on the logico-mathematical basis of kin reckoning (Read 2001)[3]; Robert McKinley on grounds of kinship as the basis of morality and obligation (McKinley 2001). Martin Ottenheimer offers a humanistic pluralism blending attention to cultural specificity and awareness of the need for cross-cultural categories of analysis

(Ottenheimer 2001). (Our own view corresponds well enough to Ottenheimer's formulation.) Ward Goodenough accuses Schneider of misinterpreting "genealogy" as a term in order to attack supposed biologically based theories. Goodenough rightly points out that "genealogy" is itself a culturally constructed category (Goodenough 2001: 207). Our readers can refer back here to our own depiction of the Duna category of *malu*, where a chain-like pedigree of agnatic ties leading to an ancestral figure is the backbone or genealogical charter legitimizing claims of named categories of people to their territory or *rindi* (Strathern and Stewart 2004). Such a genealogy is only one of a whole set of variants which people *can* give among the Duna. It is unique in that only some people are keepers of it and authorized to cite it or use it to assert their own special roles (or person-hood, as we might put it) in crucial social contexts. Absolutely, then, *malu* are culturally (and politically) constructed; and they leave out at least as much as they include, for instance quite often they omit the spouses of agnatic males in the pedigree. Yet Duna groups in general are cognatically founded. And genea-logy is a simplified version of history: a charter, in the Malinowskian sense of the term (Malinowski [1948] 1984).

Susan Montague's chapter in Feinberg's volume ambitiously uses Schneider's idea of relativity in distinctive features of kinship to produce yet another analysis of the famous Trobriand "kinship system," discussed earlier in this book and in the work of Annette Weiner (Montague 2001; Weiner 1988). In order to carry out her analysis, Montague concentrates on what Schneider would have called "codes for conduct," one dimension of "kinship," the other being the definitions of the ways in which people enter into a kinship status (stereotypically via sexually based procreation). However, Montague maintains that her definitions are also based on ideas of shared substance. It is just that these ideas are not ones of shared "blood" but initially are about "milk," and about the "bodily blood" of the genetrix of a child, which is built out of the foods the genetrix has consumed. Moreover, Montague suggests, the term *ina* in the sense of "social mother" has to do with the giving of processed foods to a child rather than with parturition of the child as such. She also argues that *tama* (father, mother's husband, pater) is seen as the one who provides food to a child while the child is young, and the child in turn provides food to the *tama* when the *tama* is old (Montague 2001: 171). All this is code for conduct again. Here, Montague does not address notions of procreation, reincarnation, or the molding of a child's appearance in the womb by repeated acts of intercourse. The outcome of Montague's study is that she points interestingly to a broaden-ing of focus on indigenous theories of bodily *substance* and how these interact with, or define, kinship. This is a topic we have ourselves looked at in detail in our book *Humors and Substances* (Stewart and Strathern 2002). The concept of "substance" has indeed provided a gateway into a broadened definition of kinship which nevertheless recognizes its rootedness in embodied existence.

Laura Zimmer-Tamakoshi's chapter in the Feinberg volume parallels Montague's approach, at least by stressing the importance of actions in defining kin as against a straightforward application of genealogical calculi (2001). However, it is important to remember here Ward Goodenough's caveat that genealogy is a cultural construct. Zimmer-Tamakoshi points out that among the Gende of Papua New Guinea contributors to funeral payments that validate or create claims to land rights may be recognized "biological" (i.e., genealogical) descendants of the deceased, but they may also be "affines and unrelated persons" (2001: 187). Such persons are rhetorically described in terms of filiative relationships, but these also refer to achieved aspects of status, based on performance of nurture and care. A child who does not meet obligations to its parents is in this sense, in Gende ideas, not a child at all (p. 188). Zimmer-Tamakoshi also recorded the manipulation and altering of genealogies due to people's wishes to claim compensation for introduced mining operations for chromite and cobalt-nickel (2001: 193). Old stories of migrations were brought into play to justify claims to clan memberships that were different from those previously claimed but would be needed as a means of asking for compensation payments (p. 195). Zimmer-Tamakoshi found her head spinning at the ingenuities with which these manipulations were pursued (2001: 198). She also notes that these actions are in line with a stress on individual agency, referring here to older literature that argues the same (see, e.g., Strathern 1971, 1972; see also Strathern and Stewart 2000). And she wonders how such fluidity of ideas affects the possibility of comparisons. Actually, her findings are quite in line with those of many others in the Pacific, especially Papua New Guinea. And she also finds that alongside this manipulation "biological [i.e. again genealogical] kinship does matter to a certain extent . . . It is recognized among the Gende that biological parents contribute blood, semen, bone, and other physical matter to a growing fetus, while mothers provide milk for growing children" (p. 199). And the key point is that the gift of these substances must be reciprocated over time (in parallel with the Trobriand case). Exchange and substance are thus brought into alignment. Gende ideas in this respect are actually very similar to notions held all over the New Guinea Highlands region. This is the rationale based on which, for example, payments to matrilateral kin are sometimes required, as among the Wiru of Pangia in the Southern Highlands Province of Papua New Guinea. The points involved here are the following:

1. There is an *interplay* between ascribed and achieved aspects of kinship relations.
2. This interplay is effected through the notion of transactions in substances and for substances.
3. There is an equation between wealth forms (pigs, shells, etc.) and persons; and
4. Substances are tied to embodiment and also to the placement of persons in the landscape. Thus, if the growing, giving, and sharing of food is important in defining kin ties, then whose food it is and where it is grown are important matters. Food grown on ancestral land may well be seen as carrying ancestral substances. Certainly the Duna would recognize this point (see Stewart and Strathern 2005).[4]

These considerations enable us to turn to a further range of studies.

RELATIVES AND RELATEDNESS: SUBSTANCE AS A KEY

Susan Montague, whose work we have discussed above, partly took her stand on the difficulties of defining who "a relative" would be in the Trobriands (2001: 173). Similar difficulties and ambiguities, however, could be found elsewhere, which does not negate the fact that there are notions of kinship at work; it simply shows that in the clash between obligations and opportunities many ambiguities can and do arise. What still holds is that within the discursive domains that develop around key concepts such as kinship or genealogy, broader ideas of relatedness still define the boundaries of definition. Janet Carsten is among those anthropologists who have explored this point. In her edited work *Cultures of Relatedness*, Carsten included essays by a number of well-known anthropologists (Carsten 2000). Sharon Hutchinson analyzed how Nuer people of the Sudan, studied earlier by Evans-Pritchard and also by herself (see Evans-Pritchard 1940, 1951; Hutchinson 1996), had been coming to terms with adapting their ideas of blood, cattle, and food as symbolic media, with problems arising out of the uses of money, guns, and paper (i.e., literacy). Nuer traditionally said that blood and food go together because food is continually transformed into blood (a processual model, and one that helps to illuminate the Papua New Guinea materials cited above from the Trobriands and the Gende; see also Strathern and Stewart 1998a for a comparison of Nuer and Melpa ideas of life and death). For the Nuer, this combination of food and blood constitutes relatedness ("kinship"). Cattle can also stand for kinship in this way, because cattle are given in bridewealth and define rights of paternity ("cattle beget children"). Nowadays money, guns, and paper transactions are perceived as threatening the values encapsulated in the domain of blood and food. The notion that cattle mediated the transmission of blood over time was the result of their use in bridewealth payments. Ideas of substances (food, blood, etc.) are thus at the heart of Nuer ideas of kinship, but these become operational only in conjunction with transactions involving cattle (see Hutchinson 1996: 172–176). And they are put at risk by new transactions, such as the sale of cattle for money, and the increased killing of persons with guns, as well as by introduced courts with new rules and words on paper (Hutchinson 2000).

The idea of transaction is also key in a study by Helen Lambert in the same volume, on "sentiment and substance" in North India (Lambert 2000a). Lambert deals with adoption procedures of a particular sort. In these, a bride, especially one from a distant place, may be ritually taken into his lap by her adoptive father in her affinal place. The adoptive daughter is called *jholi*. The primary significance of the ritual act is that her new adoptive kin perform vital life-cycle rituals for her on festive occasions, and the relationship may last into the next generation. That the act is a ritual one and is performed only in ritual occasions seems to be a vital point of detail here. Ritual action models and also plays on other contexts of action. The bride is taken on the lap in an intimate embodied act, as for a young child. And she is henceforth emplaced in her adoptive family by being relieved of observing affinal taboos, such as veiling. The provision of a bride with fictive agnatic kin in her affinal place finds its parallel in traditional practices recorded by L. Langness among the Bena of the Eastern Highlands of Papua New Guinea, occurring for the same practical reasons: the provision of support and the emplacement of a bride from a distant, perhaps hostile place in her new home (Langness 1964). Lambert also explicitly draws attention to the South Indian idea of "an ecological conception of relations and flows of substance between person and place" (Lambert 2000a: 84). The parallel with the Highlands of Papua New Guinea is again very close. Yet Lambert further notes that "consanguineal kinship constitutes the ideal model of relatedness, and optative forms of relations invoke this model, rather than being entirely identified with it" (2000a: 85). Such an observation points to the fact that while we can certainly recognize a class of "relatedness" beyond genealogy and consanguinity, not all types of relatedness may be of equal valency. This observation is also relevant for the analysis of "substances" as a category of ideology and practice. In our book *Humors and Substances*," we argued that particular elements, such as blood, grease, and water, may be salient and symbolically important: We call these "humors," following the classic models of humoral elements in bodies familiar from the Hippocratean treatises onward. Other substances may also be identified, for example, tears or urine. We begin therefore to build a more complex and structured model of how substances enter into flows of social relationships. (See also Carsten 2004: 109–135 on this topic of substances and kinship.)

Monica Böck and Aparno Rao have edited a book, *Concepts of Kinship in South Asian Practice* (2000), which usefully adds to these perspectives, containing a further essay by Helen Lambert on Rajasthani kinship. The editors, in their introduction to that volume, include a section on "The Human Body and Bodily Substances." They refer to the ideas of McKim Marriott, E. Valentine Daniel, and other scholars who stressed the elements of fluidity in the construction of the boundaries of personhood. Böck and Rao themselves stress the processual aspects of both personhood and kin relations. The connection between substances and moral norms is also reaffirmed, and we should note that this is certainly in line with what we know about "humors and substances" in New Guinea. It is also consistent with this point that "in most South Asian cultures . . . it appears that not only do physiological concepts lay the basis for ideas about biological procreation, but that they go further to influence broad aspects of social organization and world views" (Böck and Rao 2000: 5–6). We should note that the "biological" views involved are culture specific. Not only is a child thought to resemble its genitor in many respects, but anciently this idea was underpinned by the notion that the child (son) is the reincarnation of the father (p. 6) and that the karmic balance from the father's life gives certain determining characteristics to the child (p. 6).

Other influences and "substances" are also involved in the processual creation and maintenance of kin ties. Religious and territorial ties are important and enter into the broad spectrum of "relatedness" that can define persons and groups (Böck and Rao 2000: 12). Relationships described as ones of "fictive kinship" may simply belong to this broad spectrum, and the distinction between "true" and "not true" kin may be blurred in practical usages (2000: 15).

God-parenthood, or "ritual kinship," is another case in point, as is the whole spectrum of adoption (pp. 15–20) . In approaching complexities of this kind, Böck and Rao further draw on the work in cognitive psychology by Lakoff and Johnson, which stresses the primacy of embodied experience as the source of thinking about the world, and on L. Hirschfeld's invocation of the concept of "natural resemblance" as shaping both notions of kinship and broader ideas of relatedness (2000: 24, citing Hirschfeld 1986: 227). They further endorse the point, which we have made central throughout this book, to study "kinship in practice" (2000: 28) and to take the historical dimension into account (p. 29).[5]

Helen Lambert's chapter in Böck and Rao's book is an excellent example of the study of practice. The *jholi* adoptive relationship, on which we have remarked above in reviewing Carsten's edited collection, was constrained by caste rules: The adopted in-marrying bride must come from a caste from which the adopters can drink water. This is because the bride and her adopters must be able to live commensally. Lambert pertinently notes that "the process of sharing substance [such as water] itself helps to establish relatedness" (Lambert 2000b: 86). A taboo on sharing, by contrast, establishes nonrelatedness. A special ritual is performed at the time of creation of the *jholi* ties by the mother of the bride. The mother places a lump of brown sugar as a gift into the *jholi*, or pouch, in the clothing of the bride's mother-in-law. Then the two women embrace. The bride in a case cited by Lambert was only two years old, so this custom is comparable to the famous instance discovered by Arthur Wolf in his fieldwork in the Ilan area of Taiwan of the adoption of girls destined to be brides to sons of the family (Wolf 1966). Lambert notes that the term *jholi* or "pouch" also refers to the womb. The adopted bride is thus treated as a gift transferred from one womb to another and so "reborn," we may suggest (p. 97*).*

Substances are also involved in sacrifices to ancestors of the lineage and to ghosts. Troubled spirits of the deceased are thought to make milk go sour or the cows become dry, so such a spirit will be given a permanent place in the local home and fields and will be offered milk-rice pudding, shared with living household members, and the figure representing the new ancestor is also bathed in milk. Here, cow's milk is ritually used to create an honored ancestor out of a troubled spirit or ghost (Lambert 2000b: 91). What is operative, it seems, is the power of milk, as also the power of sharing this prime nurturant substance. Lambert takes a very balanced view here. She acknowledges the importance of transactions in substance and places these alongside notions about biological procreation, seeing kinship as supported by both of these elements.

Böck and Rao's edited volume represents a careful, ethnographically backed, revision of ideas about kinship in South Asia, reviewing and evaluating the models of Marriott and others that were taken over wholesale into Oceanic contexts and offering a middle way between competing perspectives deriving from the work of David Schneider. Pacific specialists would do well to take note of this newer work in South Asia. With this in mind, we now turn to another consideration of kinship debates in Oceanic materials.

FILIATION, AFFILIATION, SOCIALITY: REWORKING PACIFIC MODELS OF KINSHIP

Harold Scheffler is a distinguished kinship theorist who has led a rearguard action on behalf of careful definitions and rigorous attention to ethnography in Pacific studies. His book *Filiation and Affiliation* (Scheffler 2001) constitutes a detailed reexamination of analytical terms such as "filiation," "parent," "descent," and so on, with reference to how writers use these as terms of comparison in ethnography. In discussing the question of recruitment to groups, Scheffler points out that relationship is not the same as recruitment. Recruitment to clan groups may depend on residence as well as filiation. He distinguishes between three possibilities in a logical fashion:

1. filiation is necessary and sufficient for recruitment;
2. it is necessary but not sufficient;
3. it is sufficient, but not necessary (Scheffler 2001: 13).

This yields a useful matrix for sorting out cases. Scheffler also recognizes that different kinds of paternity and indeed maternity may be at work in the same society, so filiation itself may not be a simple term (2001: 19). In Meyer Fortes's usage, however, there is little doubt that by filiation he meant something normative, jurally recognized (Fortes 1969).

Scheffler places the New Guinea Highlands cases into his category 3, patrifiliation sufficient but not necessary. He includes the Melpa in this set of Highlands cases (also Enga, Chimbu, Siane, and Mende [this should be "Mendi"] and also the Wola need to be included here; e.g., Sillitoe 1979 and many innovative and thoughtful further contributions by Sillitoe). Building on this classification and briefly noting that there are instances where a person brought up outside of their father's patrifilial place will or can belong where they grew up, Scheffler proceeds to write that "unless patrifiliation is a necessary condition for affiliation, relations of patrilineal descent need not even occur within a group" (2001: 29). He follows Fortes's usage that descent must refer to a rule of affiliation and only groups whose constitution is by unilineal descent should be described as "descent groups" (p. 31). He elaborates his position in chapter 8 of his book (pp. 132–159), using J. A. Barnes's concept of "cumulative patrifiliation" (Barnes 1962: 134). Again, following his definitional guidelines, Scheffler argues that the groups identified by anthropologists as clan groups in the Highlands are invariably local groups with bounded territories, and that talk of "descent" in relation to such groups refers to no more than the people's own talk of "extended" brothers, fathers, sons, and so on (2001: 135ff.).

Scheffler's treatment of the data here is in line with his definitional position. It is also supported by Sillitoe's work on the Wola (1979). And certainly in effective terms, clan groups are closed by residence as well as by participation in exchanges. But, to take the Melpa case, group structure is not tied simply to filiation. Filiative links do provide the building blocks in which models and images of group segments and their solidarities or conflicts are developed. Myths of origin provide an overarching framework for each large group, defined with reference to sky-beings as ancestors and a sacred item, the *mi*, on which oaths are sworn. A pervasive ideology of male procreation suffuses origin narratives. Scheffler has bypassed all this in pursuit of a clean analytical definition. Yet, if he were to extend his own argument, he would have to recognize that territory and shared obligations *in fact* determine why many African groups also define themselves in terms of descent. (See also on a Polynesian case, Anuta, Feinberg 1990.)

A brief comparative look at the Melpa and Duna cases will help to elucidate how both filiation and descent, following Fortes's broad delineation of these terms, can be usefully deployed in relation to the Highlands societies. In the Melpa case, recruitment, as we have earlier noted, is filiative, normatively via patrifiliation but acceptably also via matrifiliation. But solidarity based on origins is always expressed in terms of descent-related dogmas that stress agnatic ties, and this is in line with wider relations in the society at large, tied in with bridewealth, residence, leadership, and so on. Descent here is a dogma applied to the long-term historical structure of groups; filiation applies to the processual, short-term minutiae of how people come to belong to these structural frameworks. In a performative sense, calling these groups descent groups or sets of fathers and sons is what actually creates them in discursive terms, and this has little to do with actual processes of recruitment but everything to do with gender and politics and their expression in the language of agnatic ties of descent.

Melpa ideology, then, is agnatic with regard to group solidarity while in recruitment groups are cognatically composed. With the Duna, the ideology is cognatic with regard to rules of recruitment, but in addition to this there is a jural assertion that lines of agnates have custody of important origin stories (*malu*) and disposition over land rights. (e.g., Strathern and Stewart 2004). In each case, we have to see the practical domains of life in which descent-based or filiation-based discourse is employed. In addition, general ideas about substance, food, locality, and the ancestrality of the ground itself are deeply involved in determining how kinship ties are achieved and articulated. Böck and Rao's collection of South Asian studies reestablishes the possibility of connecting South Asian and Pacific materials in a way that goes beyond the specifics of McKim Marriott's work, with his use of the term "dividual" and the idea that persons are not "bounded" entities. Certainly, they are not; but they are also not *just* bounded entities in so-called Western contexts, nor are they *entirely* without definitional boundaries in Oceanic societies. Scheffler's careful typological work suffices to show us this point, with his delineation of the jural concomitants of different kinds of filiative rules. A sustained application of a practice theory approach could yield further dividends in this sphere. It is important to break free from the constraints of earlier formulations of what "the problems" are in this sphere, for example whether groups "are" descent groups or not, and whether they are "loosely structured" or not. Groups may perfectly well "be" descent groups from one viewpoint and not from another. They may be loosely (i.e., flexibly) structured in one domain and not in another. What matters is process and practice and how practices relate to universes of being that we ourselves have identified analytically as cosmological worlds (see, e.g., Stewart and Strathern 2001, 2002).

Edvard Hviding has reexamined the problem of how cognatic kinship operates in Oceania, with his case study of the *butubutu* kin group in New Georgia (Hviding 2003). Hviding refers to the enlarged analytical umbrella of "relatedness," which we have been discussing here as the context of "kinship in action." He notes that *butubutu* as a term is polyvalent. It is not restricted to one meaning such as "descent group." The same can be said for terms such as *reklaep*, a "row" or "line" in the Melpa language of Papua New Guinea. Such a concept of a row or line as an image-schema of group activity is derived from the embodied practice of men dancing in a row at a *moka* exchange. It can also be used "vertically," as well as in this "horizontal" usage, to refer to lines of connections with ancestors. This concept of the *reklaep* can thus be seen as a comparative example of an image of "structured sociality" corresponding to a cognitive schema which Hviding invokes here, citing among others G. Lakoff's work on "prototypical categorization" (Hviding 2003: 73, citing Lakoff 1987). Hviding is also interested in indigenous theories of "sociality" (2003: 73 again)— a topic which was by no means absent from the earlier flow of work on the New Guinea Highlands (e.g., Strathern 1972) and has continued through into more recent writings (e.g., Stewart and Strathern 2002; Strathern and Stewart 2004 on the Duna).

In this vein, Hviding announces that he will examine the concepts of *kale* ("side") and *huana* ("path") in the Marovo Lagoon area of the Solomon Islands, New Georgia (2003: 74). He enters first, however, into the old problem of cognatic groups and how these overlap in principle but may be bounded in practice (p. 75). Hviding refers to Peter Lawrence's study of the Garia of Madang Province, Papua New Guinea (Lawrence 1984). He quotes from Meyer Fortes's foreword to this volume, in which Fortes reports that his response in 1950 to Lawrence's material was "cautious" (Fortes 1984: ix) (not "disbelief," as Hviding 2003: 76, appears to suggest). Fortes himself points out that regardless of the mechanisms by which "order" was achieved in Garia social relations, the production of an overall socio-cosmic order was what Lawrence was analyzing. Fortes in fact adopted the Garia concept of *nanunanu* ("thinking of others") as a hallmark of kinship amity, and he identified the "all-pervasive character of the cognatic structure and morality of Garia kinship institutions" (1984: x). These two observations are thoroughly in line with the ethos of Fortes's own presentation of his Tallensi materials, if we substitute "patrilineal" for "cognatic" in his sentence quoted here (Lawrence also notes in his preface that both Meyer Fortes and one of the present authors, AJS, "read and commented on the final draft of his book," Lawrence 1984: xxiii). The Garia ethnography was thus not simply a product of an encounter with a new Melanesian ethnography of "cognatic societies" (Hviding 2003: 76). It stemmed from the much longer-term search for indigenous concepts of kinship and their relationship to social order in general.

Furthermore, the "cognatic societies" in question need to be differentiated, between those with ego-based ramifying *kindreds* (like the Garia) and those with *ancestor-focused* groups in which cognatic ties of descent/kinship are premised on genealogical ties with such ancestors. Further, we need to recognize that multiple forms of grouping, including at minimum both kindreds and ancestor-focused groups, may easily be found together in a single case. (Incidentally, Meyer Fortes recognized the existence of wider groupings and cross-cutting networks in the Tallensi case itself, see Fortes 1945, 1949).

What, then, of the *butubutu* as a concept and a set of practices? First, land disputes are common and people quote genealogies to support their claims. These genealogies contain both male and female links and are therefore nonunilineal. Second, people have for long been used to encountering and dealing with strangers and no doubt with setting up connections with such strangers (Hviding 2003: 81). A persistent difference is also made between "coastal" and "bush" people, who were in precolonial times "linguistically and politically distinct" (p. 81). *Butubutu* is applied as a term primarily to "kin-based groups" that claim "delimited territories" (*puava*) (2003: 82). *Butubutu* + *puava* thus equates to the Duna concept of *rindi/tindi* which encompasses both kin and land (Strathern and Stewart 2004). The Marovo say, Hviding reports, "the *butubutu* guards the *puava*" (as the agnatic lines do among the Duna). Since the name of the *butubutu* may be in fact the name of its ancestral territory, the parallel with the Duna *rindi* concept seems very close here. Marovo genealogies are also comparable to Duna ones: 10–15 generations deep. (Duna genealogies tend to be curtailed at 14 generations, because of a prevailing notion of the cyclic ending and renewal of the earth, see Stewart and Strathern 2002 with references to similar ideas in neighboring areas.) "Male hereditary leaders" (agnates?) hold the customary knowledge (=Duna *malu*) that justifies each *butubutu*'s inalienable claim to its territory (land and sea). Filiative rules, operating through the parent of either gender, determine access to rights of guardianship over territory (p. 83). Genealogical strings plus histories of settlement validate all claims (p. 84).

Hviding notes that *butubutu* is often rendered in Solomon Islands Pijin as *laen* (=*lain*, in Papua New Guinea Tok Pisin, with the same extension of meaning as in Melpa *reklaep*, remarked on above). *Laen* is a general term, and so is *butubutu*. It can refer to any ancestor-focused set of people, to a bilateral kindred or extended family, or to a corporate, localized lineage—we may take the latter perhaps as a prototypical usage. Hviding does not hesitate, *pace* the kinds of restrictions of usage advocated by Harold Scheffler (2001; but see Scheffler's own earlier ethnography in 1965 on the Choiseulese of the Solomons) to use the term "cognatic descent" here (2003: 85).

He goes on, however, to recognize complexities. A localized *butubutu* has a "core" of people (Hviding 2003: 86) whose membership is strong, that is, is backed up by genealogies and long residence. These genealogical strings tend to stress "unilinearity," and to favor "cumulative patrifiliation," although some female links are included. Connections with *puava* by whatever historical links are described as *soto*, "being joined" (2003: 88). Writing in a way that brings the Marovo case into clear alignment with both the Duna and the Melpa (as well as the Choiseulese and the Kwaio of Malaita, Keesing 1971, 1972, also cited by Hviding), Hviding notes the paired significance of "being born of" a man or a woman in terms of attachment to a group, but adds that "certain unilineal biases go hand in hand with the dominant cognatic notion" and the associated "counting of attachments" (2003: 89). These biases go with the taking of "sides," he says (p. 89).

Nowadays, leaders are often described as "chiefs," and chiefly genealogies show a patrilineal emphasis in many cases (Hviding 2003: 89). Coastal groups show the patrilineal bias most clearly, linking it to *binangara*, "leadership substance" (p. 89). This is an idea of succession, or ideally male primogeniture (bringing it close to, but going beyond, the Duna idea of *anoagaro*, "man-standing," lines of succession in the *rindi*; Strathern and Stewart 2004: 28–29). By contrast, bush people show a matrilateral or even matrilineal bias (p. 90), referred to as *vuluvulu* (p. 91). *Vuluvulu* refers to a kind of female-based "blood core," which may be counterposed to male-based *binangara*—A sense of structural balance is given here. Overall, the numerous possibilities of tracing ties and links through filiative chains provide people with much flexibility of choice; yet in practice people generally know in detail only the genealogies of their effective *butubutu* membership (p. 92).

In a broader sense, "side" (i.e., paternal, maternal) and "path" make up a kind of cosmic duality referring to male/female and bush/sea categories. "Path" concepts lead outward not only to histories of migration and journeyings, where people came from and what places they went through, but also to all customary ways of being. Side and path together define the field of affiliations of people. Hviding notes further how these concepts have come into play in, and been modified by, contemporary indigenous experts on local custom in relation to the activities of a mining company from Australia (2003: 101; compare also the Duna case in Stewart and Strathern 2002: 163). A shift toward unilineal claims may represent a tendency to restrict the numbers of groups or people who can make compensation claims (2003: 102), as has been found elsewhere also. Hence, we must agree that "fluid relationality" (Hviding 2003: 108) can sometimes be transformed into "rigid demarcation" when arguments about the commoditization of land and about state-introduced money come into play. Perceptions of "flows of power" (p. 108) are certainly involved; and questions of individual agency must also be considered.

Kinship and personhood are always closely bound up with each other, and often through the perspective of the constraints of morality as well as through assumptions about power, wealth, and entitlement. Hviding's study does not broach this topic directly. But it does make it clear that there is a great scope in the *butubutu* concept *both* for the formation of corporate groups *and* for the exercise of personal (read "individual") agency. We have discussed these kinds of issues many times before (e.g., Strathern and Stewart 1998b, 2000, 2008; Stewart and Strathern 2000, 2001). Here, we note that attention to multiplicity and complexity in relationships corresponds to our concept of the "relational-individual," a concept that crosscuts the stereotypical and dichotomous dividual/individual contrast that has been deployed in depictions of "Melanesian sociality" (Hviding does not rely on this dichotomy). It is particularly at the level of practice that the relevance of the relational-individual concept becomes evident; yet we would venture to say that it also operates at an ideological level; and the polysemous character of the *butubutu* category suggests that this is so. One point should be made clear. The relational-individual concept is emphatically not a derivative of the "dividual" category. "Dividual" as a term implies an opposition to the notion of the "individual," negating it. Our concept rather recognizes both poles of personhood, reflecting ultimately self and group, *both* relational concepts.

We have referred to Meyer Fortes and his assistance with Peter Lawrence's work and Lawrence's book *The Garia* in particular. There is a further profound insight (among many) in Fortes's work, far transcending the narrow definitional question about "descent" and "descent groups." This insight has to do with Fortes's conjoining of the topics of religion, morality, and the person in his posthumously published collection of studies on the Tallensi (Fortes 1987). In particular, in this book, which comprises essays from many different phases of his writings, Fortes stresses the significance of ritual. In considering how "flexibility" as well as fixity is achieved in kinship ties, it is pertinent to note that rituals are generally very important. In other words, choices may be exercised, but often they are made socially effective by ritual means. A clear case of this process at work is found in Lambert's study of *jholi* custom in Rajasthan. Another instance can be found in the custom among the Melpa of planting a cordyline plant surrounded by a small fence in the birthplace of a child, during which the father also buries the child's navel-string there and later throws the infant's feces into the little enclosure to protect it from being consumed by pigs (the enclosure is called the *kangambokla te pakla*, in the Melpa language). The child is thus attached to the ground where its father lives, but also via a part of maternal substance. Attention to practices of this ritual kind, which punctuate the flow of life and its substances, can greatly help us to understand how the intersection of kinship, ritual, and personhood is created and imaginatively brought out in many societies. For a thoughtful review of similar issues for the Tolai people of Papua New Guinea and their concept of *gunantuna*, "person," see Epstein (1999). *Gunan* primarily refers to "land" and *gunantuna* to "person," showing the significance of embodiment and emplacement in the definition of the person. Epstein refers to "the powerful sentiment that attached to the burial of the umbilical cord in the *gunan* of one's birth" (1999: 32)—in this case as a mark of matrilineal identification, while in the parallel case from Hagen the father's act of "making the fence" for the child gives the act a paternal significance. In fact, there was a related custom among the Tolai, Epstein notes, in which "a father or grandfather may specially prepare a cordyline plant with the roots wrapped up, circle it around the infant and afterwards plant it in ancestral land, as the 'rooting' of the child" (p. 32). The parallel with the Melpa use of the cordyline is here exact, across an otherwise wide divide between a coastal Austronesian context and a highlands Non-Austronesian one. The power of the cordyline as a boundary marker of land claims and as a long-lasting keeper of the vitality of the person or group with which it is associated, energized in human ritual actions, is abundantly evident, and this underlines our point about the significance of ritual and its capacity to transform social relationships.

While with this example we bring our discussion of Oceanic kinship in action to a close, we also suggest that it marks a further horizon in which the theorizing of ritual and the theorizing of kinship relations could be explicitly brought into mutual articulation. A volume of studies on birth customs in Taiwan, the Philippines, and Indonesia, focused on Austronesian-speaking groups, recognizes in its title the connections between kinship, the cosmos, and gender (Yamaji 1990a). One study in this collection recognizes special ritual procedures surrounding the navel, including acts of divination regarding the child's life trajectory (Kawai 1990: 113). Cases from the Taiwanese indigenous Rukai, Amis, and Tsou groups equally show elaborate ritual rules and precautions that both protect the child at a vulnerable stage and establish its identity in various embodied and emplaced ritual ways (Kasahara 1990; Lin 1990; Ogawa 1990; Yamaji 1990b). The comparative ethnography of the Taiwanese indigenous groups in relation to the wider Pacific world, including their kinship systems, is a study that must wait a while; but a pursuit of ritual themes and their anchoring in the lived landscapes of environmental belonging would richly repay the time invested in it.

We began this book by recounting (see Chapter 1) the plot of Sir Walter Scott's novel *The Fair Maid of Perth*. We will close it by recounting the story of a film, *Jean de Florette,* based on the novel by the French author Marcel Pagnol, and the sequel film *Manon des Sources.* The story deals with kinship, land, greed, village life, and hidden circumstances that are not revealed until the end of the two films.[6]

An old bachelor César Soubeyran living in a village in Provence has acquired land and some money. His family is old-established in the area, but he has no wife or any children to whom he can pass on his name and perpetuate the name of the Soubeyrans. His nephew (brother's son) Ugolin Soubeyran comes back from military service and begins secretly to work on a project to grow red carnations. The land is dry and needs plenty of water from his cistern. César knows of the location of a partially blocked up spring on neighboring land, and he and Ugolin go to offer to buy it. The owner, who is of a rival family, refuses and they get into an altercation with him, in which he dies. They leave his body by a tree, and later they find the spring and plug it up with cement.

The farm of the neighbor goes to his sister, Florette, but she dies and in turn it is inherited by her son Jean and his wife and daughter. As it happens, Florette had been a sweetheart of César in earlier times. He remembers her by a decorative comb of hers which he keeps as an intimate source of memory without showing it to anyone else. Florette had left her village and gone in marriage to a blacksmith in the village of Crespin while César was away as a soldier and wounded in a military hospital in Morocco.

Jean and his family turn up at the farm, and to the discomfiture of Ugolin and César, he sets about vigorously to plant vegetables and raise rabbits for sale, rejoicing in the rural life and determined to overcome all difficulties. The family has a little money Jean has inherited from his mother to tide them over while trying to set themselves up. Jean is a hunchback. The villagers note this and scoff at his chances of succeeding. Ugolin pretends to befriend Jean, and conceals from him the fact that rain rarely falls on the farm even though it falls nearby. A drought ensues and Jean and his family are exhausted with hauling water from a distant spring. Their plants wither and their rabbits have nothing to eat. In despair, Jean sets them free.

Ugolin tries to get Jean to sell the farm now, but instead Jean goes to get a mortgage. César steps in to fund this loan, expecting to profit thereby. Jean sets about using dynamite to blast open an area where he has identified water by a dowsing rod, but he is killed when the dynamite explodes and he is hit by a propelled rock.

Now the widowed mother Aimée and her daughter Manon are forced to leave the farm and César buys it. As they are leaving, César and Ugolin gleefully unplug the spring and César "baptizes" Ugolin with its water (an "unholy" baptism); but Manon secretly comes and observes them. She shrieks out, but the two men think this is just a buzzard that has made a kill.

In the sequel film, *Manon des Sources*, we find that time has moved on. Aimée has taken up work elsewhere as an opera singer, but her daughter Manon has lived with an old Piedmontese (Italian) squatter couple who were in the area of the farm before. Manon tends goats, tripping lightly over the hills and calling to them in a lilting voice like their own bleatings. She harbors her memories of what she had seen as a child. Ugolin has made a successful business of growing carnations, using water from the spring. He becomes aware, however, of the presence in the vicinity of Manon and spies on her, and fancies himself in love with her. From then, he becomes besotted with desire for her. But Manon knows he and César tricked and betrayed her father and will have nothing to do with him.

One day she follows a young goat into a crevice in a hillside and stumbles on the source of the spring that feeds water to the local farms and the whole village below. She blocks its point of outflow, and the farmers and villagers are driven to desperation and believe that some great power has done this to punish them for their complicity in the misdeed of Ugolin and César against the hunchback Jean. Manon herself has formed a romantic attachment to a young local teacher, Bernard. She publicly accuses Ugolin and César of blocking and then unplugging the spring on her father's land. Ugolin declares his love for her and asks her to marry him, but she spurns him and in despair he goes home and hangs himself on the tree from which Manon had swung in play as a child when her father was still alive. The villagers meanwhile hold a religious procession to ask for the flow of water to be renewed. Manon and Bernard secretly go to the source and unblock it, so that the water gushes back into the village fountain just as the procession passes by, and a miracle is accordingly declared.

César carries a bunch of carnations to Ugolin's gravesite and meets an old acquaintance of his, Delphine. She now tells him that Florette had written a letter to him long ago, when he was away in Africa during the fighting there, telling him she was pregnant with his child. Receiving no reply to this letter (that César never received), she tried to forcibly abort her child, but went at length in marriage to the blacksmith in Crespin. The child was the hunchback Jean.

César realizes that in trying to prolong the Soubeyran family via his nephew Ugolin and in driving Jean effectively to his death, he had actually been the instrument of the death of his own immediate son. With this revelation, he determines to leave all his belongings to Manon, who is herself now pregnant, and to die in his sleep, which he does, holding Florette's comb in his hand as a last mode of contact with her memory. The pursuit of family has led to the destruction of family and its re-creation in descendants through the woman who turns out to have been his own granddaughter. It is a story activated by the aims of kinship in action, of César Soubeyran's sense of self within his group, of profound contingency and biological complexity, involving ideology, sentiment, misrecognition, and a final, if incomplete, reconciliation or at least resolution in which kin ties are realized in the devolution of property. Personhood, agency, passionate emotions, attachments to the land, and the vagaries of fortune, all these are woven into an intricate narrative in which the power of renewal in water is juxtaposed with the power of blockages exercised by greed.

Andrew J. Strathern in front of the authors' long-established field house among the Kawelka people of Kuk, Mount Hagen, Papua New Guinea (1990s). The fieldworker wears a colorful headnet of the kind worn locally by men in Hagen. His jacket comes from an agricultural show held in Ayrshire, Scotland.   (Photo: P. J. Stewart/A. Strathern Archive)

Pamela J. Stewart in a small local church at Kuk, Mount Hagen, Papua New Guinea (1990s). The fieldworker is listening to a sermon along with a set of boys and senior men. The man with his hand contemplatively over his face is Ongka, a famous leader among the Kawelka people, who died in April 2003. See Andrew Strathern and Pamela J. Stewart. 2000. *Collaborations and Conflicts: A Leader Through Time.* Fort Worth, TX: Harcourt College Publishers.   (Photo: P. J. Stewart/A. Strathern Archive)

Conclusion

Throughout this book, our aim has been twofold: to discuss kinship relations and structures as processes—hence the idea of "kinship in action"—and to link these processes to ongoing ideas about people's perceptions of themselves and their identities as group members—hence "self and group." The narrative of *Manon of the Spring* abundantly illustrates these two universal themes, plus some twists of its own in line with Greek tragedy (recognition, reversal of role, suffering, and learning). It also demonstrates the tight connection between kinship and land, whether seen as property or as identity, or as both: land that provides both a source of livelihood and a sense of the perpetuation of life, as kinship itself does.

Questions to Consider

1. What are the advantages and disadvantages of adopting either a broad or a narrow definition of kinship? Use examples in this chapter to support your view.
2. How can you relate the recent Oceanic studies reported here with those from India? What does their juxtaposition tell us about making comparisons?

Notes

1. We say here that this point is at the most "elementary" level. It is also the most fundamental matter, because it can be taken as the source from which other distinctions are drawn. "Blood ties" may be "given," although they too are the product of arrangements by choice that were not simply given, that is, they are the products of sexual relations. People have to "make" or "take" what they can on the basis of these givens and the multiple circumstances in which such a "gift" comes. Sometimes the "making" may also involve "breaking" the ties of relationship, even if those of relatedness cannot be changed. Marriage, as a relationship designed to create relatedness, is the opposite of consanguinity; and divorce is the context in which it is broken, while other aspects of relatedness flowing from it may not be.

2. Nuer ghost marriage was a means by which lineage descendants could be provided for a man who had died without issue. The deceased's close brother would marry a woman to the name of his dead brother. The wife would speak of the dead man as her husband and his brother, with whom she had sexual relations, as her brother-in-law. This was done partly to appease the ghost of the dead man and ward off sickness that the ghost might inflict. From the Loess Plateau in the Yellow River region in China comes another custom, which takes the idea of the agency of the dead a step further. In the case of a male teenager or young man who dies as a bachelor, the ghost is thought to be unhappy. His parents may then, it appears, "search for a dead woman to be his bride, and once a corpse is obtained, bury the pair together as a married couple" (*New York Times*, Thursday, October 5, 2006, pp. 1, 12). The custom "was described as a parental duty to a lost child that reflected Confucian values about loyalty to family" (p. 12). Families of girls who have died unmarried, perhaps by drowning, can receive the equivalent of USD $1,200 for the body if it is purchased for this purpose. The price stands as the equivalent of a brideprice payment which they would have received had the daughter lived (p. 12). The custom is called *minghum* marriage. Families too poor to buy a *minghum* bride "make a figure of straw and bury it beside a dead son as the spouse he never had" (p. 12).

3. More recently, Read has provided an ambitious mathematically based account of kin terminology systems, utilizing the idea that these form logically integrated matrices and make up cultural ontologies of relatedness. Read calls his method "cultural instantiation." It looks for formal, implicational relationships between kin terms that can generate genealogical, but also other, bases of kinship. Read uses American kin terms to exemplify his new paradigm. It would be interesting to see the method employed on other cases, for example, from New Guinea. Read provides references to some Pacific Island cases to support his viewpoint (Dwight W. Read, "Kinship theory: A paradigm shift," *Ethnology* 46, no. 4 (2007): 329–364).

4. Feinberg, in a characteristically sensible and thoughtful review of materials in the introduction to his co-edited volume discussed here, notes that Schneider's attempt to deconstruct American kinship by arguing that it cannot be distinguished from politics or religion fails because in American ideas kinship is indeed genealogical. He goes on to point out that there can be *different* ideas of substance linking people together. Thus, land may be different from biogenetic ties (Feinberg in Feinberg and Ottenheimer 2001: 13). Of course, in some cultures, notably in New Guinea, land and kinship are linked, as in the Duna concept of the *rindi* (see Stewart and Strathern 2002).

5. See also Nitya Rao, "Kinship matters: Women's land claims in the Santal Parganas, Jharkland," *JRAI,* n.s., 11 (2005): 725–746.
6. One of our peer reviewers questioned the inclusion of this example in our book. We include it because it reveals the passions that run in counterpoint to structures of kinship. In New Guinea, such passion appears in the guise of magic, sorcery, and witchcraft, in the intimacies of conflict, as well as in the camaraderie of amity. In this book, we have often been concerned with structures, but kinship structures are ones through which rivers of passion run, sometimes shallow, sometimes deep. This French narrative reveals this fundamental, and indeed universal, point very clearly.

References

Bamford, Sandra, and James Leach, eds., 2009. *Kinship and Beyond. The Genealogical Model Reconsidered.* Oxford: Berhgahn.

Barnes, John Arundel. 1962. African models in the New Guinea Highlands. *Man* 62: 2–9.

Barnes, John Arundel. 1971. *Three Styles in the Study of Kinship.* Berkeley, CA: University of California Press.

Böck, Monika, and Aparna Rao, eds. 2000. Introduction. In *Culture, Creation and Procreation. Concepts of Kinship in South Asian Practice,* ed. M. Böck and A. Rao, 1–52. Oxford: Berghahn.

Bonaccorso, Monica M. E. 2009. *Conceiving Kinship: Assisted Conception, Procreation and Family in Southern Europe.* Oxford: Berghahn Books.

Bowlby, John. 1969. *Attachment and Loss. Volume 1: Attachment.* London: Hogarth Press.

Bowlby, John. 1973. *Attachment and Loss. Volume 2: Separation.* London: Hogarth Press.

Bowlby, John. 1980. *Attachment and Loss. Volume 3: Loss, Sadness, and Depression.* New York: Basic Books.

Browne, Jude, ed. 2007. *The Future of Gender.* Cambridge: Cambridge University Press.

Carsten, Janet, ed. 2000. *Cultures of Relatedness: New Approaches to the Study of Kinship.* Cambridge: Cambridge University Press.

Carsten, Janet. 2004. *After Kinship.* Cambridge: Cambridge University Press.

Cohen, Myron L. 2005. *Kinship, Contract, Community, and State.* Stanford, CA: Stanford University Press.

Edwards, Jeanette. 2000. *Born and Bred: Idioms of Kinship and New Reproductive Technologies.* Oxford: Oxford University Press.

Epstein, Arnold Leonard. 1999. *Gunantuna: Aspects of the Person, the Self, and the Individual among the Tolai.* Bathurst, NSW: Crawford House Publishing.

Evans-Pritchard, Edward Evan. 1940. *The Nuer: A Description of the Modes of Livelihood and Political Institutions of a Nilotic People.* Oxford: Clarendon Press.

Evans-Pritchard, Edward Evan. 1951. *Kinship and Marriage among the Nuer.* Oxford: Clarendon Press.

Feinberg, Richard. 1990. New Guinea Models on a Polynesian outlier? *Ethnology* 29: 83–96.

Feinberg, Richard, and Martin Ottenheimer, eds. 2001. *The Cultural Analysis of Kinship. The Legacy of David M. Schneider.* Urbana, IL: University of Illinois Press.

Ferguson, James. 1999. *Expectations of Modernity. Myths and Meanings of Urban Life on the Zambian Copperbelt.* Berkeley, CA: University of California Press.

Fortes, Meyer. 1945. *The Dynamics of Clanship among the Tallensi.* Oxford: Oxford University Press, for the International African Institute.

Fortes, Meyer. 1949. *The Web of Kinship among the Tallensi.* Oxford: Oxford University Press, for the International African Institute.

Fortes, Meyer. 1969. *Kinship and the Social Order*. Chicago, IL: Aldine.

Fortes, Meyer. 1984. Foreword. In *The Garia*, ed. P. Lawrence, ix–xii. Melbourne, VIC: Melbourne University Press.

Fortes, Meyer. 1987. *Religion, Morality, and the Person. Essays on Tallensi Religion*, ed. Jack Goody. Cambridge: Cambridge University Press.

Fox, Robin. 1967. *Kinship and Marriage*. Harmondsworth: Penguin Books.

Fox, Robin. 1997. *Reproduction and Succession. Studies in Anthropology, Law, and Society*. New Brunswick, NJ: Transaction Publishers.

Franklin, Sarah, and Susan McKinnon. 2003. *Relative Values: Reconfiguring Kinship Studies*. Durham, NC: Duke University Press.

Goodenough, Ward H. 2001. Conclusions: Muddles in Schneider's model. In *The Cultural Analysis of Kinship*, ed. R. Feinberg and M. Ottenheimer, 205–222. Urbana, IL: University of Illinois Press.

Griffiths, Anne M. O. 1997. *In the Shadow of Marriage: Gender and Justice in an African Community*. Chicago, IL: The University of Chicago Press.

Hayden, Corinne P. 2004. Gender, genetics, and generation: Reformulating biology in lesbian kinship. In *Kinship and Family: An Anthropological Reader*, ed. Robert Parkin and Linda Stone, 378–394. Oxford: Blackwell.

Hirschfeld, Larry A. 1986. Kinship and cognition: Genealogy and the meaning of kinship terms. *Current Anthropology* 27(3): 217–242.

Holy, Ladislav. 1996. *Anthropological Perspectives on Kinship*. London: Pluto Press.

Hutchinson, Sharon E. 1996. *Nuer Dilemmas. Coping with Money, War, and the State*. Berkeley, CA: University of California Press.

Hutchinson, Sharon E. 2000. Identity and substance: The broadening bases of relatedness among the Nuer of Southern Sudan. In *Cultures of Relatedness*, ed. J. Carsten, 55–72. Cambridge: Cambridge University Press.

Hviding, Eduard. 2003. Disentangling the Butubutu of New Georgia: Cognatic kinship in thought and action. In *Oceanic Socialities and Cultural Forms*, ed. I. Hoëm and S. Roalkvam, 71–114. Oxford: Berghan.

Kasahara, Masaharu. 1990. Parturition, child recognition, and social stratification among the Rukai of Taiwan. In *Kinship, Gender, and the Cosmic World*, ed. K. Yamaji, 3–28. Taipei: SMC Publishing Inc.

Kawai, Toshimitsu. 1990. The navel of the cosmos: A study of the folk psychology of childbirth and child development among the Bukidnon. In *Kinship, Gender, and the Cosmic World*, ed. K. Yamaji, 105–130. Taipei: SMC Publishing, Inc.

Keesing, Roger M. 1971. Descent, residence and cultural codes, In *Anthropology in Oceania: Essays Presented to Ian Hogbin*, ed. L. Hiatt and C. Jayawardena, 121–128. Sydney: Angus and Robertson.

Keesing, Roger M. 1972. Simple models of complexity: The lure of kinship. In *Kinship Studies in the Morgan Centennial Year*, ed. P. Reining, 17–31. Washington, D.C.: Anthropological Society of Washington.

Keesing, Roger M. 1975. *Kin Groups and Social Structure*. Fort Worth, TX: Harcourt Brace.

Lakoff, George. 1987. *Women, Fire, and Dangerous Things: What Categories Reveal About the Mind*. Chicago, IL: University of Chicago Press.

Lambert, Helen. 2000a. Sentiment and substance in North Indian forms of relatedness. In *Cultures of Relatedness*, ed. J. Carsten, 73–89. Cambridge: Cambridge University Press.

Lambert, Helen. 200b. Village bodies? Reflections on locality, constitution, and affect in Rajasthani kinship. In *Culture, Creation, and Procreation*, ed. M. Böck and A. Rao, 53–80. Oxford: Berghahn.

Langness, L. L. 1964. Some problems in the conceptualization of Highlands social structure. *American Anthropologist* 66(4, part 2): 162–182 (special public, ed. by James B. Watson).

Lawrence, Peter. 1984. *The Garia: An Ethnography of a Traditional Cosmic System in Papua New Guinea*. Melbourne, VIC: Melbourne University Press.

Lin, Meirong. 1990. Traditional customs of childbearing and childrearing among the Rukai people. In *Kinship, Gender, and the Cosmic World*, ed. K. Yamaji, 29–48. Taipei: SMC Publishing, Inc.

Lustig, B. Andrew, B. A. Brody, and Gerald P. McKenny, eds. 2008. *Altering Nature, Vol. 2: Religion, Biotechnology, and Public Policy*. London: Springer.

Malinowski, Bronislaw. 1984 [1948]. The role of myth in life. In *Magic, Science, and Religion*, ed. B. Malinowski, 96–111. Westport, CT: Greenwood Press.

Markens, Susan. 2007. *Surrogate Motherhood and the Politics of Reproduction*. Berkeley, CA: University of California Press.

McKinley, Robert. 2001. The Philosophy of Kinship: A reply to Schneider's *Critique of the Study of Kinship*. In *The Cultural Analysis of Kinship*, ed. R. Feinberg and M. Ottenheimer, 131–167. Urbana, IL: University of Illinois Press.

Montague, Susan P. 2001. The Trobriand kinship classification and Schneider's cultural relativism. In *The Cultural Analysis of Kinship*, ed. R. Feinberg and M. Ottenheimer, 168–186. Urbana, IL: University of Illinois Press.

Meillassoux, Claude. 1981. *Maidens, Meal and Money*. Cambridge: Cambridge University Press (Translation of *Femmes, Greniers et Capitaux* 1975).

Ogawa, Masayasu. 1990. Symbolic implications of the Tsou house. In *Kinship, Gender, and the Cosmic World*, ed. K. Yamaji, 77–104. Taipei: SMC Publishing Inc.

Ottenheimer, Martin. 2001. Relativism in kinship analysis. In *The Cultural Analysis of Kinship*, ed. R. Feinberg and M. Ottenheimer, 118–130. Urbana, IL: University of Illinois Press.

Pasternak, Burton, Carol R. Ember, and Melvin Ember. 1997. *Sex, Gender, and Kinship: A Cross-Cultural Perspective*. New Jersey: Prentice Hall.

Peletz, Michael G. 2009. *Gender Pluralism. Southeast Asia Since Early Modern Times*. London and New York: Routledge.

Read, Dwight W. 2001. What is kinship? In *The Cultural Analysis of Kinship*, ed. R. Feinberg and M. Ottenheimer, 78–117. Urbana, IL: University of Illinois Press.

Read, Dwight W. 2007. Kinship theory: A paradigm shift. *Ethnology* 46(4): 329–364.

Robertson, A. F. 1991. *Beyond the Family: The Social Organization of Human Reproduction*. Berkeley, CA: University of California Press.

Ryan-Flood, Roisin. 2009. *Lesbian Motherhood: Gender, Families, and Sexual Citizenship*. New York: Palgrave Macmillan.

Sabean, David W. 1990. *Property, Production, and Family in Neckarhausen, 1700–1870*. Cambridge: Cambridge University Press.

Scheffler, Harold W. 1965. *Choiseul Island Social Structure*. Berkeley, CA: University of California Press.

Scheffler, Harold W. 1976. The "meaning" of kinship terms in American culture: Another view. In *Meaning in Anthropology*, ed. K. Basso and H. Selby, 57–92. Albuquerque, NM: University of New Mexico Press.

Scheffler, Harold W. 2001. *Filiation and Affiliation*. Boulder, CO: Westview Press.

Sillitoe, Paul. 1979. *Give and Take. Exchange in Wola Society*. Canberra: Australian National University Press.

Simpson, Bob. 1998. *Changing Families. An Ethnographic Approach to Divorce and Separation*. Oxford: Berg.

Stewart, Pamela J., and Andrew Strathern. 2000. Introduction: Narratives speak. In *Identity Work: Constructing Pacific Lives*, ed. Pamela J. Stewart and Andrew Strathern, 1–26. Pittsburgh, PA: University of Pittsburgh Press.

Stewart, Pamela J., and Andrew Strathern. 2001. *Humors and Substances: Ideas of the Body in New Guinea*. Westport, CT: Bergin and Garvey (Greenwood Publishing).

Stewart, Pamela J., and Andrew Strathern. 2002. *Remaking the World: Myth, Mining, and Ritual Change among the Duna of Papua New Guinea*. Washington, D.C.: Smithsonian Institution Press.

Stewart, Pamela J., and Andrew Strathern. 2005. Cosmology, resources, and Landscape: agencies of the dead and the living in Duna, Papua New Guinea. *Ethnology* 44(1): 35–47.

Stone, Linda. 2001. *Kinship and Gender: An Introduction*. 2nd ed. Boulder, CO: Westview Press.

Stone, Linda. 2010. *Kinship and Gender: An Introduction*. 4th ed. Boulder, CO: Westview Press.

Strathern, Andrew. 1971. *The Rope of Moka*. Cambridge: Cambridge University Press. (Reissued, with new Preface by A. Strathern and P. J. Stewart, 2007.)

Strathern, Andrew. 1972. *One Father, One Blood. Descent and Group Structure among the Melpa People*. Canberra: Australian National University Press.

Strathern, Andrew. 1973. Kinship, descent, and locality: Some New Guinea examples. In *The Character of Kinship*, ed. J. Goody, 21–33. Cambridge: Cambridge University Press.

Strathern, Andrew J., and Pamela J. Stewart. 1998a. Melpa and Nuer ideas of life and death: The rebirth of a comparison. In *Bodies and Persons: Comparative Perspectives from Africa and Melanesia*, ed. M. Lambek and A. Strathern, 497–502. Cambridge: Cambridge University Press.

Strathern, Andrew, and Pamela J. Stewart. 1998b. Seeking personhood: Anthropological accounts and local concepts in Mount Hagen, Papua New Guinea. *Oceania* 68(3): 170–188.

Strathern, Andrew, and Pamela J. Stewart. 1999. *Curing and Healing: Medical Anthropology in Global Perspective*. Durham, NC: Carolina Academic Press.

Strathern, Andrew, and Pamela J. Stewart. 2000. *Arrow Talk: Transaction, Transition, and Contradiction in New Guinea Highlands History*. Kent, OH: The Kent State University Press.

Strathern, Andrew, and Pamela J. Stewart. 2000. Creating difference: A contemporary affiliation drama in the Highlands of New Guinea. *The Journal of the Royal Anthropological Institute* 6(1): 1–15.

Strathern, Andrew, and Pamela J. Stewart. 2004. *Empowering the Past, Confronting the Future: The Duna of Papua New Guinea*. New York: Palgrave Macmillan.

Strathern, Andrew, and Pamela J. Stewart. 2008. Introduction: Aligning Words, Aligning Worlds. In *Exchange and Sacrifice*, ed. Pamela J. Stewart and Andrew Strathern, xi–xxxvi. Durham, NC: Carolina Academic Press.

Turner, Victor W. 1957. *Schism and Continuity in an African Society*. Manchester: Manchester University Press.

Turner, Victor W. 1967. *The Forest of Symbols: Aspects of Ndembu Ritual*. Ithaca, NY: Cornell University Press.

van Velsen, J. 1964. *The Politics of Kinship. A Study in Social Manipulation among the Lakeside Tonga*. Manchester: Manchester University Press.

Weiner, Annette. 1988. *The Trobrianders of Papua New Guinea*. Forth Worth, TX. Harcourt Brace (Thomson/Wadsworth).

Weston, Kath. 1991. *Families We Choose: Lesbians, Gays, Kinship*. New York: Columbia University Press.

Wolf, Arthur. 1966. Childhood association, sexual attraction, and the incest taboo: A Chinese case. *American Anthropologist* 68: 883–898.

Yamaji, Katsuhiko. 1990a. Female activity in the Amis of Taiwan In *Kinship, Gender and the Cosmic World*, ed. K. Yamaji, 49–76. Taipei: SMC Publishing Inc.

Yamaji, Katsuhiko. ed. 1990b. *Kinship, Gender and the Cosmic World. Ethnographies of Birth Customs in Taiwan, the Philippines and Indonesia*. Taipei: SMC Publishing, Inc.

Zimmer-Tamakoshi, Laura. 2001. Development and Ancestral Gerrymandering. Schneider in Papua New Guinea. In *The Cultural Analysis of Kinship*, ed. R. Feinberg and M. Ottenheimer , 187–204. Urbana, IL: University of Illinois Press.

APPENDIX 1

Kinship Terminologies

The study of kin terminologies has been regarded as central both to anthropology in general and to the analysis of kinship relations. This tradition of enquiry and thought goes back at least to the work of Lewis Henry Morgan (1870, 1877) and other nineteenth-century scholars, who were intent on using ethnographic evidence from around the globe to establish the early history of humans and their social systems. Morgan investigated kin terms among the Iroquois Native Americans and also compiled lists of kin term systems gathered from other sources around the world. He enshrined certain named types of systems, identified by their varying characteristics, for example, Dravidian, Hawaiian, Iroquois, Eskimo, and Crow; and mixed types such as Crow–Omaha and Dravidian–Iroquois emerged from these classifications. (For concise expositions, see Keesing 1975: 101–120; Stone 2010: 315–321; compare the earlier work of Fox 1967: 240–262; Holy 1996 notes these matters only in passing.) As descriptive and analytical categories, these classifications became part of the stock in trade of anthropological work. The terms refer to specific cases, which were then seen as types or examples found widely. So we find kin terminology classifications in the New Guinea Highlands, opened to the outside world only long after Morgan and his fellow scientists had passed away, that are reported to be predominantly "Iroquois" in form; and this, in spite of the fact that the Native American Iroquois studied by Morgan practiced matrilineal descent, while most New Guinea Highlands cases fall within the patrilineal rubric (or patrilineal plus cognatic structures such as those found among the Duna people; see Meggitt 1964; Strathern and Stewart 2004).

What do these kinds of classifications identify, and what do they signify? To answer these two questions, we need to step back and look at some technical definitions.

Morgan's empirical discovery was that there are indeed a limited number of major types of kin terminologies. He also found that kin terms were widely used in a *classificatory* way, in the pattern known as bifurcate-merging. This means that immediate lineal kin and collateral kin are classified under the same term. Typically, these usages go with group membership: For example, in a patrilineal system of descent, the terms "brother," "father," and "son" may be extended between males to the whole group. This can, and often does, happen whether or not ties involved can be traced through immediate genealogical links. The classificatory use of kin terms thus appears to be one key to social structure.

Classificatory kinship further poses the question of what the putative basis is for kinship itself. If we accept at least that it refers to some kind of significant "relatedness" (as argued, e.g., by Carsten 2000), the question becomes,

"What kind or basis of relatedness is involved here?" If we assume that the primary basis of kinship lies in what we call "immediate" or "genealogical" ties, then relatedness must stem from these ties and be extended outward from them on analogical principles (as supposed in "componential analyses," e.g., Lounsbury 1964). If, however, we were to argue that kinship begins with society-wide or group-based classifications, or on some other basis such as residence, sharing food, and so on, the translation into English of terms from systems constructed along these broad lines becomes moot. Anthropologists have historically disagreed about this fundamental issue, just as they have disagreed about whether to consider alliance by marriage between groups or descent and succession within groups as fundamental to the operation of kinship systems.

A reasonable solution to this dilemma can be offered as follows: In the operation of a given kinship universe, various principles may come into play. It is fundamental that the classifications involved form a logical grid of terms. This logic can be established in more than one way. Commonly, a distinction is made between immediate and more distant kin of the same overall type or term. Also, affines (in-laws) are distinguished clearly, both in terminology and in behavior, from consanguineal kin. Genealogies of specific consanguineal ties are cultural in form and may encompass both procreative and social bases of relationship. In the operation of kinship, ties of descent and marriage are always found together and contribute to the general workings of social relations. There is much variation in the extent to which these elements of kinship, such as descent or marital alliance, are prominent and highly structured or may be inconspicuous and flexible. The distinction between consanguines and affines is modified when a rule or practice of marriage by which kinsfolk become spouses, such as in cousin marriage, comes into play. In a fully prescriptive system, the terms for certain cousins, say, and certain in-laws would be the same.

Such a formulation does not, by any means, do away with all the debates about kinship and kinship terms. It does help us to find our way around them into more amenable matters.

First, terminologies are not immediate indicators of social roles. This holds across the board. A person may stand in a classificatory sense to another as a "father," but may not fulfill a role consonant with that term, other than in certain group contexts where solidarity is displayed.

Second, peoples who use classificatory terms are well aware of this first point. They recognize the sliding scale of obligations that operates in practice.

Third, if genealogy is a major component of kin relatedness, it is always combined in practice with other criteria: propinquity, cooperation, shared property, and the like. It is not an abstract diagram or blueprint that people follow. It belongs, rather, to their embodied practices, that is, to the domains of performance or nonperformance.

Fourth, kinship ties are important for people because they are a locus or site of matters vital to social reproduction and continuity, including gendered roles, generational roles, socialization, senses of identity, emplacement, desire, conscience, restraint, self-expression, shame, and honor.

Fifth, kin terms can provide us with a partial guide to the operation of the factors just listed here. When we know the society, we can understand what the terms mean. Just looking at the terms themselves will not give us all the answers.

We have frequently discussed the Hagen and Duna people of Papua New Guinea. We will now give a summary of kin terms in these two areas and point out some ways in which these fit with social forms and processes. Two points must be noted: Terms of address often differ from terms of reference, and terms used may vary with respect to the gender of the speakers (male or female). The terms are also given from the viewpoint of an individual person (the propositus, as this is called technically, or "Ego").

TABLE A1.1 Melpa Consanguineal Kin Terminology

Reference Term	Gloss	Terms of Address	Range of Application
Kouwa	grandfather–grandchild (reciprocal)	*kouwa*, also *anda* ("old man")	subclan, clan
Apom	grandmother–grandchild (reciprocal)	*ape, wend'ape,* also *ambwenda* ("old woman")	subclan, clan
tepam,[1] *rara*	father	*ta, wuö ta, rara* ("senior man")	subclan, clan. Also: MZS, FMZS[1]
mam,[2] *amb mam*	mother	*ma, amb ma*	clansman's wife; MZ to subclan level; MMZD
pam[3]	mother's brother (maternal uncle) –sister's child	*apa*	mother's clansmen; brothers of clan mothers
Ötin	father's sister (paternal aunt) –brother's child	*ata*	senior clanswoman; FMZD
öngin[4]	same-sex sibling (male or female speaking, m.s. or f.s.)	*ana, ang, ang-wuö* (brother, m.s.)	*ang-wuö* = any distant relationship classed as a same-sex sibling. Widely extended; MZS (m.s.) MZD (f.s.)
Kimun	opposite sex sibling (male or female speaking)	*aya*	widely extended, as for *öngin*
pelpam, korpel[5]	cross-cousin	*pel, korpel, apa*	members of mother's clan of same generation as ego

TABLE A1.1 Continued

Reference Term	Gloss	Terms of Address	Range of Application
Kangem	son	*ta* (m.s.) *ma* (f.s.)	junior clansman (m.s.); H's junior clansman (f.s.)
Mboklam [alt. spelling *boglam*]	daughter	*ta* (m.s.) *ma* (f.s.)	junior female of clan (m.s.); H's junior female clan member (f.s.)

(Key: F = father, M = mother, Z = sister, B = brother, W = wife, H = husband, C = cousin, P = parallel, X = cross, Ch. or ch. = children, S = son, D = daughter.)

[1]Markers can be added to make distinctions: *tepam ingk* or *tepam köndi* means true or genuine father that is, immediate father, presumed genitor who is also mother's husband; *tepam mburlukna*, "backside father" means a lineal same-generation male relative of the immediate father; *tepam komone*, "elder father" means father's elder brother; *tepam akele*, "younger father" means father's younger brother. *Tepam* also inflects according to second person, thus *tepanem* = "your (sing.) father," and number, thus *tepamal* = "fathers." In address, *ta* is self-reciprocal between father and son/daughter.

[2]*Mam* can also mean "big" in ordinary linguistic usage. Old spirit men in folktales are sometimes referred to as *wuö mam*, "big men." *Mam* as mother inflects in the same way as *tepam*. In address, *ma* is self-reciprocal between mother and daughter/son also.

[3]Inflections as for n.1 and n.2. *Mburlukna* may be used to indicate a classificatory relationship, as in n.1. "Pam" is a strongly emotive term, connoting compassion and empathy. Men will refer to the fact that their sisters gave the breast to their children in expressing the relationship with sister's children. *Pam/apa* is self-reciprocal in both address and reference.

[4]The term *amb angin wuö*, "woman same-sex sibling man" is used for WZH, and MZCh. are "siblings," expressing a closeness of relationship.

[5]*Pelpam* is the term regularly used in northern Melpa areas. Using the term *apa* in address emphasizes the link between cross-sex siblings in the senior generation that leads in the next generation to cross-cousinhood. In ordinary linguistic usage, *pel* means a cross-plank or a fence part. Second and third cross-cousins are variously termed by cross-cousin or sibling terms, often with reference not to the apical cross-sex sibling links but with reference to the gender of the immediate parental linking figure.

Source: Adapted and synthesized/modified from Strathern (1980). Some details are omitted. Emphasis is on northern Melpa usages. Authors' field notes are the primary source.

The table provides data on the self-reciprocal use of address terms. A father calls his children, for example, *kang ta* "boy child" and *ambokla ta*, "girl child." The children call him *wuö ta*, "man father." *Ta* = both child and father. The stress is on the pairing of persons in relationships, which is an overall feature of the culture. It is the relationship that is in focus in address. A father does not *refer to* his children in this way, however. In reference, they are *kangem*, "son," and *mboklam*, "daughter," and he is *tepam* to them (or occasionally *ta*, as in reference where familiarity and closeness are stressed).

Another notable feature is that most distinctions are made in ego's own generation or in generation +1 or −1. F is distinguished clearly from MB, and FZ from MZ. Parallel cousins are siblings, whether FBCh. or MZCh., and are distinguished from cross-cousins. The terms *pam* for MB and *pelpam* for FZCh. or MBCh. are linguistically related.

Extensions to the clan level are widely employed, especially for sibling terms.

Immediate relationships are, however, clearly distinguished from classificatory ones. "Kinship" for the Melpa is based on *both* genealogical criteria *and* wide extensions of terms as category words suggesting moral components of meaning.

Except for H and W, all terms can be used self-reciprocally. All therefore represent reciprocal pairings, stressing the duality of the dyadic relationships involved. This is a very important feature of both the consanguineal and the affinal terminology. Obviously the effect of this pattern is to point indexically to the bonds between those involved. Cross-sex relationships are recognized widely in ego's same-generation relationships also, and a cross/parallel distinction is also most important at this generational level. In a general way, this fits with the creation of exchange relationships along affinal and cross-cousin ties; but relationships with matrilateral parallel kin are also important for exchange

TABLE A1.2 Melpa Affinal Terms

Reference Term	Gloss	Term of Address	Range of Application
Ambom	wife	*amb-e*	not extended
Wam	husband	*Wuö-e*	not extended
amb wölik[1]	co-wife	*amb-e* or by name or food name	not beyond immediate co-wife
Koklom [alt. spelling *koglom*]	wife's brother–sister's husband (m.s.) (reciprocal)	*pöi, kopa*	extended to some collaterals
kimöm, kimum	wife's sister, (m.s.) brother's wife (m.s.) husband's brother (f.s.)	*kopa*	extended to some collaterals
kulpam[2]	spouse's parent (reciprocal)	*kopa*	numerous collateral extensions: daughter's or son's wife's mother
Mönin	brother's wife, husband's sister (f.s.)	*amb man*	BWZ, cross-cousin's wife and other collaterals
Apom	husband's mother (f.s.) (reciprocal)	*ape*	HMZ, MBW, and numerous other collateral extensions

[1]*wöl-ik* literally means one who spins jealous talk or magical talk against another. Co-wives are expected to be very jealous of each other. To establish friendship, they may share a special food and declare that they will not use their personal names or relationship terms but will reciprocally call each other by the name of the food. (see Stewart and Strathern 2001; Strathern 1977). This is a very common practice among consanguineal kin and also between friends who are not kin.

[2]Gender markers are used to refer to the gender of the referent, that is, *wuö kulpam* = father-in-law, and *amb kulpam* = mother-in-law, for both m.s. and f.s. For spouse's grandparent, an age marker can be added, for example, *wenda kulpam*, "wife's mother's mother."

purposes, as they also are traditionally among the neighboring Tombema Enga people (see Feil 1984). Many kin types can also be brought under the rubrics of types whose primary referents do seem to be the genealogically immediate ones. Melpa kin terms fit with a view that *both* primary classifications *and* extended usages are structurally significant for the universe of kin ties.

Duna consanguineal kin terms thus operate in ways quite similar to those among the Melpa. The greatest number of distinctions in terms is made in ego's own generation. However, there is one difference here: Whereas for the Melpa "same-sex sibling" is represented by the same term (*öngin*) for

TABLE A1.3 Duna Consanguineal Kin Terminology

Term	Gloss[1]	Range of Application
Mamane	grandfather–grandchild	includes great-uncle and great-nephew
Auwene	grandmother–grandchild	includes great-aunt and great-niece
Ame	father	includes paternal uncle and classificatory kin
Antia	mother	includes maternal aunt, MZ and FW
auwene[2]	maternal uncle nephew/niece	includes, e.g., FBDS
Arane	paternal aunt nephew/niece	includes, e.g., FFBD
Keni	same-sex sibling (male speaking [m.s.]) "brother"	includes, e.g., FBS and MZS
Hagini	same-sex sibling (female speaking) "sister"	includes, e.g., FBD and MZD
Kane	opposite-sex sibling "sister" (male speaking) "brother" (female speaking)	includes, e.g., FBS or D; MZD or D
Hanini	cross-cousin	includes, e.g., FFBDS or D, MFBSS or D
Ngini	son	includes, e.g., MZSS
Wane	daughter	includes, e.g., MZSD
apa[3]	remote cross-cousin, distant cousin	includes the agnatic descendants of a brother–sister pair in earlier generations (marks limits of recognized consanguineal ties)

[1]All these terms can be used self-reciprocally, except for F, M, S, and D in reference forms.

[2]We report usages in the Aluni Valley area. Modjeska (1980) reported terms for Horaile, nearer to Lake Kopiago station.

[3]*Apa* usages indicate an extension of cross-cousin relationships over a number of generations. *Apa* are at the "limits" of kinship.

Source: Adapted from Strathern and Stewart (2004: 34–35) with authors' field notes as the primary source of information.

both male speakers (m.s.) and female speakers (f.s.), thus creating a consistent parallel universe of terms for both genders, among the Duna males and females use different terms for same-sex siblings (*keni* = brother, m.s., and *hagini* = sister, f.s.). Duna males and females do, on the other hand, use the same term for opposite sex sibling, *kane*. Duna are thus picking out gender-specific roles more sharply than the Melpa. Exchange ties between affines are less important for the Duna than for Melpa, and Duna women do not have much formal autonomy in regard to affinal prestations. It is possible that these role differences are reflected in the kin classifications we have noted.

Duna affinal terms also resemble Melpa terms in their structure. Melpa does not have special step-kin terms, however. The Duna *yakini* term does pick these out. Since cognatic ties of all kinds can be used for group affiliation among the Duna, it becomes important for them to delineate breaks or boundaries in such ties. They would agree with Freeman (1961), who excluded affines from his definition of the "kindred" in the more restricted sense of the term.

Differences between Duna and Melpa social structures are not precisely marked by these kin and affinal usages, although such differences that do appear in the terms are consonant with the structural differences we have noted here. Terminology is a clue, but only one clue, to social structure in the broader sense.

TABLE A1.4 Duna Affinal Terms

Term	Gloss[1]	Range of Application
iwane[1]	Wife	not extended
Noni	Husband	not extended
Hakalini	co-wife (female speaking)	HW, HBW
Kiane	brother's wife–husband's brother	not extended
Arane	sister-in-law (female speaking)	BW, HZ
mbaluni[2] / *paluni*	brother-in-law	ZH, WB, WZ
aruni[3]	female in-law, daughter-in-law	includes MBW and cross-cousin's W
yakane[4]	mother-in-law, father-in-law, daughter-in-law	wife's cross-cousin
Yakini	step-father, step-child	includes also MZH, WZch.

[1] All terms except W and H can be used self-reciprocally. W and H generally use personal names in address. *Iwa-* means "to plant."

[2] A commonly used term in the Aluni Valley is *imanggu*, which means "wife-giver/wife-given."

[3] Used widely for husband's kin. See Modjeska (1980: 324).

[4] *Yakane* is an emotive term, conjuring up a mother's influence over her daughter in the case of the mother-in-law.

References

Carsten, Janet, ed. 2000. *Cultures of Relatedness. New Approaches to the Study of Kinship.* Cambridge: Cambridge University Press.

Feil, Daryl K. 1984. Beyond patriliny in the New Guinea-Highlands. *Man,* n.s., 19: 50–76.

Fox, Robin. 1967. *Kinship and Marriage.* Harmondsworth, Middlesex: Penguin Books (a Pelican Original).

Freeman, J. Derek. 1961. On the concept of the kindred. *Journal of the Royal Anthropological Institute* 9: 192–220.

Holy, Ladislav. 1996. *Anthropological Perspectives on Kinship.* London and Chicago: Pluto Press.

Keesing, Roger M. 1975. *Kin Groups and Social Structure.* Fort Worth, TX: Harcourt Brace Jovanovitch.

Lounsbury, Floyd C. 1964. A formal account of the Omaha and Crow-Type kinship terminology. In *Explorations in Cultural Anthropology,* ed. W. Goodenough. New York: McGraw-Hill.

Meggitt, Mervyn J. 1964. The kinship terminology of the Mae Enga of New Guinea. *Oceania* 34: 101–200.

Modjeska, Nicholas. 1980. Duna kinship terms: An atrophied Iroquois system. In *Blood and Semen: Kinship Systems of Highland New Guinea,* ed. Edwin A. Cook and Denise O'Brien, 305–328. Ann Arbor, MI: The University of Michigan Press.

Morgan, Lewis Henry. 1870. *Ancient Society.* New York: Holt and Co.

Morgan, Lewis Henry. 1877. *Systems of Consanguinity and Affinity of the Human Family.* Washington, D.C.: Smithsonian Institution.

Stewart, Pamela J., and Andrew Strathern. 2001. *Humors and Substances: Ideas of the Body in New Guinea.* Westport, CT: Bergin and Garvey (Greenwood Publications).

Stone, Linda. 2010. *Kinship and Gender: An Introduction,* 4th ed. Boulder, CO: Westview Press.

Strathern, Andrew. 1977. Melpa food-names as an expression of ideas on identity and substance. *Journal of the Polynesian Society* 86: 503–511.

Strathern, Andrew. 1980. Melpa kinship terms. In *Blood and Semen: Kinship Systems of Highland New Guinea,* ed. Edwin A. Cook and Denise O'Brien, 329–370. Ann Arbor, MI: The University of Michigan Press.

Strathern, Andrew, and Pamela J. Stewart. 2004. *Empowering the Past, Confronting the Future. The Duna People of Papua New Guinea.* New York: Palgrave Macmillan.

APPENDIX 2

Incest and Exogamy: Sex is Good to Prohibit

Human populations depend on sexual reproduction for their biological continuity, and this in turn has historically depended on the act of sexual intercourse between females and males. Our formulation here may sound rather elaborate. It is designed, however, to recognize that with new reproductive technologies the standard practices of the past are no longer the only ones possible. In evolutionary terms, though, pair-bonding has gone with sexual intercourse, and the family of cross-sex parents and children has generally resulted. Commonly, partners for such pair-bonding are sought outside of the domain of close family ties, that is, outside of the ties of parenthood and siblingship. This pattern corresponds to the widespread institution of an incest taboo, specifying that such sexual relations within the parent–child and sibling sets of dyads are strongly disapproved of, and often there are legal, moral, and social sanctions applied to any act that transgresses such a taboo.

This widespread—but not completely universal—pattern has in turn led to two opposed tendencies in anthropological analysis. In one trend, associated with the work of Sigmund Freud (e.g., in his *Totem and Taboo* 1918), the taboo was explained as the social repression of an unconscious desire, which had to be curbed in order to allow an orderly and clear set of kinship arrangements in the society. Apart from its psychological underpinnings, this theory is clearly functionalist in tone: Incestuous sexual relationships are viewed as repressed because of social needs. Freud was most concerned with the taboo on intercourse between parents and children, and he supported this idea with his theory of the Oedipus complex, in which he argued that sons unconsciously wish to kill their fathers and have sexual relations with their mothers; and correlatively, but with perhaps less emphasis, daughters wished to have such relations with their fathers, removing their mothers from the scene (the "Electra complex"). Presumably, the theory would require wishes of this kind also on the part of the mother and the father, so that each person in the family complex would have to suppress their desires. Freud further backed up his theory with a hypothesis that in the "primal horde" structure, the primitive form of human groups, sons had turned on their father and killed him, expiating their sin by subsequently instituting practices of ritual respect toward the father's spirit (Freud 1918). However, Freud's notion of the primal horde has largely been discarded.

His idea of the basic psychological complex, by contrast, has enjoyed a long scientific life; was advocated by the psychoanalyst Ernest Jones (1924) and carefully reconsidered and reshaped by the anthropologist Meyer Fortes (1987, especially Chapters 6 and 8, see also Strathern and Stewart n.d.); and was attacked by the anthropologist Bronislaw Malinowski in reference to data from the Trobriand Islands of Papua New Guinea (1927), while it was reinstated and strongly defended by the anthropologist Melford Spiro (1982) in a further consideration of Malinowski's fieldwork data. Freud's ideas are referred to briefly by Linda Stone (2010: 58), noting how the "primal horde" theory has been removed from consideration. Robin Fox (1967: 60–61) remarks that it is not clear how Freud's theories are supposed to work, but praises him for asking "the right questions" (p. 61) about the transition to "humanity" in early times. Roger Keesing (1975) and Ladislav Holy (1996) appear not to have mentioned Freud at all in the course of their discussions of incest rules.

The opposite approach to Freud's was one put forward by Edward Westermarck prior to Freud's publication of *Totem and Taboo* in 1918 (Westermarck 1891). Westermarck, like all his contemporary theorists, was concerned with the evolution of human societal forms and took marriage to be a central institution to think about in these terms. He quite sensibly rejected current theories of "primitive promiscuity" and "group marriage," which were perhaps based on a misconception of the working of sections in Australian Aboriginal marriage systems (Buchler and Selby 1968: 3). Westermarck also suggested that the childhood association of parents with children and opposite-sex siblings with each other leads to a lack of sexual interest. This is not a "familiarity breeds contempt" argument. It is an argument that familiarity goes with a different kind of emotional predisposition, based on the idea of amity between familial kin. Amity is thought to exclude or reduce sexual desire. Siblings thus learn to look for sexual partners outside of the family as they grow up. The argument in fact must apply primarily between siblings, explaining why there is an inclination for them to move out of the family circle when seeking a sexual relationship. Freud's theory might conceivably be held to apply between the generations, and Westermarck's to cross-sex siblings.

Work by primatologists and ethologists was brought into play, long after Westermarck's time but largely in support of it, or rather in support of the idea that in nonhuman animal societies there is a tendency to avoid sexual relations within the small familial groups that implicitly emerge in primate societies (see, e.g., Stone 2010: Chapter 2; Kortmulder 1968 also examined the problem of both incest and exogamy from the viewpoint of ethology, i.e., the descriptive field study of patterns of animal behavior and their functional correlates in terms of survival, dominance, hierarchy, reproduction, etc.). Criticism that if there is a natural tendency to avoid a practice, why would strongly sanctioned taboos against it be brought into play may give some pause here; but there is no reason to suppose that human social practices should not build on preexisting dispositions: that is, dispositions toward prosocial behavior, for example, grooming, in-group amity, aggression toward others, and the like. So the criticism is not necessarily valid.

The most detailed ethnographic work in general support of a position akin to Westermarck's ideas stems from studies carried out in Taiwan by Arthur P. Wolf. Wolf's early research was reported on in three notable publications (1966, 1968, 1970). He carried out his fieldwork in Hsiachichou, a village near the town of Hsulin [Shulin], populated by Hokkien [Hoklo] speakers, whose ancestors migrated from Fukien [Fujian] Province of China to Taiwan in the seventeenth and eighteenth centuries (Wolf 1966: 883, 1970: 504). In his 1968 article, perhaps the one best known, Wolf broadened his discussion to parts of mainland China, indicating that the practices he found in his field area were by no means restricted to it. The practices themselves he describes as consisting of a "major" and a "minor" form of marriage, with a particular interest in the minor form (Wolf 1970: 504). In his 1966 article, Wolf describes these practices as follows: In the first (major) type of marriage, which he designates the "grand patrilocal" form (p. 883), "the bride leaves her natal home and relinquishes membership in her family of orientation [natal family]; she steps over the threshold of the groom's home and becomes a member of his household; and she is presented to the groom's [patrilineal] ancestors and thereby acquires the status of wife." All this was supposed to happen in a single ritual sequence on the same day (p. 883).

By contrast, in the alternative or minor type of patrilocal marriage, the two events of entering the future husband's home and being presented to the lineage ancestors "are separated by 10 to 15 years. Dressed in the traditional red wedding costume, the bride enters her future husband's home as a child. She is seldom more than three years of age and often less than a year" (Wolf 1966: 884). She is then brought up as a member of her new affinal household and takes its family name as her own, placing her natal family name second to it, in the same way as for major marriage. The bride and her future husband are brought up together and, Wolf says, "are free to behave as though they were siblings until they are designated husband and wife" (1966: 884).

Wolf took the enterprising opportunity offered by these different practices to assess the likely validity of Westermarck's theory of sexual aversion between those brought up together in the same household as siblings or like siblings. His basic hypothesis was that the partners brought up together from an early age as siblings would in some way experience a less "successful" marriage, in terms of a sexual relationship, than those who came together as strangers and were united immediately as spouses in the "major" marriage form (even though, from another perspective, we might also expect problems for the couple brought together in the major form, because they had not chosen each other).

In the local language (shared by the villagers with others in the same valley as far as Sanhsia city to the north of Shulin), the bride brought into the household in the minor form was called a *sim-pua*, "little daughter-in-law" (compare Wolf 1968: 864). Genealogical data that Wolf collected of males born before 1910 showed that in 22 out of 48 examples, the parents decided to take in a *sim-pua* as a future bride, and in 16 cases, the arrangements went through to completion. So the "minor" form was originally quite common. Wolf argues, however, that it was unpopular with youths themselves by comparison with the major form. In other words, they did not mind so much marrying a bride chosen for them from outside, but they did not like marrying a girl with whom they had been brought up. Wolf further argues, and continued to argue in the 1970 paper, that *sim-pua* marriages were less sexually satisfactory, perhaps for both partners, than the grand major type. He based his findings on village gossip and case histories, on the supposed frequency of men's resort to prostitutes, on divorce rates, on reports of adultery, and on numbers of children born to a marriage.

Wolf's reasoning throughout is careful, and he takes into account historical changes in the community. Economic changes in Taipei brought more chances of independence to young men. They could leave home and work elsewhere. Missionaries of Christian churches and government authorities saw the minor marriage as a kind of oppression (Wolf 1966: 886–887). Young people were reluctant to marry in the *sim-pua* form and referred to it as being forced together (p. 887). Besides, the major form was accompanied by much ceremonial festivity and the transfer of a dowry, ensuring a network alliance between the in-laws so brought into association (p. 888). Apparently, this did not hold in *sim-pua* marriage.

Wolf also notes that the number of children registered as born to a marriage is not necessarily a reliable guide to sexual relations within marriage, because men could register children by their mistress as children of the marital household. The overriding concern was that there should be sons to perpetuate the lineage and "inherit the family prosperity and carry on the rites of ancestor worship" (Wolf 1970: 508). If this does not happen, Wolf says, the ancestors are condemned to be hungry, wandering ghosts. They would be without a home, because there would be no one to sacrifice to them. In such circumstances, any aversion to sexual relations could be overcome by the social and moral imperative to perpetuate the line of succession in the family.

Social learning and social pressures could conceivably account for the patterns of behavior whether there was an initial aversion to sexual relations or not. The *sim-pua* arrangement was in the past appreciated by the parents of the groom-to-be since "a girl who is raised by her husband's family makes a better daughter-in-law than a girl who joins the family as a young adult" (Wolf 1970: 509). Mother-in-law and daughter-in-law were expected to be in conflict in the major marriage form, because of competition for the affection and loyalty "of the young man who is the older woman's son and the younger woman's husband" (Wolf 1968: 869). From Wolf's remarks here, it appears that conflict overtly centered around cooking. The mother-in-law scolded the daughter-in-law for not knowing how to cook properly or stealing money, or being greedy or lazy. The daughter-in-law in turn would try to persuade her husband to leave the extended family, thereby increasing the level of conflict. Bitter accusations of intent might follow such suspicions, exacerbated by the fact that the incoming wife was usually an outsider to her husband's family; and indeed this was the preferred situation, since the bride would not have her own kinsfolk as allies nearby. "A volatile triangle of strife ensued" (Wolf 1968: 870). All this was obviated when a family took in a *sim-pua* bride. The young girl would obey the senior woman as a daughter, and would later have a less close relationship with her husband, Wolf says, adding, "The effect . . . is to drive a wedge between husband and wife and thereby take the strain off the bonds between the generations" (1968: 870).

Clearly, these arrangements represent a kind of trade-off in kinship relations. The trade-off is not perfect, and this is apparently because of an aversion between the partners. It would be interesting to know more about the total gender and authority dynamics involved. Also, what about the actual siblings in the family? How does the *sim-pua* fit in with them? Further, social learning could explain the patterns observed or imputed. A *sim-pua* would see that actual siblings were prohibited from marrying, and her position would possibly give rise to a feeling of cognitive dissonance: she is a sibling, but not a sibling. Finally, as Wolf notes, the whole thing would depend strongly on parental authority, either in giving away a daughter as a *sim-pua* or in ordering a son to take her as his bride. When parental authority decreased, the practices also predictably decreased in frequency (Wolf 1966: 888–889, 1968: 873). The considerable complexities involved in theorizing the problem of the incest taboo from both biological and sociological perspectives are explored further in a volume that Arthur Wolf and William Durham co-edited and published in 2005 (Wolf and Durham 2005).

In this volume, Hill Gates refers readers back to the work of Bronislaw Malinowski (notably Malinowski 1927, 1929), on the Trobrianders of Papua New Guinea. Malinowski explains how, in traditional Trobriand thinking, everyone belonged to one of four named autochthonous totemic matrilineal clans (*kumila*), divided into local subclans (*dala*) (Malinowski 1929: 494–495). From a man's viewpoint, all women of the same clan as himself are classified as his sisters and are not to be married. The clan is an exogamous unit. People do, however, make a distinction between clan and subclan membership. Clan relatives are *kakaveyogu*, which Malinowski translates as "spurious kinsman" (1929: 496). Subclan relatives are *veyogu*, "kinsman." The term *lubaygu*, meaning "sweetheart or lover" (p. 501), can never be overtly applied to a woman of the same clan. Women of other clans, by contrast, are described by the root form *tabu-*, meaning "father's sister" and by extension all women of the father's clan, or any clan other than the speaker's own. This term *tabu-* means that such women can lawfully be married (p. 502). Breaking the rules prohibiting "clan incest," that is, sexual relations within the clan, is called *suvasova* (p. 502); and Malinowski noted that informants equated the application of incest rules and exogamy: no sex or marriage to be permitted within the clan.

However, Malinowski also noted that sexual relations with *kakaveyola*(pl.), kin of the same clan but outside of the subclan, "though officially forbidden, ruled to be improper, and surrounded by supernatural sanctions, is yet everywhere committed" (p. 512). However, marriage within the clan, as distinct from sexual relations, was strongly forbidden in practice as well as in ideology (p. 512). Men who committed clan incest were also supposed to have magical powers to protect themselves against the expected harmful effects of indulging in it, that is, disease and death.

This example shows two things. First, classificatory terms do not imply exact equality of relationship. The strongest taboo among the Trobrianders was on intercourse with the immediate sister. Subclan sisters were also forbidden and this rule was maintained strongly because the *dala* was the effective unit of social reproduction within the sphere of matrilineal ties. Clan sisters were at the outer end of shared group identity, on the borders between the possibility of sex and of marriage. *Suvasova* with them was covertly permitted, but marriage was not. No clearer demonstration of the difference between incest and exogamy could be made than in this famous Trobriand case.

It is an important distinction to make, because most social theorists have recognized that a rule of exogamy belongs more to the conscious design of things by humans, whereas the incest taboo is often, perhaps following Freud, seen as belonging to the unconscious. Of course, extended rules couched in terms of incest can coincide with rules of exogamy. Lévi-Strauss (1949) indeed argued that the incest taboo itself should be seen as a positive injunction to marry out, and that therefore the basic unit of reproduction from early times in human societies would include the mother's brother, who putatively "gives" his sister in marriage to another man. He thus argued that the basic rule is as much positive as it is negative. Rules of exogamy, however, can vary enormously. Marrying a cross-cousin in a patrilineal system means marrying outside of one's clan or lineage, but it also means marrying back into the place where the mother came from, that is, mother's brother's daughter (from the male viewpoint). Marrying a "stranger" outside of the total nexus of cognatic kin would be very different from marrying a cousin. The considerable variation in exogamic rules tells us clearly that they need to be considered comparatively and in sociological terms for their implications. For this reason, conflating the explanations of incest and exogamy may not be the best strategy. Kortmulder (1968) attempted to bring the two together by arguing that not only is there a possible aversion from sex with close kin, but that sexual relations themselves are characterized by a certain level of aggressiveness. If persons are socialized into not showing such aggressiveness—the obverse, we might say, of Meyer Fortes's axiom of amity between kin—then they will not be inclined to have sex with one another, according to the basic form of this argument.

Kortmulder's suggestions chime with those made subsequently by Paul Roscoe (1994), who argued that whereas in childhood there may be incestuous play between siblings, when the children grow up they prefer to seek sexual partners elsewhere, and he refers to a close ethological association "between sex and aggression" (p. 54). He suggests further that "sexual and aggressive excitation are *experientially conflated*" (p. 56). Correlatively, he argues that "incest avoidance is connected to something akin to familial amity" (p. 57). Roscoe recognizes that although a social value such as amity "may have a biopsychological substrate, it also must be learned as a part of a cultural repertoire" (p. 68). His approach has the merit of incorporating "culture" and "nature" in a single framework of theorizing. We can conclude that such theorizing is compatible with a more sociologically oriented theory of exogamy, with one important caveat: There can be too much aggression.

In a more balanced formulation, we may suggest that many social ties are compounded by both aggression and amity; and this can profitably be applied to the arena of sex and marriage (as well as, indeed, to intrafamilial ties). While an initial boldness may be required to initiate sexual relations, longer-term relationships may come to depend on something close to amity as well. Indeed, we might argue that such a transformative process is significant for the degree of achievement of what most theorists, following the early formulation of E. B. Tylor, have seen as the major positive rationale for exogamy: that is, the creation of friendly ties of alliance between families and clans, thus mitigating hostilities and promoting cooperative ties between them.

Tylor's basic ideas along these lines have been much quoted in texts on kinship (e.g., Fox 1967: 176, see also Fox 1980; Holy 1996: 125–126; Keesing 1975: 78; Stone 2010: 59–60). Tylor produced his statement on the functions of exogamy in the course of expounding a method of establishing cross-cultural correlations of practices and their concomitants. He rejects (Tylor 1889: 265) the hypothesis that exogamy is a result of wife-capture in patrilineal societies, and he notes that exogamy may be the rule in matrilineal cases also, thus placing it, in his view, earlier on in the scale of social evolution. This concern of nineteenth-century anthropology to reconstruct the pathways of the evolution of kinship structures aside, his observations led him on to note that already 20 years previously he had "noticed that in any full discussion of the subject would have to be considered the wish to bind different tribes together by friendship in intermarriage." Here, Tylor imputes conscious intentions to those who negotiate marriage ties across group boundaries; and while the rule of marrying outside of the group may be predicated on the relatively unconscious acceptance of the application of kin terminologies equating clan relatives with closer familial ones (i.e., as clan sisters, brothers, etc.), the specific *choice* of which family to draw a marriage partner from is more likely to be consciously made. Moreover, exogamy is a broad term indicating marrying "out" but not what one marries "into." Cousin marriages may be exogamous (or indeed endogamous in cases where a father's brother's daughter is the normative category to marry); its implications of a close-knit connubium, perhaps perpetuated over the generations, is very different from the case of a society in which the rule of clan exogamy is combined with the prohibition of marrying any recognized cognatic kin, a rule which would result in a wide dispersion of ties through marriage and correspondingly larger networks of affines and kin. Marriage rules have different effects where polygyny is practiced, allowing one man to have affinal ties with numbers of different groups, thus facilitating the use of these ties to raise wealth for the purpose of competitive exchanges of goods, such as in the Central Highlands societies of New Guinea.

In his discussion, Tylor goes on to range over a number of matters, including exogamy and totemism, that is, the idea that a group is descended from a particular animal or other creature or plant in the environment or that its members regard that creature as sacred and taboo its consumption, or consume it only on special ritual occasions. He notes that Robertson Smith argued that exogamy derived from totemism (Tylor 1889: 268). This would imply, interestingly, that just as people should refrain from eating their totem, so they should refrain from sexual relations with their clan kin, thus suggesting the well-known cross-cultural likening of sexual relations to the consumption of food. Tylor, however, does not pursue this point, but adverts again to his main point, with a caveat: "As to the law of exogamy itself, the evidence shows it in operation over a great part of the human race as a factor of political prosperity. It cannot be claimed as absolutely preventing strife and bloodshed . . . Still by binding together a whole community with ties of kinship and affinity, and especially by the peacemaking of the women who hold to one clan as sisters and to another as wives, it tends to keep down feuds and to heal them when they arise . . . " (p. 268).

The passage from Tylor that is most quoted comes a little earlier in his text: "Again and again in the world's history, savage tribes must have had plainly before their minds the simple practical alternative between marrying-out and being killed out" (p. 267).

Tylor's formulation is a piece of speculative history, of the kind that later structural-functionalists like Radcliffe-Brown eschewed. It is also, however, very functionally oriented itself. And it does not just impute a function to exogamy; it implies conscious agency on the part of those who first adopted it. At the same time, Tylor is careful to note that the function is not realized one hundred percent. Groups that intermarry do sometimes fight; but if they do, they are relatively easily able to settle their disputes, and this is partly because of the active go-between and peacemaking agency of the women who form the links of alliance. It is not only the male act of arranging a marriage but also the female capacity to help build peaceable ties that is involved. As producers of children who link kin of both groups together and as producers of wealth such as pigs that can be exchanged, the women in Papua New Guinea societies are preeminently important in the practical constitution of alliance. With Tylor's early prescience, then, we can move beyond "exogamy" and into gendered roles, the intersection between kinship and politics, the importance of ceremonial exchanges, and the like (see also Williamson 1984).

"Sex is good to prohibit," we have suggested. Obviously it is also "good to practice," for without it reproduction would not take place. In adopting this phrase, we have consciously referred to the concept of taboo. We have also invoked a play on the meaning of sex and the meanings of eating (noted earlier in the context of totemism). On the Micronesian island of Yap, David Labby notes, incest was equated with both animal behavior and cannibalism. Incestuous acts were called *ku'w*, a term that signified "a variety of large sea bass which was notorious for its voraciousness and huge mouth" (Labby 1976: 171). In other words, incest, like witchcraft in many cultures, was likened basically to the idea of greed, appetite that does not respect social bonds of sharing and restraint. Labby concludes, "incest was ultimately 'cannibalistic,' a denial of culture, of exchange, or work, a kind of survival through self-consumption" (1976: 179).

These Yapese juxtapositions of wrongful sex acts and wrongful acts of eating may suitably remind us of Meyer Fortes's observations regarding "totem and taboo" practices. Lévi-Strauss wrote that animals in general (including totemic ones) are "good to think with" (*bon à penser*, Lévi-Strauss 1962). Fortes commented that animals are both good to think with and good to eat, and eating, or constraints on eating, is always hedged with moral imperatives. He went on:

> Animals, I suggest, are peculiarly suited to objectify these moral imperatives because they are "good to forbid." They lend themselves specially to this form of moral constraints because, being alive, they are "good to kill" and, above all, "good to eat." (Fortes 1987: 144)

What Fortes wrote about the killing and consumption of animals applies equally to the domain of sexual activity. Sexual actions become embodied enactments of the moral domain in social life, and if sex is "good to perform," it is also "good to prohibit." The rules of incest and exogamy give shape to these two statements.

References

Buchler, Ira R., and Henry A. Selby. 1968. *Kinship and Social Organization: An Introduction to Theory and Method*. New York: Macmillan.

Fortes, Meyer. 1987. *Religion, Morality, and the Person: Essays on Tallensi Religion*, ed. Jack Goody. Cambridge, U.K.: Cambridge University Press.

Fox, Robin. 1967. *Kinship and Marriage. An Anthropological Perspective*. Baltimore, MD: Penguin Books (a Pelican Original).

Fox, Robin. 1980. *The Red Lamp of Incest*. New York: E. P. Dutton.

Freud, Sigmund. 1918. *Totem and Taboo*. New York: A. A. Brill.

Holy, Ladislav. 1996. *Anthropological Perspectives on Kinship*. London and Chicago: Pluto Press.

Jones, Ernest. 1924. Psycho-analysis and anthropology. In *Essays in Applied Psychoanalysis*, vol. 2, E. Jones. London: Hogarth Press.

Keesing, Roger M. 1975. *Kin Groups and Social Structure*. Fort Worth, TX: Harcourt Brace Jovanovitch.

Kortmulder, K. 1968. An ethological theory of the incest taboo and exogamy, with special reference to the views of Claude Lévi-Strauss. *Current Anthropology* 9(5): 437–449.

Labby, David. 1976. Incest as cannibalism: The Yapese analysis. *Journal of the Polynesian Society* 85: 171–179.

Lévi-Strauss, Claude. 1949. *Les structures élémentaires de la parenté*. Paris: Presses Universitaires de France.

Lévi-Strauss, Claude. 1962. *Le totémisme aujourd'hui*. Paris: Presses Universitaires de France.

Malinowski, Bronislaw. 1927. *Sex and Repression in Savage Society*. London: Routledge.

Malinowski, Bronislaw. 1929. *The Sexual Life of Savages in North-Western Melanesia*. New York: Halcyon House (1941 edition).

Roscoe, Paul B. 1994. Amity and aggression: a symbolic theory of incest. *Man* (JRAI) 29(1): 49–76.

Spiro, Melford E. 1982. *Oedipus in the Trobriands*. Chicago, IL: The University of Chicago Press.

Stone, Linda. 2010. *Kinship and Gender: An Introduction*, 4th ed. Boulder, CO: Westview Press.

Strathern, Andrew, and Pamela J. Stewart. n.d. *Kinship, Ritual, Cosmos*. To appear in a special issue of the *Journal de la Société des Océanistes*, papers in memory of Bernard Juillerat, ed. Denis Monnerie and Pierre Lemonnier.

Tylor, Edward Burnett. 1889. On a method of investigating the development of institutions applied to laws of marriage and descent. *Journal of the Royal Anthropological Institute* 18: 245–272.

Westermarck, Edward A. 1891. *The History of Human Marriage*. London: Macmillan.

Williamson, Margaret. 1984. Incest, exchange, and the definition of women among the Kwoma. *Anthropology* 8(2): 1–4.

Wolf, Arthur. 1966. Childhood association, sexual attraction, and the incest taboo: A Chinese case. *American Anthropologist* 68(4): 883–898.

Wolf, Arthur.1968. Adopt a daughter-in-law, marry a sister: A Chinese solution to the problem of the incest taboo. *American Anthropologist* 70(5): 864–874.

Wolf, Arthur.1970. Childhood association and sexual attraction: A further test of the Westermarck hypothesis. *American Anthropologist* 72(3): 503–515.

Wolf, Arthur P., and William H. Durham, eds. 2005. *Inbreeding, Incest, and the Incest Taboo: The State of Knowledge at the Turn of the Century*. Stanford, CA: Stanford University Press.

APPENDIX 3

Further Readings

From the vast literature, both old and recent, on kinship, we provide here a few further references, indicating the broad spectrum of topics that are dealt with under this heading. The list is deliberately heterogeneous and overlaps with references given in the chapters of this book. It illustrates something of the historical depth and also the contemporary vitality of studies on kinship.

Adrian, Bonnie. 2003. *Framing the Bride: Globalizing Beauty and Romance in Taiwan's Bridal Industry.* Berkeley, Los Angeles and London: University of California Press.

Aijmer, Göran. 2007. On making fathers in Lesu: The historical anthropology of a New Ireland society. *Oceania* 77: 232–246.

Befu, Harumi. 1963. Patrilineal descent and personal kindred in Japan. *American Anthropologist* 65(6): 1328–1341.

Brandewie, Ernest. 1981. *Contrast and Context in New Guinea Culture: The Case of the Mbowamb of the Central Highlands,* vol. 39. St. Augustin: Studia Instituti Anthropos.

Brandtstädter, Susanne, and Gonçalo D. Santos, eds. 2009. *Chinese Kinship: Contemporary Anthropological Perspectives.* London and New York: Routledge.

Browne, Jude, ed. 2007. *The Future of Gender.* Cambridge: Cambridge University Press.

Deshon, Shirley. 1963. Compadrazgo on a henequen hacienda in Yucatan: A structural re-evaluation. *American Anthropologist* 65(3, pt. 1): 574–583.

Dousset, Laurent. 2008. The "global" versus the "local": Cognitive processes of kin determination in Aboriginal Australia. *Oceania* 78: 260–279.

Eriksen, Annelin. 2008. *Gender, Christianity, and Change in Vanuatu: An Analysis of Social Movements in North Ambrym.* Aldershot: Ashgate Publications.

Forth, Gregory. 2008. Miwok mysteries: The question of asymmetric prescriptive marriage in Aboriginal North America. *Ethnology* 47(1): 61–83.

Gibbs, James L., Jr. 1963. Marital instability among the Kpelle: Towards a theory of epainogamy. *American Anthropologist* 65(3, pt. 1): 552–573.

Gilberthorpe, Emma. 2007. Fasu solidarity: A case study of kin networks, land tenure, and oil extraction in Kutubu, Papua New Guinea. *American Anthropologist* 109(1): 101–112.

Goody, Jack. 2005. The labyrinth of kinship. Review of M. Godelier *Métamorphoses de la Parenté (Paris: Fayard: 2004). New Left Review* 36, November–December.

Gudeman, Steven. 1972. The compadrazgo as the reflection of the natural and spiritual person. *Proceedings of the Royal Anthropological Institute of Great Britain and Ireland for 1971,* 45–71. London: Royal Anthropological Institute.

Harrell, Stevan, and Sara A. Dickey 1985. Dowry systems in complex societies. *Ethnology* 24(2): 105–120.

Heady, Patrick, ed. 2009. *Family, Kinship and State in Contemporary Europe.* 3 vols. Chicago, IL: The University of Chicago Press.

Herman, Ellen. 2008. *Kinship by Design: A History of Adoption in the Modern United States.* Chicago and London: University of Chicago Press.

Hiatt, L. R 1996. *Arguments about Aborigines: Australia and the Evolution of Social Anthropology.* Cambridge: Cambridge University Press.

Hirsch, Jennifer S., and Holly Wardlow, eds. 2006. *Modern Loves. The Anthropology of Romantic Courtship and Companionate Marriage*. Ann Arbor, MI: The University of Michigan Press.

Ingham, John, and David H. Spain. 2005. Sensual attachment and incest avoidance in human evolution and child development. *JRAI*, n.s., 11(4): 677–702.

James, Wendy, Nicholas Allen, Hillary Callan, and Robin Dunbar, eds. 2008. *Early Human Kinship*. Hoboken, NJ: Wiley-Blackwell.

Jankowiak, William. 2008. Co-wives, husbands, and the Mormon polygynous family. *Ethnology* 47(3): 163–180.

Joyce, Rosemary A., and Susan D. Gillespie, eds. 2000. *Beyond Kinship: Social and Material Reproduction in House Societies*. Philadelphia, PA: University of Pennsylvania Press.

Keck, Verena. 2005. *Social Discord and Bodily Disorders: Healing among the Yupno of Papua New Guinea*. Durham, NC: Carolina Academic Press.

Kendall, Laurel. 1985. Ritual silks and kowtow money: the bride as daughter-in-law in Korean wedding rituals. *Ethnology* 24(4): 253–268.

Koentjaraningrat. 1966. Bride-price and adoption among the Bgu of West Irian. *Ethnology* 5(3): 233–244.

Kurtz, Stanley N. 1991. Polysexualization: A new approach to Oedipus in the Trobriands. *Ethos* 19(1): 68–101.

Lawrence, Peter. 1984. *The Garia. An Ethnography of a Traditional Cosmic System in Papua New Guinea*. Melbourne, VIC: Melbourne University Press.

Leach, Edmund R. 1957. Aspects of bridewealth and marriage stability among the Kachin and Lakher. *Man* 57: 50–55.

Leach, James. 2003. *Creative Land: Place and Procreation on the Rai Coast of Papua New Guinea*. Oxford and New York: Berghahn Books.

Lewin, Ellen. 2009. *Gay Fatherhood: Narratives of Family and Citizenship in America*. Chicago, IL: The University of Chicago Press.

Lowe, Edward D. 2002. A widow, a child, and two lineages: Exploring kinship and attachment in Chuuk. *American Anthropologist* 104(1): 123–137.

Marshall, Mac, and John L. Caughey, eds.1989. Culture, Kin and Cognition in Oceania: Essays in Honor of Ward H. Goodenough, a special publication of the American Anthropological Association number 25.

McConvell, Patrick, Laurent Dousset, and Fiona Powell, eds. 2002. Special issue: Kinship and Change in Aboriginal Australia. *Anthropological Forum* 12(2).

Meigs, Anna, and Kathleen Barlow. 2002. Beyond the taboo: Imagining incest. *American Anthropologist* 104(1): 38–49.

Needham, Rodney, ed. 1971. *Rethinking Kinship and Marriage*. ASA Monographs 11. London: Tavistock.

Peletz, Michael. 1995. Kinship studies in late twentieth century anthropology. *Annual Review of Anthropology* 24: 343–372.

Patterson, Mary. 2005. Coming too close, going too far: theoretical and cross-cutting approaches to incest and its prohibitions. *The Australian Journal of Anthropology* 16(1): 95–115.

Popenoe, David. 2005. *War Over the Family*. New Brunswick: Transaction Publishers.

Sabean, David Warren, Simon Teuscher, and Jon Mathieu, eds. 2010 *Kinship in Europe: Approaches to Long-Term Development (1300–1900)*. New York and Oxford: Berghahn Books.

Santos, Gonçalo D. 2008. On "same-year siblings" in rural South China. *JRAI*, n.s., 14(3): 535–553.

Scott, Michael W. 2007. *The Severed Snake: Matrilineages, Making Place, and a Melanesian Christianity in Southeast Solomon Islands*. Durham, NC: Carolina Academic Press.

Sillitoe, Paul, and Jackie Sillitoe. 2009. *Grass-clearing Man: A Factional Ethnography of Life in the New Guinea Highlands*. Long Grove, IL: Waveland Press.

Simpson, Bob. 1997. On gifts, payments and disputes: divorce and changing family structures in contemporary Britain. *JRAI*, n.s., 3(4): 731–746.

Stasch, Rupert. 2009. *Society of Others: Kinship and Mourning in a West Papuan Place*. Berkeley, Los Angeles and London: University of California Press.

Sutton, Peter. 2003. *Native Title in Australia: An Ethnographic Perspective*. Cambridge: Cambridge University Press.

Sweetser, Dorrian Apple. 1966. Avoidance, social affiliation, and the incest taboo. *Ethnology* 5(3): 304–316.

Taylor, John Patrick. 2008. *The Other Side: Ways of Being and Place in Vanuatu*. Pacific Island Monograph Series. Honolulu, HI: University of Hawai'i Press.

Traphagan, John W. 2003. Older women as caregivers and ancestral protection in Japan. *Ethnology* 42(2): 109–126.

Van Vleet, Krista E. 2008. *Performing Kinship: Narrative, Gender, and the Intimacies of Power in the Andes*. Austin, TX: University of Texas Press.

NAME INDEX

Morgan, L. H., 3–4, 12, 14 n4, 182
Murdock, G. P., 16 n13, 151

N

Needham, R., 32 n8, 107–109, 114 n12

O

O'Brien, D., 187–188
Ogawa, M., 172
Oliver, D. L., 38
Ottenheimer, M., 15 n8, 54, 160–161, 176 n4

P

Pawley, A., 81 n4
Peter, H.R.H. of Greece, 101

R

Rao, A., 164–165, 167, 177 n5
Read, D., 160, 176 n3
Rivers, W. H. R., 101
Robbins, J., 112 n2
Robertson, A. F., 153, 159–160
Robertson Smith, W., 196
Roscoe, P., 33 n16, 195
Ross, M., 82 n4
Rumsey, A., 81 n3

S

Sabean, D., 122–125, 143, 152
Salisbury, R. F., 27–28, 33 n20
Scheffler, H. W., 66, 131, 160, 166–167, 169
Schneider, D. M., 6, 15 n8, 39–41, 44, 53 n2,
        56 n5, 76, 114 n11, 128–132, 136, 139,
        149 n2, 151, 156–157, 160–161, 165,
        176 n4
Scott, W., 12–13, 16 n14
Segalen, M., 119–121, 141
Selby, H. A., 191
Sillitoe, P., 166
Spiro, M. E., 191
Stevenson, R. L., 18, 32 n2, 120, 122
Stewart, P. J., 15 n10, 23, 25, 32 n4, 32 n14,
        33 n15, 64–67, 70–72, 81 n3, 82 n6, n7,
        91, 95, 104, 109, 112, 112 n2, 112–113 n4,
        113 n5, n6, 124, 142–144, 146, 154, 157,
        161–163, 167–170, 175, 182, 186–187, 190

Stockard, J., 42
Stone, L., 15 n6, 86, 101–102, 131–132, 151,
        157, 182, 191, 196
Strathern, A. J., 15 n9, 23, 25, 32 n4, n5, n6,
        n7, n9, n11, n13, n14, 33 n15, n19,
        20, n21, 50, 64–68, 70–72, 81 n1, n3,
        82 n5, n6, n7, n8, 89–91, 95, 101, 104,
        109, 112, 124, 142–144, 146, 154, 157,
        161–163, 167–169, 170, 176 n4, 182,
        186–187, 190
Strathesk, J., 127
Strauss, H., 32 n14, 82 n7

T

Thomas, N., 102–103
Tylor, E. B., 4, 15 n5, 196–197

U

Uhlmann, A., 138–141

V

Valeri, V., 91–93, 113 n6, 114 n12
Velsen, J. van, 151–152
Vernier, B., 16 n11
Vicedom, G. F., 82 n7

W

Wagner, R., 55 n5, 71
Weiner, A. B., 16 n11, 37, 81 n3, 161
Westermarck, E., 191–192
Weston, K., 16 n12, 157
Williamson, M., 197
Wolf, A. P., 165, 191–194
Wurm, S. A., 81 n4

Y

Yamaji, K., 172
Yan, Y., 112–113 n4, 113 n6
Yanagisako, S. J., 16 n11, 103

Z

Zimmer-Tamakoshi, L., 161–162

SUBJECT INDEX